SELECT WRITINGS OF
JAMES EARL MASSEY

VIEWS *from the* MOUNTAIN

D1521464

ALDERSGATE
PRESS

SELECT WRITINGS OF **JAMES EARL MASSEY**
Views *from the* Mountain

EDITED BY BARRY L. CALLEN & CURTISS PAUL DeYOUNG

PUBLISHED BY:
ALDERSGATE **PRESS**
The publications arm of

HOLINESSANDUNITY.ORG

IN COLLABORATION WITH:

ANDERSON UNIVERSITY PRESS
WWW.ANDERSON.EDU/AUPRESS

Publication Design
& Management:

lamppostpublishers.com

Printed in the United States of America

Soft Cover ISBN 13:   978-1-60039-312-9
ebook ISBN-13:   978-1-60039-984-8

Library of Congress Control Number: 2018949516

DEDICATION

I dedicate this volume of my work to the future preparation
of strong-hearted servants of the Word of God.

May they lead the church in a renewal of its
understanding and possession of the blessing of holiness,
the God-intended unity of the Christian community,
and the impetus for evangelism.

James Earl Massey

Aspects *of my* Pilgrimage

An Autobiography

James Earl Massey

CONTENTS

Section V | 333
WISDOM FROM THE GREATS CROSSING MASSEY'S PATH

SELECT WRITINGS OF
JAMES EARL MASSEY

VIEWS *from the*
MOUNTAIN

EDITORIAL INTRODUCTION

by Barry L. Callen

In this 50th anniversary year of Rev. Dr. Martin Luther King's "I've Been to the Mountain" speech (April 3, 2018), the mountain imagery seemed an apt title for this book honoring Rev. Dr. James Earl Massey. Dr. King used the imagery of Moses looking toward the promised land while knowing that he would not get there himself. So it was Moses, then with King and now with Massey. Having seen and pointed the way, they have had to leave the completion of the great task to generations that will follow.

Dr. Massey was a friend and ministerial colleague of Dr. King, Howard Thurman, and so many others. He also has been to the mountaintop, peered into the land of God's promise, and been given a prophetic voice by God to report the wisdom gained. This voice has now spoken eloquently for decades to laypersons, pastors, preachers, biblical scholars, and educational leaders. As with Dr. King, the voice of Dr. Massey is most worthy of being heard today by church, academic, and national leaders. This volume hopes to enable that needed hearing.

Keynotes for the Future

It was only a little slip of the tongue, but it brought to public awareness in a humorous way much that would characterize the future ministries of our honored friend. Dr. Massey rarely slipped when speaking, nor did he on this occasion. But there was a slip and he made the most of it.

At the time, Rev. James Earl Massey was a young and obviously gifted Church of God pastor from Detroit, Michigan. He was on the campus of Anderson University. It was 1962 and he was addressing the undergraduate student body for the first of many coming times. His host was the school's admiring president, Dr. Robert H. Reardon. Here's how Massey recalls what happened after the little slip of the tongue.

> As President Robert H. Reardon was introducing me, giving details about my life and work, a *faux pas* occurred as Reardon closed his introduction with the words, "I now present to you, Raymond Massey." As I stood and walked toward the pulpit, there was a mild rumble of laughter in the packed auditorium. Both students and faculty had politely reacted to President Reardon's embarrassing mistake in calling the name of *Raymond* Massey, the well-known star of stage and screen, rather than *James*, my first name.
>
> I knew that all eyes were on me, wondering *if* or *how* I would handle the mistake before I went on with my speaking. Knowing President Reardon as I did, I was comfortable with what I felt would be appropriate on my part. I gave a mild smile and, in an unhurried pace, I said to the faculty and students, "I observe that your president is much more familiar with the world of the theater than with the world of the church!"

The previous mild rumble of laughter in the pews became a relieving big laugh throughout the crowd. Reardon accepted my levity with the grace I expected, aware as I was that the chapel crowd enjoyed seeing him momentarily red-faced.[1]

It had been such a quick and simple incident, a slip of the tongue and a clever come-back. The question now is this. What did this come-back bring to public awareness that would characterize the future of Massey's long relationship with this campus, and with God's people at large?

For one thing, the incident certainly made clear that there was a special bond between the two men involved, a college president of Irish origin with light skin and a young pastor with African origin and skin much darker in color. They trusted each other, really knew and admired each other, and were unusually at ease in public at a time when race relations were very strained in the nation, and even in the churches. Rev. Massey was comfortable with his racial heritage, in fact, proud of it without ever being haughty or defensive or demeaning of others.

The slip of the tongue was reflected on later by President Reardon. What was he really thinking as the students laughed at his little error and that the guest preacher from Detroit proceeded to address the student body for the first time? Just this: "Slowly, students accustomed to studying during chapel began to put down their books and look up attentively. They found themselves being carried along by this intense young expositor of the Word. I said to myself, 'Here is a man who could make a profound impact on the

---

1 From *Doors to Life: The Stories of Gustav Jeeninga*, Barry L. Callen, ed. (Anderson University Press, 2002), in the Foreword by James Earl Massey, 9-10. Used by permission.

campus if we could entice him to come.'"[2] He soon was so enticed and proceeded to make the expected impact.

But there was much more than a warm relationship between two men. This gifted young preacher in a Black tradition prominent in the Church of God (Anderson) could manage to stand comfortably before college students with their minds on everything but the speaker and arrest their attention for thirty minutes. He also could grab the attention and respect of the faculty without having to parade sophisticated words designed to impress their analytical minds. Massey was confident in tone, dignified in style, rich in content, and intently focused on the significance of the Word of God for the spiritual needs of the wise and simple, the young and old, whatever their race, culture, or denominational label. All heard him gladly.

And there was still more. Massey conveyed real love for his hearers and a passion for the wholeness and justice of human relationships. He knew discrimination firsthand in the major urban setting where he pastored and was leading his people there in addressing it straightforwardly and yet non-violently. He partnered with Martin Luther King, Jr., and others in Detroit on behalf of social righteousness in the name of Jesus Christ, and he did so long before it became "respectable" to do so.

Yes, there was laughter in that chapel session in 1962, but at the expense of none, not even the president he loved and enjoyed teasing. Rev. Massey could take to the pulpit or the piano with equal skill, and make real music from either place. His original professional intent had been classical piano performance, but God intervened with a call instead to the pulpit, lecture hall, classroom, and printed page.

---

2   Robert H. Reardon, in Barry L. Callen, ed., *Sharing Heaven's Music* (Abingdon Press, 1995), 225.

Within seven years of the little slip of the President Reardon's tongue, Rev. Massey would be back on the Anderson campus, now not as a guest but as a full-time faculty member, campus pastor, and eventually Dean of the graduate School of Theology. From that base, he would broaden his ministry to numerous campuses and church bodies nation-wide, and even world-wide.

Requests of Dr. Massey

This project was initiated by James Earl Massey. Nearing ninety years of age and suffering late-stage cancer, he had much time to look back, reflect, and then look ahead. He envisioned a volume of his selected writings and chose two of his colleagues whom he trusted to manage the whole project. Of these he wrote: "Special thanks are due to Dr. Barry Lee Callen and Dr. Curtiss Paul DeYoung, longtime colleagues whose timely counsel, caring presence, and editorial skills will make this anthology of my work the book I have intended."

His intent was not an ego trip; it was one more effort to share his gathered wisdom for the benefit of a new generation. As co-editors on Dr. Massey's behalf, it has been our pleasure to serve a dear mentor and friend in this special way. There is great wisdom in these writings, more than enough to have warranted our time and energy. We are honored to have been chosen for the task.

Dr. Massey explains one of the many delights associated with fulfilling his numerous invitations to speak and write over the years. Often the results became opportunities for follow-up publication. Now he asked us that a selection of these publications appear in one place. They reflect several literary styles, exposition, description, narration, biography, autobiography, some sermons, some academic articles, some interviews with him, some of his tributes to others. For the convenience of the reader, we have in-cluded an index of persons—Dr. Massey knew and is known and loved by so many.

For the most part, Dr. Massey did not wish to have included sections of his many books—see a full listing of them at the end of this volume. An exception is a chapter of his *The Responsible Pulpit*. This book in particular gained the attention of many teachers of preaching, causing them to comment favorably in their own writ-ing and to use the Massey material in their seminary classrooms across North America. We also have included a few small sections from Massey's 2002 autobiography, *Aspects of My Pilgrimage*, and other materials from the large corpus of Dr. Massey, including an undelivered commencement address, two or three milestone ser-mons, various interviews done with him, and his "final thoughts" drawn from his autobiography.

Massey's hopes for this volume included his preference for use of one professional title among the several available. His choice is "James Earl Massey, Dean Emeritus & Distinguished Professor-at-Large, Anderson University School of Theology." This school, now known now as "Anderson School of Theology and Ministry," was his chosen home, representing as it does the Church of God (Anderson), his particular and beloved church heritage. This strong identity with Anderson, Indiana, is why Aldersgate Press, this book's publisher, has collaborated with Anderson University Press.

A large oil portrait of Dean Massey hangs proudly in the foyer just outside Miller Chapel of this Anderson campus. He loves this school and it loves him as well, and is most pleased to join in spon-soring a volume that seeks to honor him and his special wisdom. It should be noted that another of the schools associated with the Church of God (Anderson), Mid-America Christian University, has also honored Dr. Massey by establishing a Massey Center on its Oklahoma campus.

The Park Place Church of God in Anderson, Indiana, was Dr. Massey's chosen home congregation for the many years the Masseys lived in Anderson. Honoring Dr. Massey's preaching prowess, for the rest of his life he has been formally known at Park Place by the title "Minister-At-Large" of this appreciative congregation. The "at-large" for this amazing minister came to involve over fifty prestigious lectureships across North America, preaching on more than one hundred college, university, and seminary campuses, being featured in prominent pulpits in Egypt, England, Japan, Australia, Europe, the Caribbean, and elsewhere, and being named in 2006 as one of the "25 most influential preachers of the last fifty years" by Christianity Today International. Detail of his many book publications is found in Appendix A.

Volume Overview

The following pages highlight key elements of the wisdom gained and shared during the long and prophetic ministry of James Earl Massey. As he wished, Curtiss Paul DeYoung and I, his chosen editors, have labored together and now present here a wide range of the insights of one of God's finest gifts to the church in recent generations. Our beloved Brother Massey has been to the mountaintop of God, listened carefully to the Divine voice, and then used his considerable gifts of preaching, teaching, and writing to proclaim widely much that God would have heard by people today and tomorrow.

We, his chosen editors, have organized the many entries of this book into themed sections, each introduced by a mature church leader well acquainted with Dr. Massey's life and work. For the convenience of the reader, we have provided a detailed Table of Contents (a subject index), the original published source of every entry, a full listing of the book publications of Dr. Massey (Appendix A), and an Index of Persons cited throughout the volume. Our desire has been to provide you, the reader, with the body of wisdom given by God and now shared with us through the discipline, obedience, and prophetic voice of God's special servant, Rev. Dr. James Earl Massey.

Barry L. Callen, co-editor
Summer, 2018

1

CONVERSION AND CALL

by James Earl Massey

Originally appeared in James Earl Massey's autobiography,
Aspects of My Pilgrimage, 28-30, 52-53, and in Barry L. Callen,
Heart of the Matter (Emeth Press, rev. ed., 2016), 12.
Used by permission.

I grew up in Detroit as a proud African-American man in a largely racist society. My conversion experience, "being saved," came when I was only six years old. I walked to a kneeling rail at the invitation of a guest evangelist from Selma, Alabama, and found my harmony with God. Although young. I had understood the call the preacher made to "come to Christ." He then asked me to stand and "testify for the Lord." I said, "I believe that the Lord has saved me!" I knew what I meant by my testimony. I felt convinced that I was in harmony with God.

That conversion experience was the beginning of my conscious relationship with God. It was more of a commitment to the sensed claim of God upon my life than any dramatic turn away from sins associated with a depth awareness of personal depravity or life-marring failures. And later God did call. I did not choose the ministry; it was divinely chosen for me. I had planned to be a musician, a classical pianist. All signs pointed to a musical career, but it was not to be, and for reasons known only to God.

My big shift from music to ministry began with a divine call that was nurtured in the midst of a strong community of believers in Detroit, especially by the mentoring of Raymond S. Jackson. My "sitting under" him helped me gain an understanding of what a solid preaching and pastoral ministry means, involves, and makes possible for people. To honor this great man of God, an early book was my 1967 biography of Rev. Jackson.

My actual experience of being called to preach happened on a Sunday morning in 1946. The morning worship service was in progress, but my attention was not on God but on a musical score I had brought with me that day. It had been my custom to carry a score with me and use any available time to study it. That day it was a waltz of Chopin, and I was deeply engrossed in it.

But this morning, during a brief let-up in my concentration on the score, I found myself being captured by the spirit of the worship occasion. As I honored the meaning of the hour and opened myself to God, I felt caught up into an almost transfixed state. I heard a Voice speaking within my consciousness: "I want you to preach!" The Voice both disturbed and settled me. The message was so forceful and the meaning so clear that I knew I would have to say "Yes," and I did.

Then, when I was nineteen, I first heard Howard Thurman speak. I was moved by his preaching, very deeply moved. I thanked him for his ministry to my life that day. As I left the sanctuary, I knew that I had found a preacher whose insights spoke to the depths of my own spirit and yearning after God. His message and manner made me sense again that wholeness of being which since a child I had come to believe belongs to the experience of hearing the word of God!

In all the years that have transpired since that holy hour, I have never had any reason to reinterpret what happened to me during that great listening moment of grace. The Voice that called me was so clear. Its bidding, though gentle, bore the unmistakable authority of a higher realm. For the first year after being called, I sometimes hungered more for the piano than I was eager for the pulpit. But that hunger was finally disciplined and my interest in the pulpit finally became keener than my retreat into music.

When much later Dr. Barry Callen graciously gathered and edited the materials for the volume about Christian preaching designed to honor me and my ministry, he was wise to title it *Sharing Heaven's Music*. The gospel of Jesus Christ had become for me the music I have played and proclaimed all of my adult life. Its lovely notes and rhythms tend to dissolve things like racism and sexism.

2

OVERVIEW OF A
MARVELOUS MINISTRY

by Barry L. Callen

Tribute by Barry L. Callen to James Earl Massey delivered
on the occasion in November, 1995, of the Wesleyan
Theological Society granting to Dr. Massey its prestigious
"Lifetime Achievement Award." Appeared the following year
in the *Wesleyan Theological Journal.* Abbreviated here and
used by permission.

I have the special privilege of presenting a man who has been a personal friend and mentor of mine for decades. More importantly, he has played the roles of teacher, pioneer, model, and prophetic spokesperson for the whole Wesleyan-Holiness tradition of Christianity in North America. This has been done from the pulpit, in the classroom, on the printed page, and in the streets with colleagues of his such as Martin Luther King, Jr.

James Earl Massey has embodied within the Christian community at large what his church of origin, the Church of God movement (Anderson), has envisioned since 1880 to be God's will for the church. The quest has been for true holiness and an authentic unity and common cause of all Christians enabled by the Spirit of God. The vision has been one of changed lives that then become effective communicators, models, and change agents of the gospel of Christ to and in the world. Our Brother Massey has shown us how to be bridge-builders among all of God's people for the sake of the credibility of the church as it is on mission for Jesus Christ.

Born in 1930, native of Detroit, Michigan, son and grandson of ministers, accomplished concert pianist, acclaimed pulpit master, James Earl Massey holds degrees from Detroit Bible College, Oberlin Graduate School of Theology, and Asbury Theological Seminary—where he has a long tenure as a distinguished trustee. He was senior minister of the Metropolitan Church of God in Detroit for more than two decades. Serving on the Anderson University campus for most of the years from 1969 until his retirement in 1995, he has been Campus Pastor, Professor of New Testament and Preaching, and Dean of the School of Theology.

Beyond the Anderson campus, he invested years as Principal of a School of Theology in Jamaica, radio speaker for the Church of God on its national program, the Christians Broadcasting Hope, and Dean of the Chapel and University Professor of Religion at Tuskegee University. He has been visiting professor, academic lecturer, or guest preacher at over one hundred colleges, universities, and seminaries. On three separate occasions, Massey has presented the William E. Conger, Jr., Lectures on Biblical Preaching at Beeson Divinity School. He has been a contributing editor for various journals, including *Christianity Today*, and was the homiletics editor for the *New Interpreters Bible*.

Massey authored several bestselling books of his own in the fields of preaching, Christian spirituality, and New Testament studies, including *Spiritual Disciplines, Designing the Sermon, The Burdensome Joy of Preaching,* and *African-Americans and the Church of God (Anderson): Aspects of a Social History*. This latter volume received the 2006 Smith-Wynkoop Book Award from the Wesleyan Theological Society.

Massey has filled distinguished pulpits from England and Egypt to Australia and Japan. A man of many campuses and of the whole church, he always has considered the Church of God (Anderson) in particular and the American holiness movement in general his home tradition. He has crossed racial and denominational lines freely, bringing with him the richness of the African-American church tradition.

Dr. Massey has intruded on the secure smugness of human prejudice with the sharp edge of the biblical word of salvation, equality, and liberation for all. A 1996 issue of the *Wesleyan Theological Journal* carries a major article by him on "Race Relations and the American Holiness Movement." As few others have been able to do, he has bridged the gulf between faith and learning, religious ideals and social realities, and the ancient biblical text and the task of contemporary preaching.

With gentle courage, our Brother Massey has broached the reluctant racial barriers in North American society and in the church. His has not been an angry call for reparations; his has been a focus on the God who calls for believers to be present agents of the new creation in Christ, courageous members of a reconciling church that, once united itself by God's grace, can bring healing to a broken world. He has taught, preached, and practiced the good news about a *holy* God and a *holy* life in the midst of real human needs and urgent social dilemmas. Prophetically confrontational without ever being angrily abrasive, he is one man of God who has made a lasting difference.

The name James Earl Massey is known and respected widely as one of the most gifted preachers of recent generations. He is referred to in many circles as the "Prince" or "Dean" of preachers. In

1995 Abingdon Press released a major hardback book on Christian preaching for the twenty-first century, written and published wholly in Massey's honor, edited by myself and authored by nineteen of the top professors and practitioners of preaching in the church today. Titled *Sharing Heaven's Music*, this book reflects a fact known so well by the line-up of its distinguished writers. James Earl, poet/pianist, expert exegete, our special holiness brother, has done much to share the inspirations and implications of the Word of God, enabling insight, new life, hope, heaven's music in the pulpit, in the soul, and in the streets.

One finds this in the introduction to *Sharing Heaven's Music*, a direct reflection of the musical and preaching gifts of Massey:

> The gospel itself has a cadence, rhythm, and joy that should be music to the world. Its non-Enlightenment dimensions of vision, imagination, and poetic approaches to grasping and sharing truth are especially relevant to postmodern sensibilities. Designing a Christian sermon is an inspired art form as much as it is a learned skill. Today's multicultural settings, usually discordant, can be transformed by the harmonizing gospel so that diversity becomes a rich melody that witnesses to the God who comes to make all things new and all disciples one (pp. 11-12).

To literally thousands of ministers and ministerial students in dozens of denominations over a span of seven decades, the cadence and courage of James Earl Massey have been heard and seen and deeply felt. He is a humble yet powerful man of God who has been model and mentor, an honored and well-heard mouthpiece of biblical truth.

While his most cherished professional title is "Dean Emeritus & Distinguished Professor-at-Large, Anderson University School of Theology," James Earl Massey's prime identity has always been an obedient and particularly articulate mouthpiece of the Most High God.

3

THE SECRET: SPIRITUAL DEPTH AND DISCIPLINE

by James Earl Massey

James Earl Massey, in dialogue with theologians Donald G. Bloesch and Georgia Harkness, in Barry L. Callen, *Heart of the Matter* (Emeth Press, rev. ed. 2016), 52, 60-61, 110-112. Used by permission.

It's obvious, Georgia [Harkness], that "mysticism" is a word that must be defined very carefully. I know, Don [Bloesch], that you're not claiming that mysticism is completely wrong, or that the many sincere Christians who have sought the mystical depths of faith should not be respected highly. Even so, you are right that real caution is warranted when considering mysticism.

An admirable example of a Christian leader who was "mystical" and still had his feet on solid theological ground is John Wesley. He sought so sincerely for "perfect love" and was influenced significantly by the mystical tradition of Christianity. Wesley initially accepted much of the mystical Christian tradition and then, Don, like you, saw the potential of its serious downsides and backed off some distance. Finally—but cautiously—he came back to some of its abiding values once the necessary theological foundations had been established.

I want to call to mind Colossians 3:1-2. We are instructed there to be serious about living the resurrected life *in Christ,* and that phrase has deep experiential and mystical dimensions. We are to be alert to what's around us and see life from Christ's perspective, through his vision as we learn to live in him. Christian spirituality is just this—because Christ lives, *so do we* with the sight and in the power of his Spirit! Galatians 2:20 is the heart of Christian spirituality. It's no longer my fallen ego that lives, but Christ who lives in and through me.

Let me emphasize the "through me" aspect of Spirit-disciplined Christian living. A particular discipline is demanded of those who would be agents of God's reconciliation in our world. It's a discipline that demands realism in the face of divisive walls, hostility, and hate; a discipline that refuses to cower before the barriers that block harmony; a discipline that properly and steadily informs, encourages, and energizes one to engage in the divine process of reconciliation, that readies one to take responsibility and, understanding the necessity for forgiveness, seeks to effect it by touching the soul, repairing the wrong that injured, and establishing the needed relationship. This discipline demands an active love, a healthy self-image, willingness to risk oneself, and a sense of being companioned in the task by God.

Wonder and intimacy with Jesus Christ are surely critical, but they are hardly attained easily. That's why I have written and preached about the discipline of meditation-prayer. I have wanted to center attention on the work of faith, encouraging believers to think of meditation as a way of enlightenment, as an openness to God in the depths of the consciousness, a process in which the wonder and engagement that we experience in life become doors into the presence of God. In my view, meditation and prayer are natural partners. Meditation keeps prayer thoughtful, while prayer sanctifies the meditation, claiming it for God.

There are times in the higher reaches of prayer when the analytical functions of the mind become suspended. The experience itself is so compelling that analysis fails, interrogation seems a sacrilege, and the only reasonable action is that of yielding oneself to the experience. Occasionally, the disciplined believer can encounter God in a way that transcends the need for words and speech, creeds and religious institutions.

Let me also say a word about the practice of fasting, a discipline practiced and encouraged by Jesus. This spiritual discipline is a reaching out for the spiritual by a temporary suspension of the material. I view this valuable practice in a "sacramental" way that is much more than giving up food. Despite the fear of many people that fasting is only a private sacrifice, a voluntary isolation from the normal stream of life, I disagree. I insist that it's a positive discipline that actually opens a person more widely and can be vital preparation for deeper living and broader public service for God.

At its best, fasting is more than abstinence, in fact hardly about abstinence at all. It's not a denying but actually an affirmative act. It's a way of waiting on God that tends to induce within us an increased awareness of the spiritual dimension of life. Fasting is not a renunciation of life; it is a means by which new life is released within us.

I have elaborated my views on Christian disciplines and the particular disciplines I see as especially valuable in my book *Spiritual Disciplines* (1972, rev. 1985, 2009). There is always something revolutionary and fundamental in the teachings of Jesus that many do not tap into because they don't have the experience of being discipled spiritually in the church. We think in terms of church membership and church activity rather than in terms of church *meaning.* When the meaning is part of our bedrock understanding, then the right activity naturally grows out of it.

Spiritual reality is the key to a serene and happy life. We must not look at the things that are seen. We must live by the things that are unseen, which calls for a true faith in God. As long as a person has that faith as life's focus, there comes a steadiness and surety by which life at its best can be lived.

> *After all, in the beginning, God.*
> *And in the end, God.*
> *And in between, God.*
> *That's the secret!*

SECTION I

WISDOM FOR
BIBLICAL INTERPRETATION
& PREACHING

EDITOR'S SECTION INTRODUCTION

by Cheryl J. Sanders

Senior Pastor of the Third Street Church of God in
Washington, D.C., and Professor of Christian Ethics at
Howard University School of Divinity

My acquaintance with Dr. James Earl Massey as a biblical interpreter and preacher began, in a way of speaking, before I was born. His relationship with the Third Street Church of God in Washington, D.C., where I now serve as senior pastor, started in the late 1940s when he visited the congregation during the tenure of the church's first pastor, Elder C. T. Benjamin. He befriended my parents, Wallace and Doris Sanders, and my grandparents, Ellis and Theodosia Haizlip, who were members of the church. A few years later he developed a unique partnership in ministry with the man who would be called to succeed Elder Benjamin, Dr. Samuel G. Hines.

Prior to his call to Third Street Church of God in 1969, Dr. Hines had exchanged pulpits with Dr. Massey, one in Kingston, Jamaica, and the other in Detroit, Michigan. Both men were revered for their preaching eloquence and skilled interpretation of Scripture. When Dr. Hines died suddenly in 1995, Dr. Massey eulogized him in the company of a vast assembly of mourners with a stellar reflection on the subject "Asleep in Jesus" (1 Thess. 4:13-18). Having now served more than twenty years as the third pastor of Third Street Church of God, I can attest to being the beneficiary of the strong influence and graced encouragement Dr. Massey has sewn into our ministry and leadership for more than seventy years. My own path as a pastor and theological educator has been illuminated by his example.

There are multiple roles and contexts in which Dr. Massey has established himself as a premier preacher and interpreter of Scripture throughout his illustrious career. In addition to his decades of day-to-day work as pastor of a vibrant urban congregation in Detroit, he also served the Church of God (Anderson, IN) at large as preacher for its international radio broadcast. Over the years, Dr. Massey has been called upon to preach for conventions, commencements, camp meetings, revivals and other special occasions for the church. He is especially cherished as a leading light among African Americans in the Church of God, often preaching and teaching at the camp meetings and conventions of the National Association of the Church of God based at West Middlesex, Pennsylvania. His sermons and lectures have fostered a significant impact on African American congregations of various denominations and historically black institutions of higher learning, notably Howard University and Tuskegee University.

Dr. Massey's mastery of ministry and scholarship is amplified by his effectiveness as a communicator and storyteller skilled in the discernment and dissemination of profound theological ideas and biblical insights using language people can understand. He has an uncanny ability to communicate Christian faith and doctrine to diverse audiences and constituencies via the spoken and written word.

In general, this section's essays on biblical interpretation and preaching illustrate three aspects of Massey's exemplary competency as a Christian intellectual: (1) his reputation as a biblical interpreter with a mastery of both classical and vernacular discourses; (2)

SELECT WRITINGS OF JAMES EARL MASSEY

his rapport as an eloquent and authentic purveyor of a distinctively Black Christian hermeneutic; and (3) his repertoire of sermons and exegetical works whose scope reflects a studied acquaintance with many mentors, colleagues and texts.

"The Perennial Power of Preaching" is a transcript of an interview wherein Massey addresses several questions about the nature and character of preaching. His responses emphasize Christ as the defining focus of the kerygmatic message of the gospel. He offers practical insights and observations regarding the preparation of sermons, the teaching of homiletics, and the future of preaching.

In "The Black Preaching Tradition: Insights For All Preachers," Massey draws from the wisdom of Gardner C. Taylor, Henry Mitchell, and others to demonstrate the scope and breadth of Black preaching as a hermeneutical undertaking. Here he examines the cultural roots of Black approaches to Scripture, highlighting the centrality of struggle as a key to understanding how Black preachers interpret the biographies of biblical figures who suffered, overcame, or endured by the help of God. He views the Black preacher as "the visible and vocal agent of the God who sends and shares the divine word."

A second essay follows on the topic of Black preaching, in this instance with special attention to the role of preaching in Black church worship. "African-American Guides to Preaching with Power" is a descriptive outline of the character of Black preaching as it operates in the Black church. Massey cites the homiletical perspectives of Howard Thurman and the poetic insights of James Weldon Johnson to illustrate the climax of impression as an essential element of Black preaching.

Beginning with a brief description of the teaching ministry of Jesus, in "The Preacher Who Would Be a Teacher" Massey captures the nature of the teaching ministry of ordained pastors. He explores four strategies for a teaching ministry: (1) by mass appeal, i.e., as a medium for the sharing of doctrine; (2) in counseling; (3) by teaching classes; and (4) by personal character and example. This essay concludes with a reflection on the measure of a great leader being the ability to teach others and develop leaders.

In "Proclaiming Holiness: The Divine Attribute and Christian Character," Massey gives explicit instructions for preaching about holiness, beginning with a biblical exposition on holiness as an attribute of God that is revealed in Jesus Christ and imparted to the believer. His approach to holiness preaching is grounded in the profound conviction that Christian holiness involves statements, expressions, and prescriptives that reveal "a clear view of human life as God wills it." He commends the study of holiness preachers such as A. W. Tozer, Paul S. Rees, and William M. Greathouse as exemplars who modeled the handling of holiness texts in their pulpit work.

This section ends with "Come Before Winter," a sermon excerpt first preached by Massey from the pulpit of Metropolitan Church of God in Detroit on the "Metropolitan Bible Hour" radio broadcast in October, 1958. His text is Paul's directive to Timothy as recorded in 2 Timothy 4:9: "Do thy diligence to come before winter." This sermon illustrates the tremendous scope of Massey's homiletical research and historically astute resourcefulness as a conscientious student of great preaching. He notes that, beginning in 1915, Dr. Clarence Edward Macartney preached annually from this same text for forty years. Massey's own sermonic reflections upon Paul's evangelical witness in the context of seasons, time, and death are enhanced by intertextual insights from Ecclesiastes and poetic embellishments from William Cullen Bryant's "Thanatopsis" and William Shakespeare's "Julius Caesar."

4

THE PERENNIAL POWER
OF PREACHING

by *James Earl Massey*

Originally appeared in Michael Duduit, ed., *Communicate with Power: Thoughts from America's Top Communicators* (Baker Books, 1996), 121-137. Used by permission.

For over three decades, James Earl Massey has captivated congregations and fellow preachers through his preaching and teaching. Recently retired as dean of the School of Theology and Professor of Preaching and Biblical Studies at Anderson University, Massey first gained a national reputation as pastor of Detroit's Metropolitan Church of God—a pulpit he filled for twenty-nine years. Later, he served as international radio preacher for his denomination and as Dean of the Chapel at Alabama's famed Tuskegee Institute. He is a charter member of *Preaching's* board of contributing editors. With an air of distinct graciousness and a voice of Christian conviction, Massey is an effective and faithful servant of the Word.

Interviewer: How do you define Christian preaching?
Massey: Christian preaching is the kind of statements, based on New Testament teachings, which highlight the ministry of Jesus

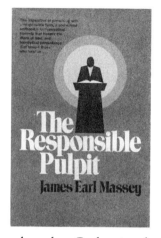

Christ in his relation to human need. Although I believe in sermons about God, which can broaden our understanding of our Creator and the One by whose providence life is ordered, I think the Christian note in preaching is different than the accent on God alone.

I make a distinction between preaching about *God* and preaching about *Christ*. I do believe that the preacher who takes God seriously must finally move to the New Testament, teaching about God *in Jesus Christ*, even if only to understand how God has made himself known through the Son. Yet there are those who preach only about God and not about Jesus the Christ. Their understanding of Jesus as Son will have to wrestle with the whole New Testament notion of Jesus as Savior. Christian preaching has to deal with that esoteric element in our Lord's ministry.

Interviewer: How do you view this as a problem in the contemporary church? Do you think that this is a particularly modern problem?

Massey: I do think this is a modern problem that is compounded by the increasing pluralism of our day. The whole notion of diversity as espoused in the seminaries has tended to level all religions in the mind of the average seminarian. Unless the professor distinctly deals with Christian particularities, the one who graduates from seminary will go out preaching *religiously*, but not *Christianly*, calling very little if any attention to Jesus in his salvific role.

This is one of the strong elements evangelicalism continues to insist upon. And it becomes a scandal in discussions between evangelicals and others. There are those who wish to leave matters of salvation to God and decline to deal with these from the pulpit, but the Christian preacher is under mandate from God to highlight the ministry of his Son.

Interviewer: As you think of the sermon in this Christocentric context, how does the message function within the Christian community to bear witness to Christ?

Massey: The sermon becomes, first of all, an invitational word to consider Christ. Second, the sermon becomes a means of expanding one's understanding of Christ. Sometimes the understanding must come before a decision can be reached. The sermon becomes a tool for helping a person consider Christ in the New Testament witness, and then the sermon takes on a teaching function. According to the New Testament, the preacher must be a teaching minister. The preacher has to lead the congregation to understand the meaning of Christ for all of life and to see all of life in the light of Christ. This tool we call the sermon is an invitational means, but also a means for increasing our understanding.

Interviewer: So, the sermon should always place a decision before the congregation?

Massey: Yes, and I as preacher must be persuaded to act upon the information placed before me in the text. All information concerning Jesus Christ presents me with a decision. As I receive this information, I must be persuaded to act upon it. All New Testament witness concerning Jesus Christ presents implications—and I must be persuaded to act upon the implications, to trust the implications.

It is not only the preacher who must heed these implications, but all those who hear the preacher's voice. I might speak a word and lack the persuasiveness to help the person who heard me to follow through. But I must leave in the hands of God the sending along of someone else who might be able to bring that persuasion, to build upon the foundation I have made. I do not expect always to see everyone who hears me believe or accept God's Word, but at least I have done my part in getting them ready for this decision.

Interviewer: How do you prepare for your preaching? Beyond that, how do you teach your students to prepare for their preaching?

Massey: Two basic ways: Either move from a human need to find what God has said with reference to that need in Scripture, or move from Scripture to that need. Whether one is sensitized by human need to move from that point to Scripture, or whether one moves from one's study of Scripture to a human need, either way God is honored and the congregation is helped. The actual manner of preparing the sermon is a different matter, but the manner of preaching must be centered in that union between the human need and God's truth.

Interviewer: Given that union between the text of Scripture and its message regarding human need, how do you move from the text to the sermon?

Massey: I place the text at one end of an ellipse, the human hearer at the other end of the ellipse, and between the two I focus on the dynamic which can help the hearer to understand the meaning of this for his or her life. The relation to the text allows the text to open up as I see one's face, someone's setting, situation, or need. The text opens up as I overhear what the Spirit of God is saying in that text and throughout the whole of Scripture.

As Donald Grey Barnhouse used to say, the text should pivot to which the whole of Scripture bears witness. Not that I pour all of Scripture into one text, but all of the Bible that I have learned is highlighted and feeds the meaning of a particular text.

Interviewer: What is the greatest threat to genuine, authentic, biblical preaching in our own day?

Massey: There are three major threats: first, the threat of generalities, second, the threat of pluralism, and third, the threat of popularity. Generalities—trying to relate all human knowledge in such a way that we do not remain particularly Christian—level everything. The whole business of pluralism, in which we wih not to offend anyone, leads many to leave off speaking as a particularly Christian voice. The global concern of our time has opened us up to the reality of differences and to the function of these differences as valid and meaningful. But the Christian preacher must always be identified with and serve the Christian particularity.

That relates to the third threat. When we want to be popular and please the crowds, we too often fall into generalities and avoid particularities, and therefore do not "sound the note" that we were called upon by God to keep before the public. There is a scandal of particularity to the Christian faith that is germane to the faith itself, and apart from that, preaching has no quickening power to change human life.

You might deal religiously with any number of notions, and may even do so devotionally. You may be spell-binding in the pulpit by way of oratory and rhetoric, but the Christian has something more to say, and that is the *kerygma*. The *kerygma* takes us beyond generalities, beyond pluralism, beyond popularity, to reach to the very reason Jesus Christ came.

Interviewer: With this issue of the *kerygma,* how does one confront the kerygmatic function of the sermon in each individual message?

Massey: This becomes a problem, because in the whole range of the pastor's work, there will be times when we should deal with other important biblical concerns. That is why we pay close attention to the Christian year. Not every sermon will appear to be kerygmatic in the same sense, but all must be informed by the *kerygma* and by the realization that the *kerygma* must ultimately be served.

Interviewer: But as you acknowledge, Christian preaching, genuinely Christian preaching, *cannot* fail to be kerygmatic. The problem is that so much passes for Christian preaching these days when, in reality, it is something else. The Christian preacher cannot escape Christ and must come face-to-face with him at every issue, and in every text.

Massey: Yes, we certainly cannot escape the *kerygma*. It has to inform us always. For instance, in dealing with Psalm 139 that is not explicitly Christocentric, Christ is not explicitly mentioned, it is nonetheless theocentric. Through that psalm, an individual has the opportunity to sense God's nearness to us.

Those verses speak of us as "fearfully and wonderfully made," known by God within the secrecy of the womb. But this passage ultimately speaks of the love extended to us by God through Jesus Christ.

All preaching gets us ready for Christ, introduces us to Christ, or helps us expand our understanding of Christ and relate more readily to him.

Interviewer: Who have been the primary models who have helped you to develop your understanding of preaching?

Massey: There were three main models. One was my father George W. Massey, Sr. My father influenced me because of his command of Scripture. He could quote Scripture at length—so well that if you quoted any Scripture, he could tell you where you were and join you in quoting it. So I learned from my father the importance of memorizing Scripture.

The second model was George Buttrick. He was a great stimulant at the level of outlining, learning how to let the Scripture unfold logically. He helped me to sense the mood in the text and then to let the sermon be shaped by that mood. Buttrick knew how to let the text shape the structure of the sermon and serve the mood.

The third person who helped me was Howard Thurman, who modeled what I thought was an excellent devotional attitude toward God and toward the text as God's Word to us, so that the preacher becomes a worshiper along with the rest of the congregation. The preacher should not just say something to the congregation, but should respond to that pressure brought to bear upon himself or herself in the presence of God in the context of worship.

Interviewer: What do you see as the future of preaching, viewed in light of the students you see day by day?

Massey: I discern on the part of my students a strong interest in how to share Christ's Word with an aching generation. They are very much aware of the hunger of the human heart, and how little has really been done by a secular society to meet those needs. Most of the students we now receive at the seminary are in their second careers. They are generally older than previous students, most are working, some have several degrees already. When they come to us, life has already prepared them to grapple with human need— much more so than the younger seminarians. The typical student of years ago came to seminary with a need to find out who they were. Today's student is more likely to have that settled, and so they have a strong sense of dedication to get about the business.

Interviewer: You have taught and influenced thousands of preachers through your teaching, preaching, and writing. What is your word to your preaching colleagues-partners in the service of the Word?

Massey: Preaching as God intended it will never lose its power nor its reason for being. Human concern will shift with every generation, but God's means of addressing human need will never change. So to find out how God has moved in history and to be open to follow that path is to remain relevant. Outside of that path, there is no relevance, even if there is, for a time, attractiveness.

The only path of success in God's eye is for us to follow what he has mandated for us to do. And that mandate, as spoken through his servant Paul, is to preach the Word, in season and out of season.

5

THE BLACK PREACHING TRADITION: INSIGHTS FOR ALL PREACHERS

by James Earl Massey

Originally appeared in Raymond E. Bailey,

Hermeneutics for Preaching: Approaches to Contemporary

Interpretations of Scripture (Broadman Press, 1992), 135-159.

Abbreviated. Used by permission.

Preachers who take their calling seriously know that hermeneutical work is an almost daily necessity, and that this regular exercise in faith and study is imperative to grant the substance, sustenance, and proper focus needed for effective pulpit work. Since the art of preaching has to do with applying the insights of Scripture to meet human needs, it is incumbent upon the preacher to know and follow the principles for interpreting Scripture rightly, fully dependent upon the sacred writings as primary source of witness about God's way with us humans.

The hermeneut—the one who practices hermeneutics—"is he who, having been addressed by the word of God and, having heard, is enabled to speak, interpret, or translate what he has heard into the human vernacular so that its power is transmitted through speech. If the minister is not a hermeneut, he has missed his vocation."[1] This chapter treats the three hermeneutical perspectives which traditionally have governed the African-American approach to the preaching task.

Perspective One: The Adequacy and Immediacy of the Biblical Witness

It is axiomatic in the African-American church that the Bible must be honored as the basis for pulpit work. The Black hermeneut, like all others, must deal with the manifold forms and genres found in the Bible, and must interrogate them for their intended meaning, using any and all skills and tools available through training and experience. Attention is centered mainly on "the life meanings of the Bible, for which it was handed down orally in the first place."[2]

The Black hermeneut seeks to escape the limitations of a skewing liberalism and avoid getting entangled in the analytical technicalities of modern critical approaches which can deaden lively imaginativeness and vital utterance. The concern is ever toward meanings for living life. In the African-American church setting, the preaching emphasis is seldom if ever upon analytical absoluteness as to concepts about the nature and scope of Scripture, but rather upon an openness to the basic message and purpose for which the Word was given and preserved.

The cultural roots of the Black approach to Scripture honor the folk appeal reflected throughout the biblical record. It is this cultural difference in the way Scripture is approached by African-Americans that has been responsible, in part, for keeping Black

---

1   Robert W. Funk, *Language. Hermeneutic and Word of God* (Harper & Row, 1966), 13-14.

2   Henry H. Mitchell, *The Recovery of Preaching*: Yale Beecher Lectures 1974 (Harper & Row, 1977), 89.

preaching free from divisive theological controversies and from deadening abstractions. In Black preaching, and in the hermeneutic by which it happens, the focus is not on concepts to be voiced and treated intellectually but upon an experience to be expected and enjoyed through an openness to the biblical witness. The Black preacher's study of Scripture for preaching is with a view to discern the experience to which the text points, and to plan the best means by which a vision of that experience can be shared in the pulpit. Gardner C. Taylor reports, "anyone who will open himself or herself to the revelation of God contained in the Bible will find endless preaching, better still, will be found by it, which demands to be delivered of the preacher by pulpit presentation."[3]

The ruling principle by which the Black hermeneutic operates in reading Scripture is to see all things in light of the deliverance theme highlighted there. The basic methodological perspective by which the entire revelatory canon is finally viewed is the biblical theme of God acting to deliver humans from their plights. This perspectival theme of freedom is a constant in Scripture. Paul's shared understanding of what God has accomplished in the human interest through Jesus Christ is best summed up in the word "freedom," since he uses it in so many connections: freedom from sin, release from subjection to the powers of the evil age, escape from bondage to the elemental spirits of the universe, freedom from confinement to legalisms, and even ultimate release from a limiting mortality by means of a coming resurrection from death.

Two related concerns merge in the African-American pulpit: liberation and community.[4] These do not allow for abstractions

---

3   Gardner C. Taylor, *How Shall They Preach: Yale Beecher Lectures 1976* (Elgin, IL: Progressive Baptist Publishing House, 1977), 59.

4   See Olin P. Moyd, *Redemption in Black Theology* (Valley Forge: Judson Press, 1979).

in preaching, nor for fruitless intellectualizing. To quote Mitchell again: "The Black devotion to the Bible is not anti-intellectual; it simply and wisely avoids intellectualisms.[5]

Perspective Two: The Importance of the Hearer's Situation in Planning the Sermon

A sermon can take its rise from a text that generates it or from musing about some human need or concern, but whatever the original occasion that shapes it, the final focus of the sermon must apply its message to the hearer's life. The truth it contains must match an end to which it is projected. This hermeneutic principle demands that the hearers be taken seriously and their life situations given due regard.

This perspective highlights the need to keep the fundamentals of the text properly wedded to the function of the sermon as a medium of intended help. The traditional emphasis in Black preaching on the importance of storytelling grows out of this concern. It is the reason story is the chief mode used by African-Americans in preaching.

Thirty years ago the scholarly religious world was in disarray, puzzled about the problems associated with speaking about God; the need was being voiced to rediscover ways and means to communicate religious meanings effectively, and many modes of utterance were being vigorously explored as the question continued to be asked about how to speak meaningfully about God in a secular and nihilistic age. It was during that questing time that Amos N. Wilder published those seminal studies on "The Language of the

---

5   Henry H. Mitchell, *Black Preaching: The Recovery of a Powerful Art* (Nashville: Abingdon Press, 1990), 59.

Gospel" and called attention to the modes, genres, and immediacy of the early Christian rhetoric reflected in the New Testament literature. One of the genres he treated was that of story.[6] There was considerable scholarly interest in his study because he directed attention back to the qualities of the language modes by which the early Christians captured the attention and, later, the recognition of a world hungry for meaning.

The strategic use of story is proverbial in the Black preaching tradition. The story mode touches everyone, leaving no hearer disengaged. This popular mode for preaching addresses the hearer at the deepest level of need because it not only interests but invites, it challenges and engages, it opens the self to new possibilities. A specimen of such story preaching will be shared as part of this chapter.

Black life in America has been the context for struggle, combat, continual pressures due to unfair treatment and unmitigated woes. Always under attack, the African-American need for spiritual resources has been acute. The Black hermeneut understands the struggle and preaches with insight because of having had a common share in it. This is why African-American preaching has appealed so often and so effectively to the biographies of struggle found in Scripture, highlighting how those who suffered in that earlier day overcame or endured by the help of God. The character of such preaching is thus more interpretative than descriptive, more pastoral and therapeutic than didactic and propositional.

The Black preacher knows that where the hearer stands in life will make all the difference for being understood and relevant. It is only out of such an awareness of the hearer's situated place in life that the sermon approach can be planned well and the sermon

---

6   Sub-titled "Early Christian Rhetoric" (Harper & Row, 1964), re-issued in 1971.

application effectively made. The Black hermeneutic always keeps this in view. From the earliest period of Black life in America until now, the preaching needed by those who are part and parcel of the African-American community must be geared to deal with "the sufferings and needs of their days."[7]

Perspective Three: The Centrality of Preaching as an Agency for Hearing and Faith

Deeply rooted in the African-American preaching tradition is the belief that preaching is an agency both for mediated meaning and a sense of divine presence. The person of the preacher is crucial because he or she is the visible and vocal agent of the God who sends and shares the divine word.

1. The preacher is traditionally and expectantly *identified with the divine word.* He or she is both an authorized handler of the sacred text and the one who applies its message to the situated life and need of the hearers. Expected to be filled with the word God intends to be uttered, the preacher is understood as the sharer of a solution. This was a part of the rich understanding out of which the late Joseph A. Johnson, Jr., wrote when he commented, "The Black preacher does not merely use the Bible, but rather he permits the Bible to use him."[8]

    The preacher is expected to be a hearer in preparation for being a speaker. This is clear from the hallowed

---

7   See Albert J. Raboteau, *Slave Religion:* The "Invisible Institution" in the Antebellum South (Oxford University Press, 1978), 213.

8   Joseph A. Johnson, Jr., *Proclamation Theology* (Shreveport, LA: Fourth Episcopal District Press, 1977), 45.

call in the Shema (Deut. 6:4) and all the other instances when God issued a summons of an attention-claiming character (see Isa. 1:10; 7:13; Jer. 2:4; 7:2; 10:1, etc.). In his teaching and preaching, Jesus knew that the people understood his call to "hear" what he was saying as invitational. "Let anyone with ears listen" (Matt. 11:15, 13:9, 43). The African-American church tradition honors the preacher as someone who has been called by God to hear, first, and who is then sent to speak for God. This view has a biblical warrant in that awesomely promising word from Jesus about those sent to represent and speak for him: "Whoever listens to you listens to me" (Luke 10:16).

2. In the African-American church setting, the preacher is understood as related by service to the highest frame of reference, *as a "man of God" or "woman of God."* This view of the preacher can make a world of difference in how the preaching can be encouraged or projected. The African-American church setting has a mind-set that conditions the freedom of the black preacher for his or her work, always associating that work with the highest frame of reference: the God who speaks.

3. The black preacher is honored as *someone intimately related to the need and future of the church.* This also makes the preaching task an honored and desired one. There is the perennial need to build bridges between the meanings in the Word and the daily concerns of the people—in a word, modeling the message. This is why the late Kelly Miller Smith commented that

communication actually begins not when the text and the sermon title are announced, but when the minister functions in the community in relation to critical social circumstances and shows social sensitivity prior to proclamation."[9]

It is quite clear that much more remains to be searched out and set forth before any definitive treatment of the African-American hermeneutic for preaching can be prepared and sent forth. My own treatment has been set down under three major perspectives, and from within the history of the tradition under review, these three are in my judgment the most central in scope and influence.

EDITOR'S NOTES

James Earl Massey completes this chapter by providing the background process he would use in developing a sample sermon for an African-American—or any—congregation based on Genesis 47:7-10. He explains the standard hermeneutical procedures and follows the perspectives above. They cause him to focus on the odd reply of Jacob after Pharaoh asked him his age: "How many are the days of the years of your life?" Jacob's reply was not in the spirit one would expect after being greeted so warmly as a guest in the land.

Massey: "The reply reeked with lament, its wording full of evident unpleasantness. Jacob's reply had no lift in it; it was moody,

---

9 *Social Crisis Preaching*: Lyman Beecher Lectures, 1983 (Mercer University Press, 1984), 80-81.

as if something other than the benefits now available to him had burdened his spirit. What was it that overshadowed his mind in this place of opportunity, a place where food would no longer be scarce? What so affected Jacob's reason that he spoke as if he had none? Whence this moodiness at a time when rejoicing was in order? Pharaoh and Joseph seemed gladdened by the old man's presence, but Jacob's mood did not match their joy."

Massey says that the story-line of the emerging sermon must be introduced in such a way "that the hearers will be gripped, as was the preacher, by the need to understand why Jacob answered Pharaoh as he did." Massey picks up biblical clues and places himself into the thought process of Jacob, observing:

1. Jacob's moodiness was occasioned in part by <u>fear</u>, fear that he might not live long enough to return to Canaan.

2. But Jacob's moodiness was stirred by another problem: remembered frustrations. His memory bank was overflowing with sad scenes from across his life: "few and evil have been the days of the years of my life."

Thus, the sermon title becomes "Looking Beyond Our Laments." Having told the story of Jacob, Massey suggests a sermon conclusion that ties the preacher and Bible story directly to the life experiences of the current hearers. Therefore, he suggests that the sermon climax by posing this question to the congregation before giving a needed assurance. Here is the question:

What frustrations make you moody? Watch how you handle them because laments can not only change your countenance, they can block your reason and distort your perspective. Laments can make us sorry company. I wonder what Joseph thought as he listened to his aged father darken the scene in the court with his moody words. I wonder what Pharaoh thought as he watched and listened to the old man.

And here are Massey's suggestions for conveying a concluding assurance and hope for God's struggling people:

There is much in life that can stir a lament within us. There are indeed conditions which make life unpleasant, unrewarding, conditions which to any reasonable mind are apparently unreasonable and unfair. You are thinking about some of those conditions as I speak, conditions that you have known. We all know what it is to lament, and we all know why we sometimes indulge in the moodiness out of which laments rise.

Any reasonable mind also knows that moodiness can make us like misfits, like Jacob before Pharaoh, so locked in the prison of his moods that his spirit lacked the openness needed to receive the hospitality being extended to him as a privileged guest in the land. Yes, moods can make us misfits. Lingering laments can affect our work, our family, our friendships, our very souls.

But there is a way out of the lament mood. There is a way out of the prison of our feelings. The road of faith is that way: faith that life is not through with us, faith that feelings are not the final facts in any case, faith that God still knows and cares about who and where we are.

This is the open secret for the courage of our slave ancestors as they faced the unyielding demands of their hard lot in life. When their frustrations seemed unrelenting, when their troubles seemed unending, when their sorrows continued to multiply beyond all counting, and when their hopes were like raisins shriveling under the hot sun, they caught a glimpse of God that helped them to look beyond their laments. Yes, they did sing, "Nobody knows the trouble I see, nobody knows my sorrow" but, having looked beyond themselves to catch a vision of the justice and mercy of God, they went on to sing, "Glory, Hallelujah!"

The Genesis record tells us that Jacob finally lifted his eyes and looked beyond himself, and as he did, God gave the old patriarch some prophetic insights for the family members gathered about his bed as he faced his end. Unless we learn to *look* beyond our laments, we will never be able to *live* beyond them!

6

AFRICAN-AMERICAN GUIDES TO PREACHING WITH POWER

by James Earl Massey

Originally appeared in James Massey, *The Responsible Pulpit* (Warner Press, 1974), 101-111. Abbreviated.
Used by permission.

Within the last few years it has become increasingly common to speak of a "black preaching tradition," meaning that style and manner of preaching that characterizes the preaching usually heard within the black churches in America. There are some significant insights to be derived from the black preaching tradition, insights which help any preacher from any tradition to sense more clearly how to keep the verbal witness of the pulpit both virile, engaging, and effective. Some of these insights follow.

Functional

First, in the black church *the sermon is functional.* That is, the sermon is never regarded as a product for its own sake, or even as an art form, but as a means to an end. And that end? The end is to initiate some person into the faith, instruct some person on how to live, inspire some person to go on living with hope despite troubles and strain, give insight into problems and possibilities within and beyond those problems. The sermon is functional in its intent to liberate the hearer's spirit, give life and sustain faith.

Festive

Second, in the black church *the sermon is festive.* Black preaching is never abstract and tangential. It deals with concrete life, with what is experienced in the daily round, and it does so without arid speculation or poised sophistry. The black sermon is usually "playful" in its measured cadences and speech liberties. The speech-result is no less true, no less sensible, even when done with "instinct" and fervid imagination. The black sermon is a kind of "soul-piece," a way of "deep calling unto deep," to use a biblical figure.

Black preaching excels in being an invitation to joy, even in the midst of sorrow and struggle. It does so by means of strong affirmation about God and through the contagious note of witnessed faith. Whatever festivity and playfulness fill the black sermon are there because they have been *won* in the midst of sorrow and lament, making the sermon itself an open expression of faith that has worked its way through, and now speaks in praise of God. This amounts to a depth theology of soul-worship. The festivity which results is never an opiate, therefore, and the playfulness is not calculated escapism. The black sermon celebrates remembered victories in the midst of raw demands.

Those who make battle daily on the many fronts of personal and public life need a worship occasion that both informs and inspires them. What worshiper can be untouched and unmoved by the preacher's recital of the victories of faith? Who does not rejoice to *sense* the truth that his present moment, however dark and forbidding, is not the last moment? Who cannot sense the joy of freedom when he realizes that the contradictions of life are not final contradictions, that the possibilities which remain are many and not yet exhausted by any means? Who can fail to anticipate victories when the assurance registers that goodness and mercy will follow him? All of this keeps the biblical tradition one of "good news" alive in the gathered church. The play element is important in it all, but it is the play of sentiment, suggestion, and a serious faith that rejoices in God.

Communal

A third characteristic in the black preaching tradition is its *communalism.* The sermon must aid the sense of group life. The well-known tradition of call-and-response should be understood in this light. Many churches of varying denominational contexts are accustomed to plan a call-response action through a reading, litany, or chant; the black sermon is itself a call for response. The black preacher usually allows for and expects acts of communalism among his hearers, even vocal expressions of praise, agreement, encouragement, and prompting. The speaker's word alerts, calls, promises, energizes, bestows, blesses, challenges, corrects, confutes, chastises, claims, convicts, convinces.

Although specific responses among black church audiences will vary in keeping with many factors (educational levels, size of church, denominational orientation, social setting, age groupings, to name a few), it is not infrequent that audible expressions of response will occur in most black settings where the preacher speaks with festive bearing, for a functional purpose, and with a sense of community with his hearers.

Communalism is also evident in the musical portion of the worship service. There is something more here than just group singing or everyone singing the same song or hymn in the harmony of sound and rhythm. There is actual and contagious engagement with each other in the music. James H. Cone has commented: "Black music is unifying because it confronts the individual with the truth of black existence and affirms that black being is possible only in a communal context."

The black sermon is itself somewhat musical at times, with a basic rhythm to its cadences and tonal variations that energize, envelope, and stir the worshipers to share their faith, even emotionally. This aspect of the black tradition is akin in some ways to the Hebrew concept of the creative power of the spoken word. This proclivity to the oral is part of an evident concern for community, with words being used to generate both vision and sense, fundamental understanding and emotional direction.

Radical

Fourth, the nature of preaching in the black church calls for the sermon to be *radical:* it must take the hearer to the roots of personal life and vital response. More often than not, this radicality demands that the preacher be a person of courage.

There is a story that has been preserved about the radicality of Dr. William Holmes Borders of Atlanta, Georgia. The story tells about a message Borders gave during the 1948 Georgia Baptist Convention, held at Pelham, a small but problematic town in that state. As principal speaker, Borders used the occasion for a major thrust against the ungodly system of segregation, urging more militancy against it and telling his black hearers that it was time for them to stand up to whites. The whole town soon heard about Borders' statements and a white mob gathered outside the church where the convention was being held. Borders preached on, seemingly oblivious to possible danger to himself and the group. He advised not only courage but politeness, wedding the radical offensiveness of his stand for rights with the reasonableness of peaceful means.

As for "radicality" on the part of the preacher, these words of Rudolf Bultmann explain and highlight that characteristic:

> Proclamation is personal address. It is authoritative address, the address of the word of God, which, paradoxically, is spoken by a man, the preacher. As God's representative (cf. 2 Cor. 5:20), the preacher stands over against the congregation. He does not speak as its voice nor does he bring to consciousness or to clear expression whatever may slumber in his hearers in the way of ideals and feeling, yearnings or even unexpressed certainties. To be sure, he can do all this, but only in order to confront his hearers with the word of God, to place them under the shifting and judging power of the word and therewith under the promise of grace.

Dr. Raymond S. Jackson preached with strong concern across his ministry about the question of birth control. His reasons were personal. Says he, "Some of my minister friends who advocate birth control asked me if I believed in it. My answer was a positive No! I added, 'And if you want my personal reason, here it is: I happen to be the fourteenth child in a family of fifteen children. Consequently, if my mother had started controlling, I wouldn't be here to tell the story.' If I, the fourteenth, had a right to life, liberty, and the pursuit of happiness, so does every other child, however large the family may be." Jackson adds, "Incidentally, I am the only minister out of that family of fifteen children!" His reasons, then, are both personal and religious.

Radicality in the sermon engages the hearer. It makes him know that he is being confronted, that necessity is being laid upon him to respond. True preaching is always confrontational. The speaking of God's word to man is a radical act; it places man before God as a "thou" but not as an equal, as one who needs to be guided, confronted, helped, taught, disciplined, forgiven, renewed. Preaching is a special process with a special goal and end in view. Radical means are essential to that process and end.

Climactic

A fifth essential characteristic of black preaching is *to produce a climax of impression for the hearer*. The sermon is a functional instrument, based upon a distinctive scriptural word, calculated in faith to win and nurture the life of the hearer. A kind of feeling-attitude is important for a proper response. Zestful speech encourages this result. The will for community, and means for nurturing it, is also essential. So are mind-engaging lines. Imagination also renders its service and continues at that service even while the process of delivery continues.

Scripture, interpretation, zestful speech, a concern for community, mind-engaging lines, controlled imagination—all these are calculated to incite the hearer to participate as well as listen, leading him to a climax of impression for faith and life. Feeling-attitude is best generated when the sermon betrays the preacher's experience with the truth he proclaims, when something presents itself as an evidence of his partnership with God, something of the supernatural flow in the gospel. Preaching is as much contagion as it is conversing; perhaps it is really more contagion than conversing.

Dr. Howard Thurman has been credited with giving a worship service some of the atmosphere of a concert hall. This was not a criticism but a compliment. The one who made the statement had often heard him preach and was quite mindful that Thurman's sermons involved him in a climax of impression. That preacher does not overdramatize his messages, nor does he depend upon mass psychology. He knows how to involve his listeners and make them share with him in a contagious moment of truth. He bends his skills to this end. Is this not what happens in a concert hall? As a servant of truth, the preacher is concerned to produce a climate for faith and a climax of impression by which that faith begins and acts to the honor of God in the human heart.

Howard Thurman recalls some of the sermons he heard in his boyhood years. The pastor of the family church was quite adept at effective preaching. Thurman reports, "Sometimes the preacher gave graphic descriptions of hell as if he had been there on a personally conducted tour."[1] That preacher had learned to use his powers of imagination in the service of biblical realities, producing intrigue, insight, and necessary caution for life. "There was not a Sunday," Thurman adds, "when the preacher did not, in some way or another, take everybody by Calvary."[2] The trip was in the service of the redemptive theme. To the sharing church, and especially to little Howard, sitting in his grandmother's lap, "the drama was exhilarating. . . . It was so real, so real . . . ."[3] A climax of impression had been reached.

In his autobiography *Along This Way*, James Weldon Johnson has recalled a similar experience in his contact with a certain

---

1   Elizabeth Yates, *Howard Thurman: Portrait of a Practical Dreamer* (New York: The John Day Company, 1964), 35.

2   Ibid., 35-36.

3   Ibid., 37.

preaching service one Sunday night in Kansas City. Johnson has, however, described the service as an exhibition, pointing up the comic and extraneous aspects of the evangelist's antics and the congregation's response. Nevertheless, Johnson admitted, "I was fascinated by this exhibition; moreover, something primordial in me was stirred.[4] Although the service, such as it was, did not dispose him to worship, it did gather him in an atmosphere of creative impression.

The preacher's abandon, picturesque speech, freedom in handling his materials, sonorous diction, native idioms, and syncopated rhythms so touched Johnson's imagination that, before the preacher finished, Johnson took a slip of paper from his pocket and "somewhat surreptitiously jotted down some ideas,"[5] which he soon shaped into "The Creation," a sermon in verse. Johnson could not commend that exhibition as a worthy service; but he could not deny the climax of impression which he had experienced.

It is true that art can be exploited and turned to the false end of exhibitionism. But the prostitution of an art must not blind us to its proper end. A preacher must not ignore the soundness of the theory that his sermon should produce a climax of impression for his hearers. Preaching at its best involves this, and more; but if it lacks this ability, no matter whatever else it has, such a sermon will make no difference.

---

4   *Along This Way: The Autobiography of James Weldon Johnson* (New York: The Viking Press, 1933), 336.

5   Ibid., 336.

7

THE PREACHER WHO WOULD
BE A TEACHER

by James Earl Massey

Originally appeared in *Preaching on the Brink,*
ed. Martha J. Simmons (Abingdon Press, 1996), 93-102.
Abbreviated. Used by permission.

T he church began under the ministry of an itinerant teaching preacher known as Jesus of Nazareth. Those who heard him teach called him "Rabbi" because of his masterful style and the engaging substance of his work. The Aramaic *rabbi,* "my master," was the title of address used when conversing with Jewish teachers of repute. It is used again and again in the Gospel accounts when persons address Jesus as he teaches.

The New Testament writings reflect the fact that the spirit of teaching was strong in the churches during the first century. Two reasons stood behind this: (1) Jesus had been "a teacher who has come from God" (John 3:2), which made the teaching ministry stand in continuing esteem; and (2) the church leaders Jesus appointed to continue his ministry knew that sound living depends upon sound teaching.[1]

---

1   See Romans 6:17-19; Philippians 4:8-9; Titus 2:1-8; and 2 Peter 1:2-8.

The early teachers of the church planned strategically, intent to guide the awakened intellect, provide religious answers for the questioning mind, and offer a systematized body of truths for the questing soul. The teaching reflected and reported in the New Testament writings mainly involves "believers," persons already won to the Christian faith through the preaching of the gospel. The Epistles show that *didache* (what is taught) was understood as necessary follow-up to *kerygma* (what is proclaimed).

By the time the Pastoral Epistles were written, it was expected that one who chose to be a pastor would also be "an apt teacher" (1 Tim. 3:2). In fact, the stipulations regarding pastoral ministry made teaching an imperative function.[2] Across the ages, the church has always needed and expected a teaching ministry.[3]

The Role of Teaching Pastor

Given the unique history and posture of American society, no professional role has been more strategic to social progress than the teaching pastor. The founding and continuing development of the nation's churches, together with their strategic impact upon the development of the character of the nation during this experiment in democracy, has depended in great measure upon the work of teaching pastors.[4]

---

2   See J. N. D. Kelly, *A Commentary on the Pastoral Epistles: 1 Timothy, 2 Timothy, Titus* (New York: Harper and Row, 1963), 766; see also 190 on 2 Timothy 2:24.

3   See Gerald E. Knoff, "The Churches Expect a Teaching Ministry," in *The Minister and Christian Nurture*, ed. Nathaniel F. Forsyth (Abingdon Press, 1957), 9-26; Floyd V. Filson, "The Christian Teacher in the First Century," *Journal of Biblical Literature* 60 (1941). 317-28; James D. Smart, *The Teaching Ministry of the Church* (Westminster Press, 1954), 13-19; Robert C. Worley, *Preaching and Teaching in the Earliest Church*, 131-51; Clark M. Williamson and Ronald Allen, *The Teaching Minister* (Westminster/John Knox Press, 1991), 47-64.

4   See especially Dewitte Holland, Jess Yoder, and Hubert Vance Taylor, eds., *Preaching in American History: Selected Issues in the American Pulpit, 1630-1967* (Abingdon Press, 1969), and the companion volume, Holland, Yoder, and

As servant-leader in a church, the pastor shares status and authority with all others called and commissioned to be "trust officers" in the service of the Lord. Called and sent to share and pass on the kerygmatic message about salvation, and to train believers in the values and implementation of the good news from God, the pastor is expected to teach what the church teaches. In this service, he or she follows the lead of the first Christian preachers and teachers, aptly described by Albert C. Outler as "traditioners-trust officers of the Christian treasure of truth, qualified judges of 'right teaching.'"[5] As a teacher, the pastor not only identifies that tradition but is identified with it and by it.

The Christian gospel is God's invitation to an experience, an experience inclusive of moral, spiritual, and social effects. The New Testament literature is the initial record of that experience as registered in the lives of distinct persons, and that record is the main sourcebook for the noble, serious, instructive, and necessary work of the teaching pastor. It is from within the province of this distinct biblical record that the Christian preacher is expected and authorized to teach what the church teaches.

The Ways a Preacher Teaches
There are at least four strategic means by which the ordained minister may teach. First, there is the *"mass appeal" of preaching.* Preaching allows moral and spiritual instruction to be shared in mass fashion, in a popular medium, but with individual impact.

Taylor, eds., *Sermons in American History: Selected Issues in the American Pulpit, 1630-1967* (Abingdon Press, 1971).

5   Albert C. Outler, "The Sense of Tradition in the Ante-Nicene Church," in *The Heritage of Christian Thought: Essays in Honor of Robert Lowry Calhoun*, eds. Robert E. Cushman and Egil Grislis (Harper & Row, 1965), 9.

According to the Synoptic Gospels, there was an evident blend between preaching and teaching in the spoken words of Jesus. There are passages in the Gospel accounts in which the terms *preaching* and *teaching* are used interchangeably, so that the action of Jesus in addressing his hearers in public appears pointedly didactic and declarative at the same time. Jesus instructed in order to inspire; he had to give content in order to share comfort. Understanding is imperative for those who seek to live out their faith, and aptness in relating biblical truths to personal questions and needs of people keeps the teaching preacher linked with them as an essential helper of their faith. The readiness and skill to instruct must surely be reflected when the congregation gathers to worship God and be addressed out of God's Word.

True religious experience is more than an emotional mood; it is a vital happening in response to something taught and caught. The climate of modernity does not inspire faith, but it does press persons to seek and locate a faith. Preaching calls attention to the Christian faith, and it does so by isolating certain facts and truths from inside the experience of that faith. Preaching that is religiously instructive will naturally be doctrinal—not doctrine for doctrine's sake but for the sake of the people's understanding and use of faith to live. In order to focus the use of doctrine, the preacher must first understand the way doctrine can help those he or she is preaching to. Doctrine then breathes life; it shows itself as more than an abstract subject and claims attention as a necessary message that attracts, alerts, and assures. The preaching that really matters does not separate inspiration from something taught.

Howard Thurman writes about how impressed his grandmother was with the preaching that she, a former slave, had heard from a certain slave preacher when she was a girl. That slave preacher had drilled into the consciousness of his Black hearers the notion that they did not have to feel inferior because they were enslaved. Thurman writes, "How everything in me quivered with the pulsing tremor of raw energy when, in her recital, she would come to the triumphant climax of the minister: 'You are not niggers. You—you are not slaves. You are God's children.' This established for them the ground of personal dignity."[6] And out of that profound sense of being children of God, those slaves could handle the pressures of their days.

A second means by which the pastor teaches is by *counseling*. Pastoral counseling ranks among the central services a pastor is expected to make available to those who seek it. Wayne E. Oates has listed several levels within the field or service of pastoral care, and one of those levels is that of teaching.[7] As an interpreter of the Scriptures, as an ordained servant of the church, the pastor's perspectives are viewed more often than not as of instructional value. The necessity to instruct seems clear when dealing with persons whose moral and religious views are problematic, or whose attitudes are unhealthy, or whose experiences need clarifying conversation. The religious care of troubled persons includes the need to share information and insights as well as the need to provide a caring presence.

As a third strategy for teaching from a pastoral perspective, the practical value of *teaching a class in the church program* should not be overlooked. Given the teaching responsibility that devolves upon the ordained minister who pastors a people, and given the investment of years in study for the ministerial role, it is not too much to expect the pastor to view the congregation as a school in

---

6   Howard Thurman, *Jesus and the Disinherited* (Abingdon-Cokesbury Press, 1949), 50.

7   See Wayne E. Oates, *The Christian Pastor* (Westminster Press, 1982, third edition), 69.

Christian living and labor. Some pastors regularly teach a "Pastor's Class" of new Christians, new members, or young people. Some engage the entire congregation in guided study under their tutelage, either to examine a biblical theme or book or to examine some issue from a biblical perspective.

The fundamental work of the Christian pastor and a congregation of believers is to interpret the significance of the Christian faith for all of life, and to develop a Christian consciousness out of which agape love, the concerns of justice, and the Christian witness can be effectively applied in the world. The concerned pastor will be alert to the need for resources, methods, and occasions for fostering an ordered approach to this perennial task, always eager to effect greater competency in this necessary work of the church.

Ultimately, however, *the pastor will teach most influentially through personal Christian character and earnest example.* The accent here is on a personal life that can instruct by its integrity and disciplined direction. Early in the twentieth century, R. P. Wyche called attention to the need for this, writing about the imperative for social uplift and advancement among the people: "The character and the ability of the [person] in the pulpit will determine its nature and extent."[8] This comment was but one from many concerned clergy reminding each other about this moral and spiritual demand for ministry.

Given the scope and import of ministry, a serious look at one's self and the potential problem areas about which ordained ministers, as both persons and professionals, must be aware has been increasingly necessary. The ultimate response a vital ministry demands of us is that of a God-committed selfhood coupled with

---

8   R. P. Wyche, "To What Extent Is the Negro Pulpit Uplifting the Race?" in *Twentieth Century Negro Literature,* ed. Daniel W. Culp (J. L. Nichols & Co., 1902), 122.

spiritual empowerment. One is not likely to rightly deliver the word of truth to others, regarding sexual morality, until one has reached a mature understanding of one's own failings and feelings in this area. Given the primary emphasis upon sex in our society, this is not an area of teaching that preachers can disregard. Nor can they live as if they are helpless against the mores of society when these mores collide with the Word and the will of God.

Developing Leaders Through Teaching

It has become rather commonplace to hear some pastor endorsed as a "great leader," meaning that he or she mixes well with people and handles leadership responsibilities with timeliness and adequacy. Many preachers view that "great leader" image as worthy of their concern and effort, as something to be attained as the capstone of their professional quest. But the serious pastor will be mindful of the need to *develop* leaders and not be content with only being viewed as one. This requires the work of teaching others.

Jesus of Nazareth showed the way in this as in all other necessary areas. Concerned about the future of the work to which he set himself, Jesus envisioned, selected, and trained a small group to expand and perpetuate his ministry as teacher, preacher, and healer. The demands upon him had become excessive and unending, and he had not come to stay. Aware that he had an impact on a growing number of followers, Jesus finally identified and isolated from within the crowds those who seemed reasonably gifted for what he would require of them.

According to Luke 6:12-13, when that time came for Jesus to single out those persons from the crowd and shape them for assignments under his direction, Jesus withdrew to pray about the choices he had to make. He prayed about it throughout the night.

The account tells us that when day came, he called his disciples and chose twelve of them. The Gospels tell us about subsequent training of the twelve, and underscore the time and guidance Jesus gave in shaping them for leadership. Jesus was sensible about the work assigned to his hands, and he chose and developed others to assist him in handling tasks that are still required in each generation. The wise pastor will think not only about the present but also about the future, and will teach others with that future in view.

The interest to become a "great leader" will certainly continue within the various church traditions and will, in some persons, obscure a clear view of the solid work required of the serious Christian pastor. But those who concern themselves as true traditioners and helpers of the people will seek to show by example and teaching the meaning and power of the Christian faith. The issues people face demand from us informational and inspirational preaching, sound biblical counsel, times of strategic learning, and an honest modeling of what the Christian faith makes possible in human experience. Those who love the Lord and are deeply concerned to help people learn to live by the will of God will be intent to "gladly teach" while following that teaching themselves.

8

PROCLAIMING HOLINESS: THE DIVINE ATTRIBUTE AND CHRISTIAN CHARACTER

by James Earl Massey

Originally appeared in *The Pastor's Guide to Effective Preaching*
(Beacon Hill Press of Kansas City, 2003), 107-115.
The NRSV translation cited.
Used by permission.

Large sections of the New Testament report how the first Christian preachers sought to help hearers learn about and appropriate the will and character of God, "the Holy One," in their personal experience. The concern of those preachers was to help believers live on God's terms, indeed to link so fully with God that sharing in God's likeness—Christ being the observed measure—would be the result.

Many texts deal with this concern. Paul says his goal in preaching and leading was "so that we may present everyone mature in Christ" (Col. 1:28). Peter's word in 2 Peter 1:4 reflects the same goal: "Thus he has given us, through these things, his precious and very great promises, so that through them you may escape from the corruption that is in the world because of lust, and may become participants of the divine nature."

Texts like these draw attention to one of the most pertinent and positive claims made by the first Christian preachers: that God has ordained that those who surrender to His love will share in His likeness. Those preachers wanted all to know that becoming a Christian not only involves a change in one's experience but also a change in one's very being. They voiced this as the goal of the gospel.

Holiness: The Divine Attribute

Every serious student of Scripture knows that the central concept among its vast teaching about God is God's holiness. God is to be understood as "the Holy One." This description about God's nature occurs with such frequency and emphasis, especially in the Old Testament, that it cannot be missed or overlooked.

As the Holy One, God is distinctly "Other." God is separated, marked-off in nature from what is ordinary, common, or human. God is so distinctive and unique, so absolute in perfection and purity, so utterly Other in being that to realize His presence is to experience a radical awe. Both Testaments supply us with multiplied instances when some human recoiled when confronted by the divine Presence.

God is holy Person, which means that His "Otherness" does more than occasion a radical awe. It also occasions a radical attractiveness that invites communion. The God about whom both the Testaments witness, the God and Father of Jesus the Christ, is uniquely separate but not remote nor utterly removed. His presence provokes awe, yet He always seeks to relate, hoping to share himself and His very life and holiness with humans.

Since this is true, it is important to understand in what way, and to what extent, God grants believers a share in His holiness.

This is a question that theological camps have debated, some claiming more than God makes available to humanity and others claiming less than God intends to bestow. Does God only *impute* His holiness to us, or does God actually *impart* His holiness to believers? Based on multiple New Testament texts that encourage believers to seek the very character of God, the Wesleyan tradition has long maintained that every believer can lay claim on God's holiness in more than a figurative manner. Christian holiness of life is far more than a figure of speech.

We who preach can proclaim that God has shown us His holiness on our human level in Jesus Christ, His Son. The Sonship of Jesus is real, and it is revelational. The character of His life as depicted in the Gospels is a manifestation of holiness in the flesh. The writer to the Hebrews reports that Jesus the Son of God "is the reflection of God's glory and the exact imprint of God's very being" (1:3). Jesus himself made the claim that "whoever sees me sees him who sent me" (John 12:45), and "whoever has seen me has seen the Father" (14:9). God has clearly revealed His holiness on our level in the unique Sonship of Jesus.

God is Jesus' Father in both mode and manner, something we are not able completely to understand or explain. The New Testament witnesses to the earthly life of Jesus and did not get side-tracked over metaphysical questions about His genesis or descent as divine Son; they rightly and wisely celebrated Jesus as Savior, giving due honor to God the Father who sent Him. John 1:18 says, "No one has ever seen God. It is God the only Son, who is close to the Father's heart, who has made him known."

Jesus as revealing Son is a necessary truth for us to keep in focus because what we are to preach about sharing in the holiness of God is related to what is exemplified in Jesus. As believers on His name, we stand related to Jesus as the one who "gave [us] power to become children of God" (John 1:12). Our adoption into God's family is derived through Jesus' relation to God.

Thus, we note Paul's praiseful words: "Blessed be the God and Father of our Lord Jesus Christ, who has blessed us in Christ with every spiritual blessing in the heavenly places, just as he chose us in Christ before the foundation of the world to be holy and blameless before him in love. He destined us for adoption as his children through Jesus Christ, according to the good pleasure of his will, to the praise of his glorious grace that he freely bestowed on us in the Beloved" (Eph. 1:3-6). Behind it all stands the holy God, working His will through Jesus Christ in our interest and to His honor. Jesus is not only God's model Son but also our means and model for a derived holy likeness to God the Father.

Christian Holiness Through Life in Christ

Our preaching should invite hearers to Christian holiness—that quality of life and those distinctive character traits made possible through openness to the indwelling Spirit of Christ. This holiness is not the product of some regional, national, or denominational influence, nor is it conformity to some pattern of conduct peculiar to some defensive group rationale. Christian holiness involves being clothed "with the new self, created according to the likeness of God" (Eph. 4:24). Christian holiness is a derived result. It is definite and distinctive.

1. Our derived share in God's holiness is, first of all, *individual*, because each believer can experience God personally. The whole self is called into the transaction with God that conversion initiates. Our human nature, marred by sin, can originally reflect only our natural

heritage of flesh, but by spiritual rebirth—by being "born from above" (John 3:7) through conversion, we can meaningfully intersect with God's will for us and live on new terms as adopted members of God's family.

But this stage is anticipatory; it is intended to usher us into a fuller share in family life with God, especially experiencing in ourselves the character of our Father and bringing honor to God through dedicated living and focused service. Preaching on Christian holiness places before the hearers the possibility, necessity, excellence, and availability of this fuller and richer experience.

2. Our derived share in God's holiness is also *identifiable*. God by His Spirit shapes new character traits. Meister Eckhart (c.1260-1327) identified Christian character as "a habitual will," by which he meant the will transformed into instinct, complete self-unity, a oneness of the self and self-interest with the will of God. Life is adjusted to God's scales. The Holy Spirit works within us with potency and immediacy as we remain surrendered to God's claim on us.

Christian character is best described as Christlikeness. The identifiable traits are set forth among the listed "fruit of the Spirit" (Gal. 5:22-23). This "fruit," these Christ-like traits of character, is produced as the Holy Spirit of God does His critical and creative work within us. He brings the many elements of personality into focus and draws tight the previously loose strings of personal life, holding them with the sure grip of God.

Irenaeus (c.175-c.195), who faithfully followed the apostolic tradition, was referring to the Holy Spirit's inward ministry when he commented that the Holy Spirit "adjusts us to God."[1] Other relations and influences in life tend to diminish the self or diffuse and dissipate the life. But the Holy Spirit works within us to shape us in conformity to a new pattern, a holy model, as we "cleanse ourselves from every defilement of body and spirit, making holiness perfect in the fear of God" (2 Cor. 7:1). The result of this is readily identifiable.

3. Our derived share in God's holiness is *intelligible*. This kind of experience, this set of results, can be expressed in the form of definite doctrines and a set of convictions. Such noble features and healthy aspects of life make sense. We can call attention to what has happened and is happening, and we can interpret to others what it means to us and for us. It has always been sensible to live by a pattern and follow a path that honors God.

4. Our derived share in God's holiness is also *instrumental*. This sharing readies us for a destiny in God's will and it enables us to fulfill the works of the law, with "love [as] the fulfilling of the law" (Rom. 13:10). That love is a divine issue "because God's love has been poured into our hearts through the Holy Spirit that has been given to us" (Rom. 5:5).

---

1   Quoted by F. W. Dillistone, *The Holy Spirit in the Life of Today* (London: Canterbury Press, 1946), 10.

Sharing in holiness deepens the believer's commitment to what is vital, what is sacred, what is necessary. The holy life is dedicated to a high and honorable standard of living, worthy values, and a sustained commitment to regard these distinctives to the honor of God. But sharing in holiness also orients us for caring. Just as there are sacred distinctives, there are social duties that are best handled through strategic services from a caring heart. John Wesley (1703-91) wrote: "The Gospel of Christ knows of no religion but social; no holiness but social holiness. Faith working by love is the length and breadth and depth and height of Christian perfection."[2]

Principles for Preaching about Holiness

Since holiness is not only a divine attribute but also a level of life, it is a vital subject for study and preaching. The earnest preacher will live daily with the Scriptures, striving to ascertain a full impact from their central message, in order to understand, live by, and wisely use scriptural themes and emphases. Holiness is one of these themes.

1. *Study the pulpit work of leading holiness exponents.* In addition to being aids to acquaint us with apt preaching styles, some of the holiness exponents can acquaint us with model ways to handle holiness texts. I have profited from reading the works of A. W. Tozer (1897-1963), whose weighted words were carefully chosen to convey the biblical vision of holiness with clarity, conciseness, and appeal. His *Pursuit of God* (1948) and *Knowledge of the Holy* (1961) are Christian classics whose biblical base, spiritual depth, and aesthetic appeal are inspirational and highly instructive.

---

2   *The Works of the Rev. John Wesley, A.M.* (London: John Mason, 1856), Vol. XIV, 305.

The same can be said about the published pulpit work of the soundly biblical and highly articulate Paul S. Rees (1900-1991). His *Christian: Commit Yourself* (1957) and *Church in God* (an expository series on Thessalonians) provide due guidance in handling the holiness emphasis in preaching. The pulpit work of William M. Greathouse must also be mentioned. This holiness advocate's trenchant for drawing meaning directly from the biblical text and for following the movement of the text in shaping the sermon made his pulpit work exegetically apt and homiletically appealing. In his book *Wholeness in Christ: Toward a Biblical Theology of Holiness* (1998), Greathouse has offered a thoroughly documented statement about biblical holiness after a lifetime of exploring the subject and reading contemporary literature.

In the late twentieth century, Beacon Hill Press of Kansas City published six volumes in a series titled *Great Holiness Classics*. The publisher conceived and launched the project "to provide a representative compilation of the best holiness literature in a format readily accessible to the average minister, thus providing: (1) the preservation of the essential elements of our holiness heritage; (2) an overview of the broad scope of the holiness message; (3) a norm for holiness theology, proclamation, and practice; (4) a succinct reference work on holiness; and (5) a revival of the best of the out-of-print holiness classics."[3]

Volume 5 in the series is a collection of sermons on holiness, sermons representing the time span from John Wesley (1703-91) to the latter part of the 20th century. Forty-four sermons are included: some deal with understanding the doctrine and emphases of holiness, some with how the experience of holiness (sanctification)

---

3   See A.F. Harper, "Understanding the Great Holiness Classics," in Vol. 5, *Holiness Preachers and Preaching*, ed. W. E. McCumber (Kansas City: Beacon Hill Press of Kansas City, 1989), 11-12.

is sought and gained, some with the Holy Spirit's ministry in helping believers live the holy life, some with the social implications of holy living, and some with proclaiming holiness. All considered, the preachers and sermons featured in the volume are fairly representative of their generations, most were from historic orthodox communions, and nearly all offer a handling of the holiness theme that is insightfully doctrinal and practical without being doctrinaire.

Throughout the volume the preachers handle the subject of holiness with clarity and tolerance. The intent of the volume is to focus light on the subject, offer angles and emphases for treating the subject of holiness, and provide documented specimens for reading and study from acknowledged advocates of Christian holiness. Holiness preachers and preaching was only one of a number of such volumes produced by publisher's intent to honor the biblical teaching of holiness, but I have highlighted this book because holiness advocates from many denominations contributed to it and because it is a resourceful compendium conveying how holiness texts have been understood and proclaimed through preaching across several centuries.

2. In planning to preach on holiness, *be mindful of the functional forcefulness of the holiness-text you choose, and let it influence your handling of the text*. By the "functional forcefulness of a text" I refer to how that text is worded and the way the biblical writer used those words. Because of our familiarity with some portion of Scripture, we often tend to miss or overlook the dynamism in the religious language the biblical writers use. When one takes time to explore and classify their sentence forms and the functions they intend the forms to achieve, the meaning and significance of their writings become all the more evident and even eventful for us.

Early in the 1970s, in the course of my career-long work of teaching seminarians and pastors to preach as servants of biblical truths, letting Scripture substance influence even the shape of the sermon, I began a fresh study of the New Testament. Influenced by semantics and studies that deal with religious language as a specialized category, I took a prolonged look at the functions the New Testament writers intend by their dynamic use of language. Beginning with the Epistles, I carefully examined the sentence units within them. I isolated and interrogated the many sentence forms and functions, intent to discern and capture more fully what was said and what was meant. I was satisfied with nothing less than the actual "meaning" and "significance" of the texts.

In time, I prepared and presented a paper to the Wesleyan Theological Society in which I categorized the treatment of Christian holiness in the Epistles using three major function-headings: "statements" about holiness, "expressions" regarding holiness, and "prescriptives" to live holy lives.[4] That paper, eventually published by the Wesleyan Theological Society, appears in fill elsewhere in this present volume.

Since the New Testament treatment of Christian holiness involves statements, expressions, and prescriptives, we gain a clear view of human life as God wills it. The New Testament expressions about holiness make clear assertions and a claim meant to gain attention and challenge us to action. The New Testament expressions about holiness convey excitement about a quality of life that is real, valuable, engaging, and progressive. The New Testament prescriptives about holiness are unsparing in what they stress for us and demand from us; the imperatives voiced in prescriptive texts

---

4   See James Earl Massey, "Semantics and Holiness: A Study in Holiness-Texts Functions," *Wesleyan Theological Journal* 10 (Spring 1975): 60-69. Appears elsewhere in this present volume.

are used with high warrant, strict realism, and decisive intent. The preacher who examines the many holiness texts from these angles cannot fail to understand that they witness about a higher level of life that God has opened to us. He or she sees that preaching about holiness is necessary to inform believers about it. God's concern is our practical holiness, the enhancement of our lives, our fulfillment of His ethical and moral demands, and our readiness for service in the world as bearers of His Spirit and character.

3. *In preaching about holiness, let the text dictate the approach to be used.* Texts that hold a "statement" about holiness suggest a doctrinal approach in the sermon, while texts that offer an "expression" about holiness can be used in an illustrative manner in treating the experience. Holiness texts that are prescriptives usually dictate, by their very nature, that the sermon be shaped to voice an unmistakable call to the hearer to enter fully into the holy life.

I have explained a holiness text as a text that utilizes one or more holiness terms in its sentence function and deals with some ethical or behavioral claim God makes upon the believer. Richard S. Taylor, a noted holiness scholar, offers a more expansive view of a holiness text. In his book *Preaching Holiness Today*, Taylor says: "A holiness text is any passage which, within itself, in its contextual relations and in its inner meaning, is related to the will of God that men should be holy."[5]

Taylor also identifies three levels of such texts: (1) those texts in which the holiness thrust is unmistakable, texts that are plainly oriented toward doctrinal statement and analysis; (2) texts in which the holiness emphasis is implicit rather than explicit; and

---

5   Richard S. Taylor, *Preaching Holiness Today* (Kansas City: Beacon Hill Press of Kansas City, 1968). See esp. chap. 7 on "Principles of Interpretation," 90–108.

(3) texts that are more or less illustrative of the holiness experience, either as picture or illustration and application of the truth about the experience. Taylor advises that, when preaching to teach about or to interpret holiness, unmistakably explicit holiness texts should be used. Texts that treat holiness implicitly rather than explicitly should be used inferentially, and texts that only illustrate holiness should only be used illustratively. The principle widely advised is that the method one uses in preaching Christian holiness should relate to the kind of text used.

9

SERMON: COME BEFORE WINTER

by James Earl Massey

Metropolitan Church of God,
Detroit, Michigan, October, 1958.[1]

Do thy diligence to come before winter. — 2 Timothy 4:21

Three figures fill my mind as I read our text, 2 Timothy 4:21. One is the Apostle Paul who wrote the letter of which this verse is a part. The second figure is the youthful and faithful Timothy, to whom the aged apostle addressed these words. The third figure is the late Dr. Clarence Edward Macartney whose use of this text did more to bring it to the attention of the church than any other preacher of our century.

It was Macartney's custom to preach once yearly from this verse and, having begun the practice in 1915, must have preached some forty times on its hidden implications. As regards his frequent use of this verse, Dr. Macartney once commented: "I suppose the chief reason is that the truth of the sermon is so evident and comes home to the experience of so many people." His voice is now hushed

---

1   Excerpted from the "Metropolitan Bible Hour" broadcast on WEXL Radio
     from the Pulpit of Metropolitan Church of God in Detroit.

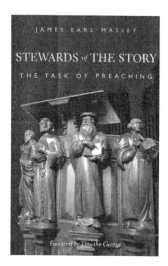

in death but the text still lives with a meaning that yet beckons.

The text reflects a personal matter from the life of the Apostle Paul. It was written during a time of severe strain. Paul was in Rome, in prison, awaiting the final hearing and action in his trial as a Christian leader. The confinement was a definite strain. His cell was small, cold, dingy, and damp. The churches for which his concern was so deep were still on his mind. This made for some of his strain. The anticipated conclusion of the trial was a means of strain. Paul already sensed that he would not be freed as before, that he would finally lose his life.

The absence of certain companions was a means of strain. Luke was with Paul at the time, but there were other matters involving situations and services about which Luke was concerned but not called upon by Paul to handle. Some of Paul's collaborators were out in necessary work for him; he was glad that he could entrust work to Titus in Dalmatia, or to Crescens in Galatia, and to Timothy in Ephesus. But now he felt the need of their presence. His most solemn and signal hour was approaching. The aged apostle needed some help. He needed that assistance administered through the presence and promise of his favored "son in the faith," Timothy.

Paul wrote to Timothy with a plea behind the pen, "Do thy diligence to come shortly unto me."[2] But the word "shortly" must not have been sufficient to carry Paul's sense of desired haste, for he repeated himself at the close of the letter and added a specific time for Timothy to come: "Do thy diligence to come *before winter.*"

---

2   2 Timothy 4:9.

The plea to come before winter is specific for a number of reasons. Two of these reasons are set forth in the body of the letter itself. Paul needed his heavy cloak to protect himself against the cold and dampness of his cell. He asked therefore that Timothy stop at Troas on the way and get the cloak from Carpus, with whom it had been left in custody. That cloak was doubtless a coarse wool blanket with a hole in the middle through which the head was inserted; the rest of the material hung down around the rest of the body. Timothy was also asked to bring the books and parchments which Paul had left at Troas. The apostle wanted some essential materials to aid his mind and soul. The cloak was needed for comfort; the books and parchments were needed for centered study.

The second reason set forth in the letter can be seen in these solemn words: "For I am now ready to be offered, and the time of my departure is at hand."[3] The apostle must have known by revelation that his death was not far away. Recall these classic words: "Comes a still voice — Yet a few days, and thee the all-beholding sun shall see no more in all his course."[4] How soon his death would take place he did not know, but Paul knew that death was ahead. So, uncertain as to what time remained for him, Paul counseled Timothy to come shortly to him, to come before the winter set it.

Long voyages on the Mediterranean Sea were not undertaken during the winter. If Timothy did not come before sea travel closed down, it was possible that he might not get to see the apostle again before spring. And by spring the trial might have been concluded and his life-course finished. To accomplish the purpose behind Paul's plea, Timothy would have to arrive before winter. In that day of slower travel, Timothy would have to get an early start on

---

3   2 Timothy 4:6.

4   William Cullen Bryant, from "Thanatopsis."

his way. I prefer to believe that Timothy did not hesitate to obey the call of the apostle.

Thus the personal matter involved in the text. But I have not chosen this verse to deal singly with Paul's plea to Timothy. This verse has prophetic overtones. It not only reveals a feature of Paul's personal life, it also reflects a fact hammered to perfection in Scripture. This verse brings a certain truth into sharp focus:

a. It tells us that there is a time of opportunity to do some things in life;

b. It tells us that the time for doing some things is a passing time;

c. It etches sharply the need for immediate action with regard to some things.

This verse has an evangelical witness. It tells us that the winter of reality closes in at a certain season, that all things left hanging and undone when the season changes must remain hanging and undone. Opportunity is a passing reality. It must be used in its season; it must be used "before winter." Winter seals us off from certain results; it hems us in or walls us out. This figurative use of winter reminds us that there is a time when we are hindered, with entrance forbidden or escape blocked, a time when things are frozen, life barren and bound.

"Come before winter." Paul wrote the words but I can hear Jesus speaking them also. He beckons with an emphasis which centers upon the wise use of opportunity. Jesus beckons with an appeal the urgency of which warms the heart, "Come." Yet the appeal warns us that the opportunity afforded to come is a limited period of time, "Come before winter." These words on the lips of Jesus invite us to come while the opportunity is unmistakably present. The call of Paul cautioned Timothy against any postponement; there was a danger in delay. The call comes at a favorable season, an opportune time. To delay involves unnecessary risk.

Come to Jesus before the winter of removal has set in upon your life. By "removal" I refer specifically to the fact of your death. Death removes life from the body. Death removes one from this world. When the winter of death has come, it is the season to go. Death is an historical event. It is a fixed season for every person. It is set within the scheme provided by God for His creation and creatures and as such is an inevitable event. The coming of death shuts off, seals off, forbids; death is a winter fact. There is "a time to be born, and a time to die."[5] Death, like inevitable winter, is a fixed season. While the earth remaineth, death certainly will come. Therefore, while the opportunity remains, you should come to Jesus before the winter of removal in death.

Those who have lived long enough or have been observant enough have learned that life is much like the seasons. There is the sparkle of delightful spring. There is the sovereign heat of a driving summer. There is the splendor of the dusky fall. And there is the saddening anger of the darkening winter. The seasons do not keep; they pass.

We tend to identify a certain season as our most beloved and beneficial. We sometimes speak of waiting for "my season" to return. The seasons are something other than ourselves, and we know that we cannot hold them. God grants seasons of opportunity. He sends out summons to invite us to Himself, and sends the invitation early enough for us to escape, if we will, the inevitable winter

5   Ecclesiastes 3:2a.

season which chills and freezes all opportunity for change. There is a time to come to God; that time is now, today. Opportunity is now afforded, but winter is on its way. Come to Jesus! Come before winter!

The beckoning apostle certainly expected Timothy to come to him. He expected Timothy to come because he had been asked. He expected him to come because of their relationship. Paul expected Timothy to come because of the necessity. Did Timothy arrive in time? I prefer to believe that he did. I believe that the young leader had a passion for the purpose set forth by the apostle. His sense of gratitude and service was so deep that he must have braved the dangers of appearing in Rome in the interest of the chained apostle.

Once Timothy had come, there must have been some dramatic moments in the life of both these servants of Christ. The aged Paul must have shared many blessings with the young man who was intent to shoulder the work among the churches thereafter. If Timothy arrived before winter, and before Paul went to his death, more meaning must have filled his future. When opportunity passes by, it is irretrievable. When winter sets in, all other seasons have been shut out. But when opportunity is seized, doors of divine grace open to the future.

The plea of Paul to Timothy was a revelation of his concern for the young man. The whole experience of meeting with the apostle would ready Timothy for more of life and labors for the Christ. The call of Jesus to the soul to "Come before winter" is a revelation of his concern for the sinner. His desire and design will involve all the interests and concerns of the life.

- Coming to Jesus will mean your salvation.

- Coming to Jesus will mean peace of soul and mind.

- Coming to Jesus will mean a new hope for you, a fresh and fertile interest in the future.

- Coming to Jesus will mean a changed life, a renewed disposition, a wholeness of being.

- Coming to Jesus will mean sharing the life and love of God.

- Coming to Jesus will mean inward and outward healing.

- Coming to Jesus can mean so much and even more.

The invitation is given: Jesus says "Come." The final result is within your power, the move is your own to make; but remember that this season of opportunity is passing. Use it with wisdom, use it while you may: Come *before winter*.

> *There is a tide in the affairs of men*
> *Which taken at the flood leads on to fortune;*
> *Omitted, all the voyage of their life*
> *Is bound in shallows and in miseries.*
> *On such a full sea are we now afloat,*
> *And we must take the current when it serves,*
> *Or lose our ventures.*[6]

---

6   William Shakespeare, *Julius Caesar*, Act IV, Scene 3.

SECTION II

WISDOM FOR CONGREGATIONS & CAMPUSES

EDITOR'S SECTION INTRODUCTION

by Ronald J. Fowler

Pastor Laureate of Arlington Church of God, Akron, Ohio,
and former Chair of the Board of Trustees
of Anderson University

This section begins with Dr. Massey speaking for himself at a key juncture in his ministry. Through an interview format, we gain valuable insights into the man, his motives, and his manner of ministering the good news in Jesus Christ. This is followed by a sensitive picture of the dignity and proper role of a minister's spouse. Gwendolyn Massey has been a loving wife and minister in her own right, a marvelous marriage companion and resource to James across all of his adult years.

During my tenure as a member of the Akron, Ohio, Public School Board, I attended a conference in San Francisco and was thrilled to have the opportunity to visit a sequoia park and the home of Howard Thurman. The sight of the giant trees served to remind me of the value of gifted teachers, including two giants, Dr. Thurman and Dr. James Earl Massey. Their instructional impact on generations of church leaders will be celebrated across the years. Samples of Dr. Massey's impact are very evident in the entries in this section of this book.

My interest in visiting Dr. Thurman's home was driven by Dr. Massey, my former pastor, and his appreciation for this man's insightful writings. Iron sharpens iron; Dr. Massey frequently shared insights gained from this mentor and friend of his. The scholarly side of Dr. Massey would often lead him to cite not merely the title of a work of Dr. Thurman, but the very page on which the quotation could be found. I longed for the time that I could visit Dr. Thurman's distribution center and spend uninterrupted time browsing through his life's work. I was delighted beyond words for the opportunity to be surrounded by the aura of this distinguished theologian/teacher. We owe a great debt of gratitude to those who have functioned as theological and moral teachers and "lamp lighters." As Thurman was one, so Massey is another.

You will find a paraphrasing of one of Dr. Massey's favorite Thurman quotations in the opening paragraph of the entry "Teaching That Points to Truth." It reads: "For those of us entrusted with the blessed privilege to teach, such tributes keep us mindful that a crown of trust has been placed above our heads and we must continually grow taller if we are ever to reach it." Such a call and challenge have often provided others with an incentive to excel. This is what Dr. Massey has done so well for so long and for so many, including me.

Dr. Massey reminds us that good teaching enables students to realize the connection between truth and basic human needs. Oh, the joy of hearing parishioners leave study or worship and exclaim, "That message spoke to me!" That grateful witness, according to Dr. Massey, is the purpose of good teaching, enabling persons to fulfill the promise of truth, affirming one's humanity and strengthening one's will to move forward in faith. Every church needs teachers, giant trees of the faith, who are prepared and disciplined to point others to truth!

The church needs such great teaching in local congregations and also on its university campuses. Much of Dr. Massey's ministry has been in higher education. How beautifully does he define the proper goals of higher education in his commencement address prepared for the centennial of his beloved Anderson University. Naturally, I resonate especially with this exceptional address since I chaired that school's Board of Trustees for several years. I also rejoice in hearing his explanation of why the history of this university is so personal for Dr. Massey. How appreciative he is, and I also am, of the unusual openness of this school to African-American students and issues, even in decades when such openness was very counter-cultural.

According to Dr. Massey, the church is founded on integrity and "energized by truth." Truth and integrity represent the foundation of character. He recalls the priority Jesus assigned to teaching, traveling from village to village and training others to take good news to the world. Leaders must serve as "trust officers," teaching what the church has always taught. Teachers of truth are stewards and managers of what belongs to God, which makes their service sacred and central to the health of the family of God. If visionary leaders are "shapers of community," a healthy church is one that has integrity with the historic understandings of truth, links vision to behavior, and gives priority to the development of leaders.

As I departed for Detroit, Michigan, to embark on a teaching career in its public schools, I can still hear my father's voice saying, "Son, when you get to Detroit, be sure to visit Brother Massey's congregation. It will do you good." Truer words were never spoken. When Sunday came, I did as advised, not knowing how life-altering that decision would become. The sanctuary was full for worship time and the congregation was standing and singing its opening hymn. The choral master was facing the audience with robed choir members in the background. The organist filled the sanctuary with its rich embodiment of selected tones. There was gladness in the air and a feeling of kinship. It was obvious that enormous planning had gone into this service. I have vivid memories of Dr. Massey transitioning from the piano to the pulpit. He was master of both.

What Massey captures well is the importance of partnership in the planning of worship, for the Chapel worship at Tuskegee University where he was the Chapel's Dean, and for every congregation. The worship experience is too important to be left to one perspective alone. Core convictions, cultural history, and central themes of Scripture must comprise a coordinated platform for celebrating the mighty acts of God. Dr. Massey has long championed integrity, order, reverence for God, and freedom with accountability. There must be a commitment to excellence and a genuine desire to meet the needs of the worshippers.

There also should be an awareness and use of the rich musical heritage of the African-American spirituals, wonderfully presented here. Dr. Massey, at his teaching best, shows how the theology of the church across the centuries and the particular experience of African-American Christians have shaped and been inspired by this amazing musical tradition of the church. He summarizes these spirituals this way: "They echo a biblical theology. They voice an affirmative theodicy. They mirror the African-American soul. They helped, and still help, a seeking people to face dark times and meet the exigencies of life with faith, fortitude, and essential pride."

Such an expansive and enriching evaluation also describes the ministry of James Earl Massey. Now Dr. Massey has done the church a great service by making his wisdom available for a wider audience and new generations. For his labor and love, and for his teaching and preaching ministries to the whole Body of Christ, I rejoice!

10

A CONVERSATION WITH PASTOR AND PROFESSOR MASSEY

Richard L. Willowby interviews James Earl Massey

The interview of James Earl Massey by
Richard L. Willowby, in *Vital Christianity*,
June 6, 1982, 10-13. Used by permission.

D r. Massey completes nearly six years as speaker for the "Christian Brotherhood Hour," radio broadcast of the Church of God (Anderson) [now known as "Christians Broadcasting Hope"]. He came to that position from the roles of teacher and nearly a quarter century of pastoral ministry. Dr. Massey now leaves the CBH post to resume full-time teaching duties as Professor of New Testament and Preaching at Anderson University School of Theology. This interview explores Dr. Massey's thoughts about radio ministry, the parish ministry, and the future of the Church of God movement and its ministries.

Willowby: Dr. Massey, what are some of your feelings about the radio ministry of the church?
Massey: The radio ministry is a very crucial one for the church. It is both a means of identifying with the public that needs to be helped, and a way of giving witness to our message and mission

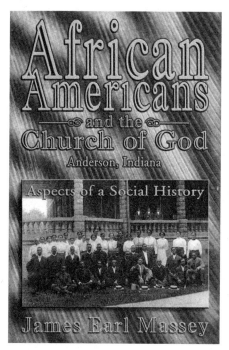

in a wider framework. The use of radio is on the upward swing again after a time when it was thought that radio would slump as television gained prominence. Interestingly, more persons now listen to the radio than ever before.

It has been very difficult to target our CBH audience with precision, but we have known for many years that we have a rather widespread listening audience. Judging from the mail received, a quite sizeable part of our audience is beyond sixty years of age, but another sizeable group is young adults.

The younger listeners have commented about the clear teaching our broadcast gives, and how they have been enlightened; older listeners write and tell us how the broadcast encourages them. It is between these two important poles of information and inspiration that I have sought to plan and preach as CBH speaker across these years.

The time has come to expand the radio ministry in order to reach and serve specifically targeted audiences and more listener concerns. Such planning has been done, and new ventures are in the offing.

Willowby: Will you continue with the Mass Communications Board after your term as speaker?

Massey: I have been asked to do so. In addition to handling a new fifteen-minute daily program devoted to Bible teaching—which will begin in early 1983—I have been asked to write for the Board and remain involved in Board-sponsored Bible study seminars held across the country.

Willowby: What prompted your decision to return to the full-time teaching ministry?

Massey: Actually, I never left the classroom when I became speaker but continued to teach on a part-time basis. But as I now return full-time to the classroom setting, it is because of my desire to be more involved in training others for church ministries. Across many years, I was privileged to teach and preach concurrently, first in the pastorate and then as a campus minister. When I became CBH speaker and my travel schedule began to interrupt my time for research and teaching, I listened to my heart and decided that I would not accept another term as speaker. This decision had freed me to travel only when I desire to do so.

Willowby: What are your major burdens in teaching?

Massey: My burden as a teacher is twofold: (1) to acquaint my classes with the scope and meaning of the New Testament writings and (2) to train seminarians for effective pulpit ministry. Thus, my two-pronged title as Professor of New Testament and Preaching.

Willowby: How many years did you serve as a parish pastor?

Massey: I served in the parish setting for twenty-four years. That includes one year as full-time associate to Dr. Raymond S. Jackson and twenty-three as a senior pastor on my own. I enjoyed the pastorate. I love people and I have appreciated the many opportunities I have had to serve in ways that count. Teaching, preaching, visitation, and counseling were steady ministries to which I gave myself as a pastor.

Willowby: Would you be able to name three or four points that you feel were most significant in your parish ministry?

Massey: Yes, I can do so. The first was readiness to help people during their times of crisis. A second was closeness to the people in daily life. Although this was not easily done in a large urban setting, I sometimes managed to visit as many as twenty homes a week, which meant that I was with the members in their home settings as well as during our congregational gatherings. There were also those times of closeness by lunching with businessmen of the church, or with schoolteachers during their lunch time.

A third thing that I found significant was maintaining contacts beyond the congregation that would aid me in helping the members of the church or the community. I could thus help someone who was out of work secure a job, or put someone who had a problem in touch with that person or agency needed to help solve it.

I especially appreciated having the trust of people who looked to me for pastoral care. I learned early how to listen to people, and I learned increasingly how to help them. Listening to the sometimes heavy and horrid problems of city folk was not easy work, but every confessing, burdened person was worth it. There were even times when someone from the community came to confess a crime. I also learned how to help in those instances.

Willowby: Is the Church of God (Anderson) concept of pastoral leadership different from that of other groups?

Massey: It is not significantly different, but I must say that our holiness emphasis does influence greatly the way we counsel and deal with our members who err and sin. I must also add that I have long sensed some significant differences between the leadership style and authority among our Black pastors on the one hand and among our White pastors on the other. The Black pastors usually enjoy a stronger position in the church and community and can deal more forthrightly with persons, families, and community issues.

Willowby: Would this be a difference in White culture and Black culture, or would this difference be in urban versus non-urban pastoral settings?

Massey: Whether in an urban or a rural setting, the Black pastor usually has more freedom to do his or her work because of the great meaning associated with being a God-called person. Black church culture is strongly influenced by religious beliefs that do not stem from socio-economic factors, and the meaning attached to those beliefs governs Black church life across the board. This has nurtured a religious tradition among Blacks in which spiritual leadership is generally respected, followed, and in some instances granted privileges that other leaders are not granted.

Willowby: Is the Church of God view of pastoral leadership adequate today?

Massey: Speaking personally, I long to see Church of God pastors become better informed about the nature, problems, and needs of our society. This is imperative if we are to bring to bear upon the social process the needed effects of radical Christian ministry. I am not referring here to any "Moral Majority" concept, but rather to our need to act out of a moral perspective toward all that affects our community life. It is not that we must become the conscience of the community, but we must learn to speak aptly and with courage to that conscience, using an informed understanding of how the gospel of Christ relates to all of life.

Willowby: What is an adequate education for pastoral ministry now and what will be adequate in the future?

Massey: An adequate education for pastoral ministry must surely engage us in learning the biblical witness on the one hand and its vital application to our change-oriented life and times on the other. Quite beyond the training secured in college or seminary, adequately trained pastors will know how to think. They will also have knowledge and competence for life beyond the church. A proper training for pastors involves more than readying men and women to "tend the store"; it includes preparation to wrestle with the larger issues of life that affect human living as God intends it to be.

It starts, as I see it, with adequate training in the biblical witness, which involves a rich working acquaintance with the forms, focus, and function of the Scriptures. It continues with a share of Scripture in evangelism, discipleship, and fellowship. Every pastor needs the training that teaches how to think beyond what one has read, and how to use one's heritage creatively in all contacts with others. By *heritage* I mean all that has shaped us culturally, racially, and spiritually. This demands that all seminary teaching must honor the inclusive anthropology in the Scriptures and understand the dimensional nature of religious experience. Only with such training can our pastors relate significantly to the wider church and the needs of our times.

Willowby: What are the educational responsibilities of the pastor in the parish now, whether or not the pastor has a seminary education?

Massey: Every pastor is responsible to be out front in thought and study, while others attend seminars made available during camp meetings they attend. A pastor might well use vacation time for serious study, doing intensive reading from book lists prepared on request by those who can wisely advise about materials of value. College and seminary professors are usually glad to receive requests for such lists, and they would share such information quite readily.

But there is another way to further one's growth: talking at length with other pastors who do serious reading and whose work shows excellence.

Willowby: What will the future pastor face as century 20 becomes century 21?

Massey: The future pastor will meet life coming at a faster pace, and hard questions that the church must try to answer. For instance, the present tampering with life in the test tube, the question of when to let an embryo live or die, the problem of job reduction through an ever-burgeoning technology, and what to do for people who lack training for the increasingly technical levels of the current job market—these are only a few of the problems of the future, and that future is already upon us.

The pastor is expected not only to preach but to help people understand how faith readies us for life. The pastor must also help people learn to relate. As our cities continue to swell in population, and as human needs press us closer together in times of crisis, leaders are needed to help persons handle relationships wisely. This is a perennial need, and the biblical witness says much about how this can happen for one and all.

The pastor also has the responsibility for interpreting Scripture, and this must be done in connection with the real needs of people in clear view. If we fail at this, people will not value our role as they should. Our work is something more than taking in new members, visiting the sick, dedicating babies, and visiting homes. Our most strategic service is helping people learn how to live, viewing life in the light of God.

Willowby: What about the future of the Church of God (Anderson)? What challenges, what opportunities, what dangers and threats lie ahead?

Massey: The big challenge as we begin our second century is how to implement the vision of unity. We will have to model our message. It has become second nature for me to be at home with other believers whose church backgrounds differ from my own. To be sure, I have a strong sense of loyalty, and I know and appreciate my roots, but at this stage of my life I am more concerned about fruit than about roots. The root system is fixed, so my energies are toward fruit-bearing. I think that this should be our concern as a movement with a unity message. We must be up and about the business of helping other believers *experience* the unity we all seek to know.

Our earliest leaders did not live long enough to see clearly how what they had envisioned can reasonably take place. The task seems clearer now than earlier, and our generation has the task of implementing that wisdom. The danger I see is that we will settle upon the limited experimentation of the early leaders as the sole method for all time. At many points, their views of the church were rather narrow. The true church is bigger and brighter than our system.

Another challenge before us is to gain a firsthand acquaintance with Scripture. All too few of our congregations are biblically alert. Our holiness tradition should be understood in its biblical base, and so taught. "Back to the blessed old Bible" is a necessary journey, but we must take that journey in order to go forward in faith and a renewed understanding of God, Christ, the Holy Spirit, the church, the world, and our necessary work in it.

Willowby: What are the great opportunities of the Church of God movement?

Massey: One great opportunity before us is the freedom to associate and share with other Christians and para-church organizations and agencies in the evangelistic mission of the church. Another great opportunity before us has to do with our invited presence and witness at the thought-level of the wider church world. We have long had a witness that is biblically sound, and we know that the time for that witness has come.

My concern is that our witness be made clearly and with conviction, but without sectarian attitudes. It is a great time to be alive. It is a great time to be active in the Church of God movement, eager to see reform happen. I value this heritage and I am busy sharing it with others. This is a major part of my ministry, and for many years now mine has been a course filled with joy.

11

DEVELOPING A VISIONARY CHURCH THAT HAS INTEGRITY

by James Earl Massey

Originally appeared in Dale Galloway, compiler, *Leading with Vision* (Beacon Hill Press of Kansas City, 1999), 27-41. Used by permission.

The Church began under a leader with the highest integrity: Jesus of Nazareth, a teaching preacher. Intent on developing an effective working group for ministry in the world, Christ fashioned a community that looked to God, trusted His judgment, and had eyes of vision for claiming the world. Our Lord planned the church intentionally based on truth. He founded the church in order to have a community with integrity to continue His work in the world when He went back to be with His Father.

The Christian minister must always remember how the church began. He or she must know what the purpose for the church was in the mind and heart of the Founder in order to follow the same lines of integrity by which Jesus established the church. In our contemporary American setting, I am wary of the business model as the best image for the pastor because it smacks of commercialism and capitalism. The Bible's focus is on the church as a fellowship, a family, and a functioning community. The pastor leads such a functioning fellowship built on integrity and energized by truth.

Jesus Inspired Vision by Teaching Truth

I said that the Church began under the ministry of an itinerant teaching preacher. The emphasis on teaching was very strong in the ministry of Jesus because He knew that those who came to hear Him needed truth—truth about God and life. So filled was Jesus with truth and so fully did He share the truth that He came to be known as the Truth, as well as the Way and the Light.

Again and again in the Gospel accounts, when persons were addressing Jesus in the midst of His teaching they referred to Him as Rabbi or Teacher. The crowds were astonished at His teaching. In our day, teaching does not seem to have the kind of allure and attractiveness that we read about in the New Testament. But when the church began, it was around the central figure of a teacher of truth.

New Testament Leaders Followed the Pattern of Jesus

The New Testament writings report that this spirit of teaching was not only in Jesus but also at work in the life of those who continued His ministry when He went to be with God. This spirit of teaching was strong in the churches during the first century for two reasons. First, Jesus as the Founder of the church had been a teacher come from God, and this kept the teaching ministry in continuing esteem. Second, the church leaders appointed by Jesus to continue His ministry knew that sound living, living with integrity, depends upon sound teaching.

The early teachers of the church planned strategically. They intended to guide the awakened intellect, to provide religious answers for the questioning mind, and to offer a systematized body of truth for the questing soul. The Epistles show that what was taught was necessary as follow-up to what is proclaimed. The soundest basis for church growth is not merely to proclaim, but to teach. Teaching the full implications of the proclamation helps to develop a church that has integrity.

By the time the Pastorals were written, it was expected that those who chose to be pastors would be able teachers (1 Tim. 3:2). In fact, the stipulations regarding pastoral ministry made teaching an imperative function. Henry Sloan Coffin has said, "A preacher who would minister in the same pulpit for a quarter of a century, or at least for a decade, and would train a congregation in conviction and ideals, in methods of intercourse with the Unseen, and in ways of serving the commonwealth, must follow a similar educational system as was followed by the Apostles."

Teaching is not always valued in our churches. The founding and continuing development of the nation's churches, together with their strategic impact upon the development of the character of the nation, has depended in great measure upon the work of ministers who could teach. But we are, I fear, weakening or altogether deserting our ministry of teaching.

Visionary Leaders Are Trust Officers of Truth

As a servant leader in the church, the minister shares status and authority with many others who are called and commissioned to be trust officers in the service of the Lord. We are called and commissioned to share and pass on the message about salvation and to train believers in the values and implementation of this good news from God. Ministers are expected to teach what the church has always taught.

We must follow the lead of the first Christian preachers and teachers, whom Albert Outler aptly described as "traditioners, trust officers of the Christian treasure of truth, qualified judges of right teaching." We are passing on something that is not novel or new. It was established by our Lord and it must continue with integrity. Teaching is one of the strongest ways by which that integrity is passed on.

The Christian gospel is God's invitation to an experience, an experience inclusive of moral effects, spiritual effects, and social effects. The biblical record is also the sourcebook for the kind of noble, serious, instructive, and necessary work that we must do as teachers. It is from within this province of the distinct biblical record that the Christian minister is expected and authorized to teach what the church teaches.

Visionary Leaders Are Shapers of Community

Along with teaching, pastors are expected to inspire and promote what generates social uplift and human advancement through freedom, justice, fairness, and the steady pursuit of community. Very little notion of the values of community are being rightly espoused in our time. We are privatized now in America. We are tribalized and competing. If this loss is to be turned back, it must be by those who understand why the tradition was established and what it is intended to do in succeeding generations.

We are sharers in that grand succession of those who have dared to proclaim the Christian faith and sought to fulfill its implications. We are linked by life and experience with people who are struggling to survive and achieve in a secularistic and otherwise problematic society. The best tool we can give people is truth, which is communicated through teaching. By teaching truth, we apply the insights of the faith and guide people whom we have won to the faith.

A church that has integrity must begin at the point of someone being taught about the meaning of salvation. The church is the community of the saved. How are they saved? Through hearing the message of truth from the preacher. It is interesting how much Paul linked salvation with the messenger bringing the good news. It is truth handled, taught, shared, lived, advocated, and modeled with integrity.

First among the strategic means for this teaching is the ministry of preaching. Preaching rightly understood allows moral and spiritual instruction to be shared in mass fashion. It allows truth to be shared in a popular medium, but always with an individual impact.

According to the Synoptic Gospels, there was a blend of preaching and teaching in the ministry of Jesus. There are passages in the Gospels in which the terms "preaching" and "teaching" are used interchangeably so that the action of Jesus in addressing His hearers in public appears pointedly didactic and declarative. Jesus instructed in order to inspire. He gave content in order to share comfort. He declared at the same time that He explained.

The pastor is to be an able teacher. The readiness and skill to instruct must be reflected when the congregation gathers to worship God. It must be there when they are addressed out of God's Word, teaching through preaching. True religious experience is more than an emotional mood. Today there is a great deal of entertainment in the midst of our worship. People judge by the excitement of the occasion, but unless something is being taught and caught, the integrity is missing.

The Visionary Effect of Doctrine

Preaching in mass fashion calls attention to the Christian faith by isolating certain facts and truths from inside the experience of that faith. Preaching that is religiously instructive must address matters of doctrine. Charles Spurgeon once said, "The most fervent revivalism will wear itself out in mere smoke if it is not maintained by the fuel of teaching." Sound teaching precedes sound living.

The concern to share doctrine must be a part of our passion—not doctrine for doctrine's sake, but for the sake of the people's understanding and use for living rightfully. Doctrine is best focused when the way it can help has been understood first by the preacher. It then breeds life and imparts a liveliness. It shows itself in more than an abstract subject. It claims attention as a necessary message that attracts, alerts, and assures.

This is the way integrity is developed in a congregation. Biblical doctrines matter for life at its best. When somebody says, "I don't want any doctrine," they do not understand the importance of shared truth. Doctrines rightly understood and rightly shared satisfy the soul's quest for truth and liberate the mind by engaging the thoughts. What a marvelous thing to leave the sanctuary at the close of a worship service and have someone say, "I've got something to wrestle with this week because of what you shared this morning." The preaching that really matters does not separate inspiration from something that has been taught.

Howard Thurman used to tell about how impressed his grandmother was with the preaching that she, a former slave, had heard from a certain slave minister when she was a girl. The slave preacher was allowed to come to the plantation and preach about four times a year, and on each occasion he had drilled into the consciousness of all his hearers the notion that they did not have to feel inferior because they were slaves. Thurman said everything in him quivered with the pulsing tremor of raw energy when, in his grandmother 's recital, she would come to the triumphant climax of the slave minister's message. He always ended the message the same way. "You," he would say, with his eyes fastened upon them, standing his full height, "You are not niggers. You are not slaves. You are God's children!"

That kind of sharing of truth gave people grounds for personal dignity. Preaching that does not involve the sharing of truth at the level of human need is not what brings the church integrity. It is out of that profound sense of being children of God that the slaves could handle the pressures of their days. They were subjects and cattle to the slave owners, but the preacher gave them that bedrock truth that brought them through. That is the foundation of the African-American faith. We must call the church back to this understanding of who we are because of God's mercy and God's grace. We must share it.

The white preacher who served the master's interest always taught them, "Slaves, obey your master." That was the training that the slave master's preacher sought to convey. He intent was to keep the people submissive. But the slave preacher applied his doctrine in the interest of his hearers. He sat where they sat. He felt what they felt, and he was intent to liberate their spirits. That is the true function of sound teaching: to liberate people. You shall know the truth, and the truth shall make you free.

A German theologian of another day had delivered a great sermon in the eyes of a person who greeted him after the service was over. She said, "Sir, I'm glad to meet a theologian who stands on the Word of God." He said, "I understand what you mean, but I want to correct you at one point. I do not stand on the Word of

God, I stand under it." When the pastor does this sort of teaching, the congregation is reminded that integrity comes by being under the authority of the Word of God.

Teaching to Build a Visionary Christian Consciousness

The fundamental work of the minister in the congregation of believers is to share the Christian faith, interpret its significance for all of life, and develop a Christian consciousness, which is sadly missing in many of the churches that are growing today. There is too much consumer consciousness, but not a Christian consciousness. Agape love flows from a Christian consciousness, the love that accepts people where they are and treats them as if they were where they ought to be.

I remember when I was given charge of pastoring in Detroit. In the first business meeting that we held as a congregation, I asked them for permission to use the first three hours of every morning free from any encumbrances apart from an emergency that might arise, and I told them why. I told them I wanted to be in study, preparing for worship, exegeting biblical passages so that I could gain the meaning of Scripture to share with them for their living. I said, "I want to spend time in prayer so that when I come among you in my visitation at the hospital or in your home, my presence will count for something. It will be more than routine."

They agreed to give me the first three hours of the early morning free from any encumbrances, and that lasted for twenty-five years. I was fresh every Sunday and never had burnout. I am talking about a way of staying vital by means of being under the truth and scheduling times in such a way that our main business remains the main business.

As a result of what happened in the midst of that kind of commitment, we did not have room for the people who came to Bible study in the midweek hour. They were standing around the walls. A church develops integrity by being in touch with truth, where everyone sees himself or herself in that mirror and we can appeal to God for change. That's integrity.

Visionary Impact of a Holy Example

By attitude and behavior, a pastor should incarnate what the church is to be and how growth will take place. A pastor develops integrity most contagiously through his or her own personal Christian character and earnest example. The accent I am placing upon a personal life that can appeal to others is very important because, unless we instruct out of a sense of integrity that is granted by the graciousness of the Lord, unless we do our work out of a disciplined direction by being under our Master in heaven, then whatever we do will not matter. The character and ability of the person in the pulpit will determine the nature of its work and the extent of its helpfulness.

Harold Carter, pastor in Baltimore, Maryland, and well-known scholarly preacher, devoted a whole chapter to pastoral integrity in his book *Myths That Mire the Ministry*. He warned against concupiscence, the desire for temporal ends that has its seat in the senses. He said, "Sex presents such a formidable problem in ministerial ranks, and since this is so, an in-depth study of its impact on our calling would be a blessing in seminary circles." Many seminaries now include the study of human sexuality among their required courses. Male and female seminarians taking these courses are guided in studying themselves existentially, with a focus on understanding temptation, entanglements, the influence of moods, the problem of viewing other persons as objects, and the problem of a low self-esteem that seeks to control other people. We must come back to that biblical notion of holiness, which in the Greek really means wholeness. We must be of one piece.

Given the scope and import of ministering, a serious look at our own selfhood is increasingly necessary. The ultimate response that vital ministry demands is that of a God-committed selfhood, coupled with spiritual empowerment—more than methods, more than techniques. The need is for the self that is dominated and directed by the Holy Spirit. The Lord requires clean hands and honest hearts for His work. A church that has integrity usually grows out of a minister who has integrity.

When the time came for Jesus to single out those persons from the crowd and shape them for assignments under His direction, He withdrew to pray about the choices He must make. He prayed about it all throughout the night, exploring His options with God, with a God-illumined thought process. And the account tells us that when day came, "He called his disciples and chose twelve of them, whom he also named apostles" (Luke 6:13).

The pastor must operate according to the vision already cast by our Lord. Dream your dreams. Let them be big, but let them be the same dreams that our Lord had when He started the church, to let it have integrity and to give His life for it.

Share Your Dream of Visionary Leaders

It was a wise word that Roger Hazelton, former dean at Oberlin Graduate School of Theology, shared with his students. "The truly effective minister is not someone who can take oversight in the church, but one who can share insight with that church." It is not one or the other; it is both. If we have insight, a church is more apt to give us and let us retain oversight. "Mark this," Hazelton said, "people in our churches today need more than strength for the mastery of life; they need light on the mystery of life, and there is a positive relationship between the two. In the last analysis, you cannot have the one without the other."

I say this to pastors. Develop great leaders. Pour your hearts into them. Do not allow yourself to be the central focus. Be the figure around whom the congregation coalesces, but let them co-alesce for the right reason—receiving truth shared from the heart that is concerned about them, so concerned that you spare no pain in order to help them have integrity.

Those who truly love the Lord and are deeply concerned to help people learn to live by God's will can develop churches with integrity because they will be contented, like that parson in Geoffrey Chaucer 's *Canterbury Tales,* to gladly teach by following that teaching themselves.

12

THE ROLE OF A PASTOR'S SPOUSE

by James Earl Massey

Originally appeared in Wanda Taylor-Smith, *The Women Speak: Shared Wisdom for Women Married to Pastors* (CreateSpace Independent Publishing Platform, 2013), 101-103. Used by permission.

D r. Wanda Taylor-Smith's book has offered a platform from which women married to preachers and pastors have been speaking. As a long-time husband (over 60 years) whose wife has been at my side during my roles as preacher/pastor/professor/seminary dean, I have learned much about role adaptability by observing my wife's responses as a companion in marriage.

First, being both the child and grandchild of pastors, my wife came into our marriage with a strong respect for the ministry and a healthy view of church life. Having watched the healthy relationship of her preacher—father and mother, and that of her preacher—grandfather and grandmother, she knew that she too could relate meaningfully and supportively in our marriage.

Second, she understood, as did I, that both marriage and ministry require natural gifts and spiritual enablement, and that self-growth must forever remain a foundational concern. She recognized my pastoral gifts and supported me in further training them

for use, but she also was aware of her own gifts for service both within the church and beyond the church setting. Her occupational interests led her to become a nurse and later a professional counselor.

As a church member, she sang in one of the choirs, taught a Sunday school class, and was a counselor to young adults. As pastor and spouse, we were intentional about supporting each other in our gift-based roles, mindful that all gifts, whether natural or spiritual, contribute to meeting human need, solving problems, and aiding possibilities for people. Recognizing, as Paul explained it, that "we have gifts that differ according to the grace given us" (Romans 12:6), we both sought to "outdo one another and showing honor" (verse 10b) as we served the Lord in our distinct roles.

Third, when invitations came for me to serve in other spheres of ministry (campus minister, denominational radio voice, professor, dean of the university chapel, seminary dean), we shared openly and prayed to discern the wisest course of action—and also to secure a concurrent role for Gwendolyn with every move we agreed to make. We remained on guard against disconnection, satisfied only with our reality, always standing with each other in a simple but steadfast relationship based on loving trust and a trusting love.

What I have written here is a faithful reflection on what Gwendolyn Inez Kilpatrick Massey has contributed to me as a person and to my path as a minister. Free to be herself, and trusted as one who loves God and me, my wife helped me to develop as a person and to better offer leadership in the ways and places entrusted to me. My vocation did not deprive her of her identity and her identity did not depend on any role imposed upon her from without. We have long rejoiced that both marriage and ministry require communal actions and that both minister and the minister's spouse succeed best when neither one acts selfishly but remains free to serve and bless on the basis of their own life-enriching, grace-sustained gifts. This is not only reasonable, it also responsibly honors the trust God placed in us.

13

THE AFRICAN-AMERICAN SPIRITUALS: FAITH AND WORSHIP

by James Earl Massey

Originally appeared in Timothy George, ed.,

God and the Holy Trinity (Baker Academic, 2006), 57-68.

Used by permission.

The topic of my essay informs you that I have chosen to treat our theme from the standpoint of the faith witness voiced in the religious folk songs or "spirituals" of African Americans. Behind this choice lie three reasons. First, these historic, history-laden songs, particularly those from the pre-Civil War period, that infamous slavery era, reflect the earliest documented worldview of African-American spirituality. Second, the present hymnological tradition within most branches of the Black church is based upon and echoes the faith perspectives and worldview to which the spirituals give such poignant witness.[1] Third, I have chosen to call attention to these songs because scholars usually

---

1   See Jon Michael Spencer, *Black Hymnody: A Hymnological History of the African-American Church* (University of Tennessee Press, 1992). John Lovell Jr., writing on the contemporary use of the gospel music genre in the Black church, has explained: "What is called gospel music is hardly anything more than an effort to give the spiritual a modernity in form, content, and beat." See his *Black Song: The Forge and the Flame* (Paragon House, 1986), 467.

overlook their confessional content when they are advancing the interests of theological reflection.

I have chosen these historic creations because of their value for treating our theme. I am deeply aware that, beyond what black philosopher Alain Locke referred to as the "ingenuous simplicity"[2] of the spirituals, there lie not only social protests and aspirations but also some instructive and inspiring theological beliefs and perspectives. There is far more in the spirituals than poignant poetry and plaintive music; there is also Scripture-informed, soul-engaging, prophetic musings about God, human life, Christian faith, spirituality, personal responsibility, and human destiny.

The Spirituals

In referring to these songs as "spirituals," I honor a respected tradition. While they are by category religious folk songs, they are by content and intent "spirituals." Influenced by the heart-wrenching history that inspired these songs, W. E. B. DuBois called them "sorrow songs."[3] Mindful of the settings in which they were fashioned and used, during and after slavery, Booker T. Washington referred to these songs as "plantation melodies."[4] After researching the history of these creations and the strivings and aspirations they voice, historian Miles Mark Fisher discussed them as "Negro

---

2   See Alain Locke, "The Negro Spirituals," in *The New Negro: An Interpretation* (1925), 199-200; idem, repr. in *Freedom on My Mind: The Columbia Documentary History of the African American Experience*, ed. Manning Marble (New York: Columbia University Press, 2003), esp. 587.

3   W.E.B. Dubois, *The Souls of Black Folk*, ed. Henry Louis Gates and Terri Hume Oliver, Norton Critical Edition (New York: Norton, 1999), esp. 154-64.

4   Booker T. Washington, "Preface" to *Twenty-Four Negro Melodies: Transcribed for the Piano by Samuel Coleridge-Taylor* (Bryn, Mawr, PA: Oliver Ditson, 1905), viii.

Slave Songs."[5] Impressed by the number of these songs, their folk origins, topical range, and transforming applications, musicologist John Lovell Jr. honored those who fashioned these songs when he referred to them collectively as "Black Song."[6]

The deep substructure of the spirituals, the foundation on which they rest and from which they rise, is faith. These songs reflect and promote black beliefs, hopes, and aspirations rooted in faith: faith in the creative, all-powerful, delivering, sustaining, energizing, and fulfilling activity of a just and loving God. This faith content gave strength to their intentions for use: to inform, encourage, sustain, and inspire. Thus, Howard Thurman makes a convictional comment: "The clue to the meaning of the spirituals is to be found in religious experience and spiritual discernment."[7]

A response of dynamic African sensibilities to teachings drawn from both Testaments of Scripture, insights from the processes of nature, and raw experiences in life, the spirituals are songs of faith content sung and used with intent. They were originally expressive instrumental agencies to give witness, to teach, to nurture, to remind, to encourage, to sustain, to convict, to convince, to inspire.

---

5   Miles Mark Fisher, *Negro Slave Songs in the United States* (New York: Citadel, 1935).

6   Lovell, *Black Song.*

7   Thurman, *Negro Spiritual Speaks of Life and Death,* 12.

God in the Spirituals

In 1938, Benjamin Elijah Mays published an important study entitled *The Negro's God*. The purpose of that study was "to tell America what the Negro thinks of God."[8] That book was a first of its kind. It was based on Negro literature dating from as early as 1760, and the researched corpus included slave narratives, biography, autobiography, addresses, novels, poetry, prayers, sermons, catechetical productions for church use, and spirituals. While the entire book is informative, it is particularly valuable as the first attempt by any scholar to study the development of the idea of God in the literature of African Americans. I call attention to what Mays discovered and reported about ideas of God as expressed in the 122 spirituals he examined:

> The ideas reflected in the Spirituals may be briefly summarized: God is omnipotent, omnipresent, and omniscient. In both Heaven and earth God is sovereign. He is a just God . . . . God is revengeful . . . . God is a warrior and He fights the battles of His chosen people . . . . God takes care of His own. He will see to it that the righteous are vindicated and that the heavily laden are given rest from the troubles of the world . . . . God is near and there is a feeling of dependence upon Him. In times of distress, He is ever present . . . . He answers prayers . . . . God is observant. He sees all you do and He hears all you say.[9]

---

8   Cited from the preface, Benjamin E. Mays, *The Negro's God: As Reflected in His Literature* (1938; repr., New York: Atheneum, 1969). With a new preface by Vincent Harding.

9   Ibid., 21.

These ideas in the spirituals regarding God are traditionally biblical. The spirituals appropriated some ideas directly from the Bible, such as God being a warrior and deliverer, as illustrated in "Go Down, Moses" and "Joshua Fit de Battle of Jericho." Statements and accounts reported in the Bible stimulated other ideas, such as God being always near and observant. In any instance, these God ideas are in agreement with what the Bible expresses about God.

The spirituals devote special attention to God as deliverer. Some of the most vibrant lines treat God's dramatic work in changing situations for certain biblical characters, or using chosen characters to change situations for others, as in this reference:

> "Thus spoke the Lord," bold Moses said;
> "Let my people go,
> If not I'll smite your firstborn dead,
> Let my people go."[10]

Or this reference to Joshua in the well-known song that honors him:

> You may talk about yo' king of Gideon,
> You may talk about yo' man of Saul,
> Dere's none like good ole Joshua,
> At de battle of Jericho.[11]

In connection with this Joshua song and its message of a sovereign God who acts to deliver the oppressed, John Lovell Jr. has

---

10   "Go Down, Moses," in *The Books of American Negro Spirituals*, compiled by James Weldon Johnson and J. Rosamond Johnson (New York: Viking, 1969), 1:15-53.

11   "Joshua Fit de Battle of Jericho," in Johnson, *Books of American Negro Spirituals*, 1:56-58.

commented: "Only the most naive reader [or singer or listener] misses the point that what Joshua did can be done again and again, wherever wrong and evil are to be overthrown, wherever promised good and right are to be established."[12] The same message comes through in the spiritual "Didn't My Lord Deliver Daniel?"

> He delivered Daniel fom de lion's den,
>
> Jonah fom de belly of de whale,
>
> An' de Hebrew chillun fom de fiery furnace,
>
> An' why not every man?[13]

The dominant view expressed in the spirituals about God is of a sovereign Creator who has the whole of life under his care, and that, being God, he will make things right in the end:

> God is a God!
>
> God don't never change!
>
> God is a God
>
> An' He always will be God!
>
> The earth His footstool
>
> an' heav'n His throne,
>
> The whole creation all His own,
>
> His love an' power will prevail,
>
> His promises will never fail.
>
> God is a God!
>
> An' always will be God![14]

---

12   Lovell, *Black Song*, 229.

13   "Didn't My Lord Deliver Daniel?" Johnson, *Books of American Negro Spirituals*, 1:148-51.

14   "God Is a God! God Don't Never Change," in Lovell, *Black Song*, 238.

Jesus in the Spirituals

The most important thing one can say about the representation of Jesus in the spirituals is that they never view him as a distant figure, or only an object of faith, but always as a living person whose warmth, concern, love, trustworthiness, helpfulness, power, steadiness, example, and availability we can experience. The spirituals understand that Jesus is Son of God and Christ. Although these titles basically describe his personhood, they do not adequately convey his personality as the singers experience and regard him.

By "personality" I refer to the personal attributes and traits that allow us to anticipate and value his behavior toward those who in openness and faith approach him. The spirituals evidence a relationship with Jesus, a valued familiarity and companionship with him as religious subject. Jesus is one who knows life as the singers knew it, and one who knows them as suffering supplicants as well.

We can readily trace the impact of the circumstances and plight of the Hebrews upon those who created and sang the spirituals. Knowledge of that nation's deliverance by God from struggles helped the singers discern the nature of God and trust God's power. But, while Old Testament narratives provided dramatic resources for faith, the New Testament story about Jesus sensitized the slave singers, especially accounts of his arrest, trial, and crucifixion. Jesus' approach to his experiences informed them for facing and handling their experiences. They identified with Jesus, deeply aware that he had already identified himself with them:

> Dey crucified my Lord,
> An' he never said a mumbalin' word.

Dey crucified my Lord,

An' he never said a mumbalin' word.

Not a word—not a word—not a word.[15]

Among the many other oft-sung elegies about our Lord's ordeal as suffering Savior, there is that unique and universally beloved spiritual that asks, "Were You There When They Crucified My Lord?"[16] In that spiritual, the singers confessed their understanding and voiced their lament concerning that event Jesus underwent. They speak of Jesus being "nailed to the tree," "pierced in the side," and "laid in the tomb," and they responded to the meaning of it all with full openness of soul:

Were you there when they crucified my Lord?

Were you there when they crucified my Lord?

Oh, sometimes it causes me to tremble, tremble, tremble.

Were you there when they crucified my Lord?

In his autobiography, Howard Thurman tells about the visit he and his wife, Sue, had with Mahatma Gandhi while in India in 1935. After a long visit with deep conversation, Gandhi asked the Thurmans not to leave before favoring him by singing one of the Negro spirituals. He specifically requested that they sing "Were You There When They Crucified My Lord?" with the comment, "I feel that this song gets to the root of the experience of the entire human race under the spread of the healing wings of suffering." Mrs. Thurman, an Oberlin Conservatory of Music graduate, led

---

15 "He Never Said a Mumbalin' Word," in ibid., 261.

16 Johnson, *Books of American Negro Spirituals*, 2:136-37.

in singing that spiritual as Gandhi and his associates bowed their heads in prayer.[17]

Although Gandhi sensed something of universal import in the undeserved suffering Jesus underwent, we lament that he missed the expiatory meaning of Jesus's death. The slave singers, however, did not miss that meaning. They understood his death as an atoning deed, and they rejoiced about it as a completed task:

> Hallelujah t' de Lamb,
> Jesus died for every man.
> But He ain't comin' here t' die no mo',
> Ain't comin' here t' die no mo.

> He died for de blind, He died for de lame,
> He bore de pain an' all de blame.
> But He ain't comin' here t' die no mo',
> Ain't comin' here t' die no mo.[18]

Several spirituals treat the Lord's resurrection, but representative of the note of victory sounded in them all is the spiritual "Dust an' Ashes," also known as "An' de Lord Shall Bear My Spirit Home."[19] First, this spiritual acknowledges that death does its work on all humans: "Dust, dust an' ashes fly over on my grave." It goes on to voice faith that death is not the end: "An' de Lord shall bear my spirit home." Successive stanzas picture the Lord's crucifixion, the burial of his body in Joseph's tomb, the

---

17 Thurman, *With Head and Heart*, 134.

18 "But He Ain't Comin' Here t' Die No Mo'," in *Religious Fold-Songs of the Negro: As Sung at Hampton*, ed. R. Nathaniel Dett (Hampton, VA: Hampton Institute Press, 1927), 103.

19 "Dust an' Ashes," in ibid., 236.

descent of an angel to roll the stone from the entrance, and then death's loss:

> De cold grave could not hold Him,
> Nor death's cold iron band,
> An' de Lord shall bear my spirit home,
> An' de Lord shall bear my spirit home.
>
> He rose, He rose, He rose from de dead.
> He rose, He rose, He rose from de dead,
> He rose, He rose, He rose from de dead,
> An' de Lord shall bear my spirit home.

The point of witness is clear: what God did for Jesus, God is going to do for those who believe in Jesus.

Regarding the Christian life, the creators of spirituals were deeply concerned about the inner life of the soul. They sensed, quite rightly, that sincere religion and courageous living call for a heart that God has touched and controls. Being enslaved, oppressed, and unfairly treated, there were times when the heart's attitudes provoked alarm and dismay, times when the impulse to deal with things on a purely selfish basis was strong, so a penitent appeal was made to God or Jesus for help:

> 'Tis me, 'tis me, 'tis me, O Lord,
> Standin' in the need of prayer.
> 'Tis me, 'tis me, 'tis me, O Lord,
> An' I'm standin' in the need of prayer.[20]

---

20   "Tis Me," in ibid., 183.

The singers knew that God and Jesus give aid for character change. That was the concern behind these lines:

> Lord, I want to be a Christian
> In-a my heart, in-a my heart,
> Lord, I want to be more loving
> In-a my heart.
> I don't want to be like Judas
> In-a my heart.
> Lord, I want to be like Jesus
> In-a my heart.[21]

The insistence was always upon faith in Jesus, trust in him as a concerned helper, an understanding companion, a brother, although he is also Lord.

> Oh, Jesus my Saviour,
> On Thee I'll depend,
> When troubles are near me,
> You'll be my true friend.[22]

Given the peace and hope from an experienced relationship with Jesus, the spirituals did not even view dying as an ultimate threat:

> You needn't mind my dying,
> You needn't mind my dying,
> You needn't mind my dying,

---

21   "Lord, I Want to Be a Christian," in ibid., 50-51.

22   "I'm Troubled in Mind," in ibid., 236.

Jesus goin' to make up my dying bed.[23]

This attitude of confidence in God and sense of companionship with Jesus, including even in the hour of death, is never absent from the spirituals. Urgency of need and sincere longing of soul made these seekers strive for survival, courage, solace, stability, and meaning. To gain these benefits the sufferers had to reach for the ultimate. In seeking the ultimate, informed by biblical truths, they found the Triune God. Thus comes the Christian orthodoxy these songs reflect.

The Holy Spirit in the Spirituals

The biblical teachings about the Holy Spirit point beyond themselves in two directions: one direction is Godward, disclosing that in the Godhead a Third Person is related to God the Father and Jesus the Son; the other direction is humanward, declaring that God relates to his open and obedient children in intimate and inward ways.

According to Romans 8:1-17 and Galatians 5:16-25, the Christian life is lived "in" and "by" the Spirit. The spirituals usually assume the pervasive presence of the Holy Spirit with the believer, but they rarely make direct references to the Spirit. There are, however, many spirituals showing experience of the deep intimacy between God and the soul as a sense of divine possession that makes one feel settled and secure, settled in grace and secure in God's love.

Voiced affirmations by African-American Christians about divine grace and a sense of being filled or possessed by the Spirit are

---

23 "Jesus Goin' to Make Up My Dying Bed," in Lovell, Black Song, 319.

two of the most persistent features in African-American worship. Regarding God's grace, Henry H. Mitchell has explained: "No mere theological nicety, the grace of God was and is to the Black [person] a means of life and strength—a source of support and balance and self-certainty in a world whose approval of Blacks is still in extremely short supply."[24]

We can understand being filled or possessed by the Spirit as an experience of feeling settled, energized, and emboldened by the Holy Spirit. This is surely reflected in the spiritual "Dere's a Little Wheel a-Turnin' in My Heart":

> O I don't feel no ways tired in my heart,
> In my heart, in my heart,
> O I don't feel no ways tired in my heart.
> I've a double 'termination in my heart,
> In my heart, in my heart,
> I've a double 'termination in my heart.[25]

After the heart has surrendered to God's claiming grace, God has witnessed his approval through his Spirit. The Spirit grants a convictional knowledge to the believer that God has become intimately linked with oneself, as in lines like these:

> O, I know the Lord,
> I know the Lord,
> I know the Lord's laid His hands on me.[26]

---

24 Henry H. Mitchell, *Black Belief: Fold Beliefs of Blacks in America and West Africa* (New York: Harper & Row, 1975), 130.

25 "Dere's a Little Wheel a-Turnin' in My Heart," in Dett, *Religious Fold-Songs*, 168.

26 "I Know the Lords Laid His Hands on Me," in Ibid., 207.

Such songs witness about a life activated and controlled from a new and ultimate center.

In one of those rare instances where the lyric directly mentions the Holy Spirit, that particular spiritual understands him as one who "moves" or motivates the believer to prayer. Perhaps Romans 8:26 or Ephesians 6:18 influenced this view:

> Ev'ry time I feel the Spirit,
>
> move-in' in my heart,
>
> I will pray.
>
> O, ev'ry time I feel the Spirit,
>
> move-in' in my heart,
>
> I will pray.[27]

The simple assumption regarding the Holy Spirit is that he joins the believer's life in a sensed filling and "possession," granting an awareness of belonging (Rom. 8:16) and of being girded (Luke 24:49). I use that expression "sensed possession" purposely. Although it would be a mistake to identify the inward witness of the Spirit solely with what one can feel and physically express in shout or movement, it is likewise a mistake to overlook the fact that feeling—the deepest, most immediate, and most vivid human experience—is sometimes the means by which the Holy Spirit allows us to realize his inward ministry to us.

The singers understood this, and while some of them certainly enjoyed and expected times of "holy overwhelming" in their religious experience, they also sang about those private times when the Holy Spirit brought needed encouragement and renewal to their lives:

---

27   "Ev'ry Time I Feel the Spirit," in Ibid., 169.

> Sometimes I feel discouraged,
> And think my work's in vain,
> But then the Holy Spirit
> Revives my soul again.[28]

The human condition involves us in a range of experiences demanding that the Christian have a focused selfhood. One achieves that focus with the help of the possessing and renewing presence of the Holy Spirit within us.

Our becoming, our growth in grace, is dependent upon the goals and means exhibited in Jesus and mediated within us by the Holy Spirit. The believer, helped by the Holy Spirit, receives strengthened resolve and readiness to live for God and to face any conflicts and opposition:

> Done made my vow to the Lord
> and I never will turn back,
> I will go, I shall go, to see what the end will be.
> Done opened my mouth to the Lord
> and I never will turn back,
> I will go, I shall go, to see what the end will be.[29]

The singers understood that the steadiness and stamina needed to fulfill such a vow depends upon a believer being possessed and enabled by the Holy Spirit.

---

28 "There Is a Balm in Gilead," in Ibid., 88.

29 "Done Made My Vow to the Lord," in Lovell, Black Song, 323.

Conclusion

I have been reviewing the Christian witness in some of the historic spirituals, those worded songs about God, Jesus, the Holy Spirit, and Christian life. Biblical truths and imagery influenced these songs, and African-American sensibilities and social experience shaped them. These spirituals, with many others, reflect faith. They bear witness, reinforce meanings, inspire worship, and sustain hope. They give us poignant music and so much more. They give us prophetic musings, flavored by the history, longings, experiences, religious discoveries, and faith of a life-tested people.

These songs nurture self-respect. They echo a biblical theology. They voice an affirmative theodicy. They mirror the African-American soul. They helped, and still help, a seeking people to face dark times and meet the exigencies of life with faith, fortitude, and essential pride. These songs are an important repository of spiritual insight and, duly regarded, they stir one to faithfulness, praise, and practical theological reflection.

14

TEACHING THAT POINTS TO TRUTH

by James Earl Massey

Originally appeared in the *Asbury Seminary Journal*, 52:1, Spring 1997, 5-9. Used by permission.

U pon graduating from the University of Berlin, Dietrich Bonhoeffer expressed gratitude to his famous teachers by writing some phrases of farewell to them on his thesis. He wrote this to Professor Harnack: "What I have learned and come to understand in your seminar is too closely associated with my whole personality for me to be able ever to forget it." For those of us entrusted with the blessed privilege to teach, such tributes keep us mindful that a crown of trust has been placed above our heads and we must continually grow taller if we are ever to reach it.

The Privilege of Teaching

Teaching is indeed a privileged work. It is a fundamental activity that is filled with promise. Jacques Barzun's timely and strategic reminder that the task of teaching is to turn pupils into life-long learners, aiding them to be creative and productive persons, high-lights aspects of that promise. This process of assisting pupils to become independent learners is usually prolonged and sometimes painful. It means interacting with students who alternate in their attitudes toward us: receiving from us, then standing in rejection, usually trusting us and often testing us, curious and eager to know most of the time but sometimes hampered by resentment toward the demands placed upon them in the process of discovering and understanding, recalling matters and relating them for meaning.

Near the end of his long and illustrious teaching career, William James was probably recalling how this sometimes distressing process had weighed upon him when he rejoiced that he would no longer have to face a "mass of alien and recalcitrant humanity." Teaching is a difficult task, but the difficulties are because of the promise associated with it, the promise of benefit, life-changing benefit, to persons.

Good teaching involves far more than the sharing of facts and the concern to stimulate inquiry; it also involves an understanding of students as persons, and the need to honor their human worth. The task of teaching includes a wide range of activities such as reading, research, reflection, consultation with one's colleagues, modeling virtues and skills, promoting values, mapping the process and monitoring the progress of students in relation to a course and a curriculum. But central to our work is the spirit in which we serve. Along with the benefits that our learning and scholarly process equip us to share, students need our human touch. Gilbert Highet had this in mind when he advised that to teach well, "You must throw your heart into it, and must realize that it cannot all be done by formulas, or you will spoil your work, and your pupils, and yourself."

The Influence of Teaching

In 1897 a book entitled *Men I Have Known* was published by clergyman Frederick W. Farrar. In it he reminisced about eminent persons he had known. Poet Robert Browning was one of them, and Farrar quoted Browning's comment to him about how important it is that young people have the memory of "seeing great men." There is in my memory of my grade school years a great and unforgettable teacher, an African-American man who threw his heart into the task of teaching me. He was competent, industrious, and caring. His classroom was a virtual picture gallery, with glossy photographs lining the space between the ceiling and the blackboard along three of the classroom walls.

I shall never forget the drama we children sensed as he supplemented the class lessons with information about the persons whose pictures hung on the classroom walls. Along with the stories, there was also an increased and justifiable sense of pride in our race because the pictures on the walls were of African Americans who were grand achievers, persons who, despite the odds, had become great. That teacher knew what we would face growing up in America, and he addressed that need. But, knowing our need to wed strict guidance to the pride and hope deepening in us, that teacher cautioned us with some lines from Longfellow's 'The Ladder of Saint Augustine":

> The heights by great men reached and kept
> Were not attained by sudden flight;
> But they, while their companions slept,
> Were toiling upward in the night.

These lines, which I first heard during my grade school years at Ulysses S. Grant School in Ferndale, Michigan, still stir my spirit and prod me to be diligent in every quest and endeavor. The teacher who recited these lines to us exemplified in his character, competence, and caring the message they bear. No one should wonder, then, why teaching came to stand out in my mind as the noblest of work.

A few years ago, I joined other friends, family members, and former students at my teacher's funeral service in Detroit. He and I had remained close across the years, sharing letters, telephone calls, and visits. He died in his 93rd year of life, and we had conversed by phone during the month before his death. His last letter to me has been placed among my treasures: he sent with it a list of former students with whom he was still in contact, and beside each name was a brief description of what that person was doing. His letter to me also included a gift photograph of himself as he was at the time he taught me in grade school!

Those mementos hold deep meaning for me and keep me reminded that the central issue in both teaching and living is to touch other lives in meaningful ways. Good teaching happens when this remains a central concern. The teaching of Mr. Coit Cook Ford, Sr., issued from his heart; his work gave me inspiration, a good human influence, and essential information. Good teaching includes these three benefits, but the greatest of them is a good human influence. This is the kind of teaching that deserves tribute, the kind of teaching that God blesses to make it prosper.

The Circumstances of Teaching

Most of you are likely familiar with John Henry Newman 's classic study *Idea of a University* and will recall that, in the preface to this book, he explains that a university is "a place of teaching universal knowledge." Newman emphasized teaching as a central function in a university setting.

Several aspects of Newman's full definition of a university are still being debated, while some aspects of it are being refined—as many of you know who are familiar with Jaroslav Pelikan's recent reassessment of Newman's classic. But Newman's emphasis on teaching as a central function in the university is worthy of being underscored anew. Teaching is crucial not only to university life, but it is imperative for transmitting and preserving a clear understanding of life itself. It is not incidental that the great leaders in history, religious leaders included, have been teachers.

I began with a quote from Dietrich Bonhoeffer's tribute to Adolf von Harnack, one of his honored teachers. As I conclude, I must mention something else Bonhoeffer wrote about his teachers. Writing from Tegel Prison to his parents on Reformation Day, 1943, seven months into his confinement there because of his political resistance to Hitler, Bonhoeffer was still aware of the rhythm of the church year and shared with them some of his meditation about the meaning of that day. He also shared his wonderment about why Martin Luther's actions and teachings had been followed by consequences which were the exact opposite of what he had intended.[1]

Luther had worked for unity between Christian people, but both the church and Europe had been torn apart. He had worked for the "freedom of the Christian believer," but the unexpected consequence was licentiousness among the masses. Luther had worked to bring about a secular order freed from clerical privilege and control, but the result was insurrection, the Peasant's War, and general disorder in society. Luther was so affected by the turn of events that tormented his last years of life; again and again he doubted the value of his life's work.

---

1   Dietrich Bonhoeffer, *Letters and Papers from Prison*, Eberhard Bethge, ed. (New York: MacMillan Publishing Co., 1972), 123.

Bonhoeffer thought about all this on that Reformation Day, and he recalled a classroom discussion in Berlin when two of his teachers had debated whether the great historical, intellectual, and spiritual movements made headway through their primary or their secondary motives. One had argued that such movements went forward due to their primary motives, while the other countered that the secondary motives moved them forward. While first hearing them debate, Bonhoeffer had thought the first to be right and the second wrong. But later, in prison, reflecting on what had happened to Germany under Hitler, and on his own situation as a political prisoner, Bonhoeffer turned more to the view that the second was right.

All teaching, even in the best of settings and in the interest of the best of students, involves us in the circle of circumstance, and our approach to our task must be tempered by an understanding that much of what we formulate and treat in teaching is not fixed and final truth, but pointers to the truth. There must also be the awareness that much of what we do will bear consequences we did not intend. Some of what we teach out of a primary motive will fall short of our intended purpose because of circumstance, and some secondary effect will become prominent. This conditional factor should keep us reminded that what we *are* is as crucial in teaching as what we *know.* This circumstantial factor to our work should keep us sensitive to our need for help from beyond ourselves as we teach.

The Discipline of Teaching

So, as we return to our work, let us continue our scholarly pursuits to stay fresh for our task, remaining eager, as well, to assist the learning process of those who look to us. Let us have a framework that encases what we do, and a focus to what we do. Let us believingly trust that there is a future in what we do. Let us anchor our dreams in prayer and bolster our deeds by a daring trust. Let us give ourselves to study, thought, planning, discipline, prayer, tears, sweat, and persistent work, doing what is ours to do, but trusting God to bless it all to the highest good.

15

PLANNING WORSHIP AT THE TUSKEGEE CHAPEL

by *James Earl Massey*

Originally appeared in *Review & Expositor*, vol. 65, no. 1
(Winter,1988), 71-78. Used by permission.

At 9:30 every Sunday morning during the school year, a service of worship gathers campus persons and community people in a vital celebration of God at the Tuskegee University Chapel. During the organ prelude, the University Concert Choir waits in the chapel foyer, just beneath the "Singing Windows" with eleven favorite Negro spirituals depicted in colorful stained glass. They are ready to sing (one hundred twenty-five voices strong) the familiar. . .

> Cast thy burden upon the Lord, and he shall sustain thee.
> He never will suffer the righteous to fall; He is at thy
>   right hand.
> Thy mercy, Lord, is great and far above the heavens;
> Let none be made ashamed that wait upon Thee.

As the Dean of the Chapel issues the Call to Worship, the congregants stand and join in singing the processional hymn as

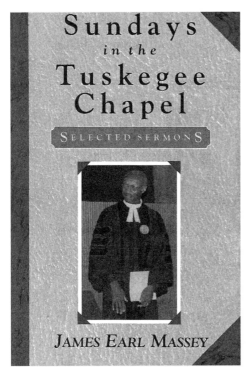

Sundays
in the
Tuskegee
Chapel

SELECTED SERMONS

JAMES EARL MASSEY

the choir enters the sanctuary. The singing is full-bodied, the atmosphere charged with sensed interest, and the place is alive with praise as the singers move up the aisles to take their places in the lofty choir space behind the pulpit area.

Thus the service begins, with "town and gown" gathered in unity and focused celebration. The Litany of Praise follows, the people still standing, and a responsive statement allows interaction between leader and people before the congregational hymn is sung. A high level of interest and involvement in worship has a long history at the Tuskegee Chapel, and the planning done to assist and bless that history takes place with a sense of privilege and responsibility.

Rationale Behind the Planning

The Chapel setting is that of a research and service university whose history dates back to 1881 when, blessed by state aid, Booker T. Washington started Tuskegee State Normal School for blacks. Washington led the development of the school until his death in 1915. The campus and city of Tuskegee are replete with many meaningful traditions and stirring legends growing out of the life, work, and influence of Booker T. Washington and George

Washington Carver, the scientist-humanitarian whose research work brought him into international prominence.

It is necessary to mention this because the educational and training opportunities for which the University is now known (agricultural technology, aerospace science, engineering, etc.) continue to attract American Blacks, some Whites, and nationals from as many as forty different countries. In 1987, ten percent of the student body of 3,300 were internationals. Given this kind of student mix, the planning for worship must not be limited to what is singularly local.

The Chapel family includes many townspeople, retired university personnel, active staff and faculty persons, and current students. Many former students attend service while visiting on the weekend. Guests from other schools in the area also attend on occasion. All these make up the congregation for which worship planning must take place.

Serious concern for spiritual nurture is traditional at Tuskegee University, and this is the case although the school is neither church-sponsored nor churchrelated. Strong chapel programs are usually associated with schools that need such activity to strengthen and extend their institutional life and mission, such as the church-controlled educational institutions.

Tuskegee University does not have such a background and orientation. It is a private university, and yet a vital chapel program has been operative in its campus life for most of its history. In 1988, the University celebrated the centennial year of having a full-time clergy person as resident chaplain. How was it that this happened? How is it that the religious emphasis continues even now with such strength and budgetary backing?

A part of the answer is in the educational philosophy of Booker T. Washington, who founded and shaped the school's programming. He initiated regular chapel services at the beginning, and soon afterward appointed an ordained clergyman to oversee the planning for the services. His view of the educational enterprise was not restrictedly intellectual but holistic. Washington asserted: "Mere hand training, without thorough moral, religious and mental education, counts for very little. The hands, the head, and the heart together, as the essential elements of educational need, should be so correlated that one may be made to help the others." Washington understood and taught that our humanity involves us all in religious and spiritual needs as well as physical, emotional, and intellectual ones. This view, and the concern to program school life in light of it, did not change after Washington died.

Another part of the answer is found in the continuing strength of religious concerns at work in Black American culture. Tuskegee University is an historically black school, with a predominantly black student body, and most of its black students have been impacted in their home communities by strong influences from within the Black Church. While it must be admitted that the cultural erosion in American life during the 1960s affected blacks as well as whites, the effects were not nearly as cataclysmic among blacks because of the strong religious sanctions at work within the black family ethos.

It is also true that student protest at Tuskegee, as at other schools across the nation, forced the removal of the compulsory chapel attendance rule in the late 1960s, allowing a student to exercise freedom of choice in the matter. This change did noticeably affect chapel attendance, but neither the University nor the Chapel suffered an identity crisis because of the change; nor did the University suffer an increased "secularization" of its life. The dropping of the compulsory chapel attendance rule only removed

a point of controversy from the campus life and freed the programming to gain strength to serve all those who voluntarily seek
its benefits.

These two explanations help to underscore why there is a continuing vitality in the life of the Chapel and a most responsible
involvement of so many in its All University Worship Services. The
societal changes were not all healthy, and many students understand this, which makes them seek All University Worship occasions to gain needed perspective for learning and life.

Design of the Worship Services

From the beginning, the religious orientation of the Tuskegee
Chapel has been decidedly Christian, and Christian presuppositions still provide the stance for the worship focus and planning.
To be sure, the University setting does embrace many others who
are identifiably active in other religious orientations, both among
the students and faculty members. The University honors their
choice and concerns by granting charters for freedom of operation on campus, but it is understood that the official orientation
of the Tuskegee Chapel is Christian. Those who study the Chapel
building cannot miss the presence of a large cross that stands at the
top of it, right over the front entrance section. Given this distinctive orientation, the planning for worship occasions in that building purposely follows the Christian worldview, honors Christian
claims, and keeps both vitally manifest in the celebration of God.

The planned format for this experience usually involves about
one hour and ten minutes. The usual Order of Service printed in
the Chapel Bulletin for the day is as follows, with occasional modi-
fication: Organ Prelude, The Choral Invitation, The Processional
Hymn, The Litany of Praise, The Congregational Hymn, The

Scripture Readings, The Morning Prayer, The Offertory, Special
Music, The Sermon, The Melody, The Recessional Hymn,
Benediction, Choral Amen, and Organ Postlude. The music selected for the singing worshipers is decidedly celebrative and confessional. The *Pilgrim Hymnal* has been used across many years;
its ecumenical spirit and wide range of materials make its contents
very suitable for this setting.

In selecting and presenting its special music, the University
Concert Choir deepens the celebrative and confessional emphasis
in worship. Professor Roy Edward Hicks, the choir director, is long-
term Chairman of the Department of Music, College of Arts and
Sciences, and is supremely dedicated to his craft and ministry. His
training and prowess, allied with a genuine concern for students,
have kept him at the growing edge. Professor Hicks favors and uses
a wide range of musical tastes in his planning of the special music,
and he will vary the offerings: sometimes scheduling an anthem,
a hymnic arrangement, a stylized Negro spiritual, a masterpiece
from the Classical era, or a contemporary sacred gospel creation. In
each instance, the spirit of the work blesses and engages rather than
merely entertains. Hicks wisely eschews selfish showmanship and
empty entertainment as a worship leader and participant.

The Melody, as it is called, which is sung after the sermon of
the day, is customarily from the black music tradition, and it blesses the meaning of the sermon at an affective climax of impression
that music best achieves. Well chosen, well sung music has always
played a major part in shaping and sustaining Chapel worship at
Tuskegee University.

Since 1932 there has been a printed Chapel Bulletin in use for
each worship service in the Chapel. Started under the ministry of
Dr. Harry V. Richardson, chaplain during 1932-1948, this custom has exacted early and regular planning for worship services.

Dr. Richardson also began the use of meditational materials on the back of the Sunday bulletin. His successors in ministry at the Chapel have continued this practice, and there is ample evidence among the worshipers to indicate that such devotional focus in print helps to prepare the climate for worship when the message is read before the service begins.

The Selection of Worship Materials and Participants

Music. In addition to what was reported above about the musical side of the service, this too must be said: the choir members show maturity and loyalty in their relationship and role. Singing every Sunday of the school year exacts its toll of time for rehearsing, and this is all on a volunteer basis. Modest academic credit is awarded for their service, but there is no financial benefit, nor is there a music major toward which such credit can be applied.

As for loyalty, although the University Concert Choir does not sing during the Summer Term, within recent years those members attending summer school have voluntarily formed a Summer Ensemble to enrich the Summer Term services. Here again one senses the vitality and the commitment which mark the students who value the ministry of the Chapel for their lives.

Scripture Reading. The Scripture readings for worship are selected with the Christian year calendar in mind, but usually in keeping with what the scheduled speaker asks to be listed. The lectionary is consulted, but its offerings are not followed slavishly. The readings are usually two, one from each Testament. With President Ronald W. Reagan expected on campus the next Sunday to give the 1987 Commencement Address, I chose to honor that expectation and preached about "God and Our Social Order," using 1 Timothy 2:16 as the New Testament lesson. The lectionary texts prescribed for that day, if used, would not have allowed for this focus.

The Pulpit Schedule and Focus. The pulpit schedule at the University Chapel brings to campus some of the nation's most notable and respected pulpit voices. The sanctuary pulpit is not only prominently placed, jutting out into the sanctuary like the prow of a ship in the water, its ministry is seriously promoted. The worship services at the Chapel have made it one of the outstanding preaching posts among campuses that have a chapel building.

The pulpit schedule for the school year involves the Dean of the Chapel, who is the resident university preacher, and those speakers he selects and secures. The Dean always begins and closes the Chapel preaching schedule and speaks on those special Sundays when a campus focus is traditional. The Dean's ministry as a regular preacher in worship allows for a greater sense of continuity as a worshiping community, such as a local church experiences under the ministry of its pastor; it also allows the congregants to receive from his preaching service in a more systematic fashion through serial planning.

The sermons delivered from the Chapel pulpit are expected to address the hearers intelligently, informatively, and inspirationally with a needed word from God, speaking to worshipers at the point of their individual pilgrimage and need. In the university setting, the meaning of faith and religious experience needs to be treated, and moral and spiritual values need to be reviewed and reinforced. The university sermon sometimes deals with what it means to be human, to be individual, to be a decision maker, and how to handle the awesome burden of being free in a threateningly contingent world of circumstances.

The theme of divine guidance must also be treated, and attention given to help students and others relate new knowledge to the established truths, so that faith and learning can serve each other in the head and heart of a responsible self.[1] The preaching done in the Chapel services is expected to address the w[ill] as well as the intellect, and those invited to preach are usually those who have homiletical effectiveness in doing so. More often than not, the persons invited to preach in the Chapel will be leaders who have had prolonged or periodic contact with university students whose setting and levels of awareness offer a hard challenge to a preacher.[2]

The Planning Team. Three persons plan the weekly services: Professor Roy Edward Hicks, Choir Director; Ms. Valerie R. Reese, University Organist; and the Dean of the Chapel, who coordinates the planning.

The planning staff is well-integrated. We talk and share with care, respect, openness, candor, and trust. A high sense of imaginativeness prevails when we do our long-term planning for the school year, and we experience great anticipation when expecting a return visit by certain speakers who have endeared themselves to our campus community. We candidly assess previous services, and we benefit from the counsel of each other and the worshiping community.

---

1   For printed examples of the kind of preaching described here as essential in a campus context, see: Willard L. Sperry, *Sermons Preached at Harvard* (New York: Harper & Brother, 1953); Howard Thurman, *The Growing Edge: Sermons in Worship Patterns* (New York: Harper & Row, 1956); idem, *Temptations of Jesus: Five Sermons* (San Francisco: Lawton Kennedy, 1962); George A. Buttrick, *Sermons Preached in a University Church* (Nashville: Abingdon Press, 1959).

2   George A. Buttrick, one of the most sought-after preachers for college and university audiences, who served at Harvard as Preacher to the University from 1955-1960, characterized university students as persons with "mingled idealism and realism, self-disparagement and self-assurance, naivete and sophistication, turmoil of emotion and keenness of mind." See his *Sermons Preached in a University Church*, 7-8.

When I am scheduled to preach, I visit with the choir during one of their rehearsal days; hearing the music readies me to complete my sermon and to prepare the morning prayer for the service. Our concern is worship. We plan with spiritual ends in view. A singular contribution to the life and heritage of Tuskegee University continues to be made by the worship ministry at the Chapel. Blessed with a setting in which religious concerns are officially promoted, but in a non-denominational way, and proud of a building of architectural dignity that lends itself so readily to awe and praise before God, those of us who regularly worship there gladly give a responsible and lively witness to our faith.

There is a deep sense of reverence as we gather, and a strong sense of community as we sing, praise, pray, hear the preaching, and experience inward renewal. Engaged as we are in a transaction with eternal import, it is a distinct privilege to plan for such times together and to review and revise that planning for a richer experience before God. *Soli Deo gloria.*

16

INSTALLATION STATEMENT AT TUSKEGEE UNIVERSITY

by James Earl Massey

September 9, 1984
The Tuskegee Chapel

President Payton: I accept the responsibilities of being Dean of this Chapel. My acceptance is not out of self-seeking pride nor vaunting ambition, but out of a prayer-anchored concern to serve.

Mr. President, your summons to ministry here makes me feel honored. It is a high privilege to share in the "Tuskegee Spirit" and to be teamed with so many able partners in the work. Across more than a century, this has been a place of high vision, exemplary leadership, noble service, and distinctive achievements. It is a heritage widely known and honored, and I feel deeply about sharing in its continuance.

In one of the books he wrote to report on the progress of Tuskegee Institute under his leadership, Booker T. Washington explained how religious concerns were being honored in this educational venture. Among the many ways he listed, Washington mentioned first, and proudly, that since almost from the start, "a regularly appointed chaplain, an ordained evangelical minister, has been connected with the school, which is non-denominational but by no means non-religious."[1] I feel privileged to take my place here in what has been a long and fruitful succession of appointed chaplains. Thank you for asking me to join, continue, and augment the noble religious tradition here. With strong trust in God, I have come to serve his cause in this great place.

I am doubly privileged to bear responsibility with others here in the ministry of teaching. In chapel, classroom, counsel sessions, and common togetherness I want to help all to see, understand, and follow what Booker T. Washington once termed "the force and inspiration of a religious motive."[2]

Dr. Washington knew something about the force and steady inspiration of religion. He knew it as a continuing influence from those early years of his life under a "mother kneeling over her children and fervently praying that Lincoln and his armies might be successful, and that she and her children might be free."[3] But he also knew religion as a personal experience which helped him to face and handle the certainties and uncertainties of his days. It was a strong religious motive that helped him to continue selfless labors in the face of great odds.

It was a strong religious motive that sustained Washington in the fight against hate, unfairness, and things that demean personhood. It was the strong and steadying force of a religious motive that kept fire in his soul, hope in his heart, and patience in his spirit as he kept making tracks of proof about Black possibilities under

---

1   *Working with the Hands* (New York: Doubleday, Page & Co., 1904), 192.

2   From "The Religious Life of the Negro," an article in the *North American Review* (1905), reprinted in *The Booker T. Washington Papers*, eds. Louis R. Harlan and Raymond W. Smock, Vol. 8 (Urbana: University of Illinois Press, 1979), 335.

3   Booker T. Washington, *Up from Slavery: An Autobiography* (Garden City, N.Y.: Doubleday & Co., 1953 reprint), 7.

God. He believed in and promoted human possibilities, but he had a prior belief: that there is a divine providence at work in life, and that the experienced power of religion gives that underlying purpose freedom to work in and through us.

Dr. Harry V. Richardson, a former chaplain here, wisely declared that "everything depends upon our understanding of religion and the faithfulness with which we apply it."[4] I certainly affirm that. This is my commitment to fulfill the pastoral and theological duties here as Dean of Tuskegee Chapel and the Institute Professor of Religion.

As I take my place in this community as part of the Tuskegee team, I gladly acknowledge those ministers who have served here as chaplains before me. The list is an impressive one:

John William Whittaker

Edgar James Penney

George Lake Imes

Harry V(an Buren) Richardson

Raymond Francis Harvey

Carleton Lafayette Lee

Daniel Webster Wynn

Andrew Lincoln Johnson

All of these minsters labored tirelessly and honorably in their chaplaincy here. I humbly enter into their labor. The duties I assume seem less forbidding because of what my noble predecessors accomplished; their services not only shaped a worthy tradition but also generated a continuing momentum. I am honored to follow their

---

4   *Dark Salvation*: The Story of Methodism as It Developed Among Blacks in America (Garden City, N.Y.: Anchor Press/Doubleday, 1976), p. ix.

lead, and I do so with commitment, intent to serve as needed and lead as required.

Booker T. Washington once lauded John William Whittaker, Tuskegee Institute's first chaplain, as "a thoroughly earnest gentleman and perfectly loyal," meaning that his character and commitment to this cause were unquestioned.[5] Some others on the scene lauded Whittaker as well, sometimes for having preached "an extra fine sermon,"[6] and usually for making his hearers feel "drawn upwards."[7] My prayer to God is that my life and labors can enable all whom I serve here to feel "drawn upwards." It is to that end that I stand committed, in honor of your inviting call and the Lord Jesus who stirred me to accept your summons to serve. I am here in His name to labor with you.

---

5 *BTW Papers*, III: 1889-1895, 62.

6 *BTW Papers*, VIII: 1904-1906, 513.

7 *BTW Papers*, III: 1889-1895, 104.

17

ANDERSON UNIVERSITY'S CENTENNIAL COMMENCEMENT ADDRESS

by James Earl Massey

Originally scheduled to be delivered as the Anderson University commencement address, May, 2017. Dr. Massey prepared the address but, because of illness, could not be present. Not previously published. Used by permission.

T hank you, President John Pistole, for the invitation to be the speaker on this hallowed occasion, and to enjoy once again being with you, Provost Marie Morris, our devoted trustees, distinguished faculty members retired and active, eager graduates, family members of this graduating class, and friends of Anderson University. Again, I say thank you!

The Shifting Soul of Higher Education

Some years ago, I was a guest speaker at the Westwood Christian Church in Los Angeles, a church attended by many students and faculty members from the adjacent campus of the University of California. At an early point before I spoke, the pastor gave me a guided tour of that church and its well-appointed facilities. I was

153

especially impressed by the large stained-glass window that adorns the sanctuary. When I spoke so admiringly to the pastor about this window, he informed me that it was their "University Window."

This required some explanation. He told me that the first minister of the church, a learned Scotsman, had designed the window with eighteen panels bearing coats of arms from 96 noted colleges and universities, both in the United States and abroad, all of which had begun under Christian auspicious. That minister and church had planned their window to acknowledge the relationship that had existed, and ought to have endured, between the church and academy, between faith and learning.

Alas, the pastor and I experienced a mood of sadness, mindful as we were that many of the schools represented in that wonderful window are no longer related in vision and service to Christian faith. Institutions which began so nobly and productively under Christian auspicious eventually fell victim to secularization and the sterility that follows when academic culture moves away from a vital religious center.

As many of you know, some of America's oldest and most notable and pace-setting colleges and universities were established with a vital religious center, and they promulgated an educational system calculated to address the need for human experience being anchored in and guided by Christian spirituality. The pattern by which this religious rootage changed in some of our nation's most elite schools has been traced most adroitly by George M. Marsden in his book *The Soul of the American University*, and by James Tunstead Burtchaell in his book *The Dying of the Light*. These men have provided detailed and provocative reports about how many of the prominent colleges and universities in our nation became disentangled from their religious identity and ecclesial affiliation.[1]

Naturally Sentimental

As I now speak about this particular school's beginning, I am both proud and sentimental. I was converted to Christ under the preaching of an evangelist who was a member of the first entering class of this institution in 1917. I was six years old and accepted wholeheartedly the message of this evangelist who came to preach at our church in Detroit, Michigan. In 1969, thirty-three years later, that evangelist was still in ministry, and when I came to teach on this campus, he was one of those who encouraged my choice to come here and serve.

That evangelist was Charles F. Jacob Jones from Alabama, the first African-American student to enjoy the openness and

1   See George M. Marsden, *The Soul of the American University* (Oxford University Press, 1994) and James Tunstead Burtchaell, *The Dying of the Light* (Wm. Eerdmans, 1998).

graciousness of this wonderful campus. In 1977, when Anderson College celebrated its 60th anniversary, Rev. Jones was one of five persons remaining alive from that first entering class. They were given special recognition. God bless that good brother and this campus that served him so well. [Editor's note: For a fuller account, see James Massey's *African Americans and the Church of God*, 105-106.]

Anderson Bible Training School, as this institution was originally named, has continued across a century. It always has been aware of alien voices and alternate views but, as has not been the case with many others, it has continued in the Christian course that influenced its original purpose and direction in 1917. The story of how this course has been maintained can be traced in some of the writings published by the school. There are five strategic historical accounts which have particularly highlighted how Anderson's presidents, trustees, and faculty members have rightfully stayed on course during times of crisis, and how Anderson Bible Training School became a college, and now holds a revered university status in the Christian tradition.

President John A. Morrison's autobiography, *As the River Flows*, is the first of these five accounts. It reports how controversy within the Church of God over educational concerns was such a divisive factor across several years. Referring to the sessions of the church's General Assembly in 1934, when the liberal arts curricular emphasis at the college was hotly debated, Morrison commented, "not all of the brothers could see their way clear to support the educational program of the church, but those who could not support it decided that they could at least tolerate it."[2]

---

2 John A. Morrison, *As the River Flows: The Autobiography of John A. Morrison* (Anderson College Press, 1962), especially pp. 163-182.

President Robert H. Reardon, who followed Dr. Morrison in the presidency here, has provided additional insights into that controversy in his book *The Early Morning Light*.[3] He looks closely at the personalities on both sides of the issue during the debate over what kinds of learning this school should rightly offer and promote. The 2004 biography of Dr. Reardon authored by Dean Barry L Callen, is titled *Staying on Course*.[4] It details the determination it took for that president to keep this school properly focused, especially during the tumultuous social upheavals of the 1960s and 1970s.

Two more recent accounts of the school's history are now available. Barry L. Callen's 1992 *Guide of Soul and Mind*, commissioned for the school's 75th anniversary, is a richly detailed survey of the college's first three-quarters of a century. The other is Merle D. Strege's *The Desk as Altar*, the centennial history offering a kaleidoscopic narrative of how campus leaders and the supporting church dealt with the issues, meanings, and motives which affected the educational scene across America during Anderson University's century of life and service.[5]

It is the stability and continuing status of this University that we celebrate today, and for these we give honor to God who has been and continues to be our Guide, both of our souls and minds. Desks have been well used, sometimes as altars before God.

---

3   Robert H. Reardon, *The Early Morning Light* (Warner Press, 1979), pp. 62-75.

4   Barry L. Callen, *Staying on Course: A Biography of Robert H. Reardon* (Anderson University Press, 2004).

5   Barry L. Callen, *Guide of Soul and Mind* (Anderson University and Warner Press, 1992), 472 pages, and Merle D. Strege, *The Desk as Altar* (Anderson University Press, 2016), 438 pages.

Avowedly Christian Institution

Anderson University is an "avowedly Christian institution of higher learning." This claim can, should, and must be true to more than a nominal extent, and it is our continuing responsibility and that of our supporters to see to it that it is.[6] Given our context, the nature of these times, the background history of our beloved school, and its continuing concerns as an institution of Christian higher learning, my emphasis during this celebration is strategic and timely.

The concerns of higher learning in early America had in view not only granting students competency skills for a career but also guidance for shaping their character for a good life. The spiritual dimension figured largely in each school's educational vision, and the institution's head usually was a chief leader in the process. Early on, there was an emphasis on faith, discerning right from wrong, self-discipline, courage, forthrightness, due consideration of others, and interest in the larger political issues that advance human good.

All of these emphases were considered central in the mission of higher education. The schools sought to instill and reinforce spiritual and ethical principles. No one who reads the histories of the many early schools of higher learning in America can miss their commitment to shape and pass on a culture of practical and moral regard for life's spiritual dimension and the importance of living a responsible life.

Robert Maynard Hutchins, a prominent leader in twentieth-century American higher education, recalled that his student years at Oberlin College helped to develop him as a "non-conformist

---

6 See Jonathan Raymond, *Higher Higher Education: Integrating Holiness into All of Campus Life* (Aldersgate Press, Barry L. Callen editor, 2015).

conscience" with a "willingness to die for one's principles."[7] A valid and vital campus experience is expected to make a difference for those who surrender to its aims. A vital campus context for adequate learning should be a place where scholarship, spirituality, and service are honored, modeled, held in balance, and humbly promoted to produce effects in and through someone's life long after the degree's requirements have been met and even long after a career has ended.

Anderson's Beloved Alma Mater

Helping students gain what a vital teaching program is calculated to give is certainly a noble purpose. I like the trenchant way Peter J. Gomes voiced this concern: "As for those of us who teach and speak where many listen, we have the task of reconnecting knowledge with wisdom, greatness with goodness, and service with scholarship; and we have to do it through the full medium of our own humanity, for precepts must be glorified by example."[8]

There are some lines that appear in this university's alma mater that remind us about this as our proper work. Donald Smith, a student here in the 1930s, understood the task when in 1939 he penned what became our alma mater:

> Anderson, our alma mater,
> Guide of soul and mind,
> Thou hast taught within thy borders,

---

7   Robert Maynard Hutchins, *Freedom, Education, and the Fund* (Meridian Books, 1956), 14. See Mary Ann Dzuback, *Robert Maynard Hutchins: Portrait of an Educator* (University of Chicago Press, 1991), 9-20.

8   Peter J. Gomes, *The Good Life: Truths that Last in Times of Need* (HarperSanFrancisco, 2002), 352.

To aid all mankind.
So for this thy noble purpose,
May our best avail;
Friend of all that's good and upright,
Hail to thee, all hail.[9]

"May our best avail." Our "best" demands a life of faith, focus, and function that reflect more than a merely natural state and that serve a purpose more worthy than mere ambition. It is to such a level that this university's noble purpose steadily bids us to rise, displaying in ourselves such classical moral virtues as courage, self-control, trustworthiness, truthfulness, integrity, compassion, and social openness, and displaying as well such theological virtues as faith, hope, and love. It is only as we live and serve at such a level that our university can be the place—as one of its earliest mottoes voiced it—"Where Quality Learning and Christian Service Come Alive."

Keeping First Things First

Teaching is a primary human need and a privileged work. It is a fundamental activity filled with promise, and those entrusted with this blessed privilege and a place to teach should remain mindful that a crown of trust has been placed over our heads, and we must continually grow taller if we are ever to reach it.

Assisting students to become life-long learners, creative and productive persons, is usually a prolonged and sometimes painful process. It means interacting with persons whose attitudes toward us often alternate: they receive from us gladly, but also are prone

---

9   See Barry L. Callen, *Guide of Soul and Mind*, pp. 3, 125, 131.

to test us. Students are usually curious and eager to learn, but sometimes they are hampered by resentment toward the demands placed on them.

Near the end of his long and illustrious teaching career, William James was recalling how this sometimes distressing teaching process had weighed upon him across the years. He rejoiced that he would no longer have to face a "massive alien and recalcitrant humanity."[10] Teaching is admittedly a difficult task, but the difficulties are because of the promise associated with them, the promise of benefit, life-changing benefit, for persons. This is not best done by formulas but by the spirit in which we teachers serve.

Our church-related university is not inevitably doomed to go the way of many others and lose its Christian vision and orientation. We have avoided that result and can continue on our proper course if we keep "first things first" and in their proper relation, partnering and cooperating collegially with a relational concern toward God, each other, and all the lives being touched.

The concerns and effects of higher education are manifold: they are intellectual, economic, political, social, aesthetic, and religious. Christian higher education is the admittedly complicated process of educating students toward being increasingly focused disciplined and sustained by a wholesome spirituality. This happens when we are submissive to God and remain committed to God's guidance and direction.

As Anderson University enters its second century of service, it must and will continue to educate toward lives of service sustained by focus, clarity, wholeness, and godly usefulness. and surely a Christian University deserves those who model such as they go about the business of educating others.

---

10   Cited by Jacques Barzun, *Teacher in America* (Doubleday, 1959), 31.

Thank you that here is a Christian university that still puts the first thing first. May the goodness and mercy of Almighty God continue to follow it and us, fulfilling us with his glory.

SECTION III

WISDOM FOR
THEOLOGY & EVANGELISM

EDITOR'S SECTION INTRODUCTION

by Barry L. Callen

P rimarily known to many as a master communicator in the pulpit, the fact is that Dr. James Earl Massey is much more than that. As a skilled theologian, he has cared deeply about the biblical and theological quality of what is communicated through preaching. There should be no question about our special brother's commitment to serious theological work. After all, he enjoyed a quality theological education himself and for some years was the dean of a graduate-level theological seminary.

What is the nature of Dr. Massey's theological stance? He uses words like "orthodox" and "apostolic doctrine." Always assuming an authoritative biblical base for Christian believing and teaching, Massey displays the rare combination of intellectual sophistication and a practical approach to the spiritual and social needs of the common person. The sophistication is seen in his "Semantics and Holiness" entry published originally in a prominent theological journal. Here he displays the rare ability to move with ease in the diverse worlds of philosophy, linguistics, and hermeneutics, all in the service of understanding the Bible properly and thus establishing an acceptable theological foundation for our efforts at preaching, serving, and evangelizing others.

Massey displays another rare combination, that of confidence and humility. Effective preaching and evangelism require confidence in the good-news message being shared. Fairness to our human condition, however, requires the related exercise of a faith couched in a humility that keeps confidence from deteriorating into unjustified arrogance. In his entry on the role of theology in the church, Dr. Massey makes clear that creeds play both good and bad roles in the church. On the good side, they are milestone occasions when the best of Christian thinking has been captured, preserved, and holds the church together with a proper respect for biblical revelation and church tradition.

However, there is the other side. Creeds often are grasped as the ultimate wordings of biblical wisdom and then get used in ways that restrict further thought and justify deep divisions among Christians. Massey explains that this is why his own church tradition, the Church of God (Anderson, IN), has been wary of championing creeds in any formal and restrictive way. We maturing disciples must continue learning and growing, being humble before the God who, after all, is never fully comprehended by any of us. Such tentativeness about final theological articulations opens the door to possible confusion, but it also keeps available the possibilities of innovation, relevance, and progress. We are to preach and evangelize with confidence, but also with measured humility.

This tension between confidence and humility is seen clearly as Massey engages two prominent theologians (John Cobb and Clark Pinnock) to determine a properly biblical understanding of the nature of God. We are engaged, Massey insists, in nothing less than a reconsideration of the nature and results of our experience of God, "the Holy One." The result of this engagement, when biblically controlled, is the right "theism," one focused on the revealing Son, Jesus, and full of our humble gratitude.

In looking for quality examples of that kind of theology, Dr. Massey commends the theological works of two of his close colleagues, Dr. Gilbert W. Stafford, who insists that serious theology is to be biblical and for everyday disciples, and myself who has written a systematic theology built on the assumption that the heart of God is a reaching and renewing *loving grace*.

James Earl Massey is a networker, bringing together persons, disciplines, and causes. He is a deep thinker and an infectious sharer, a preacher, teacher, and evangelist. For him, evangelism happens best where agape love, reflecting God's very nature, controls the witnesses. Evangelism must involve scriptural truths and eternal meanings, but it also must display a caring spirit within the witness. The entry "Sharers in Holiness" makes this clear. Walking with God not only means a change in our *experience* but also contributes to the renewal of our very *being*. God has ordained that those who surrender to his love will then be *sharers of his likeness*.

The apostles' doctrine, still to be our believing guide, needs to be known, believed, confessed, and lived according to Massey. The church is to be a place of prescribed learning, and apart from that specific training it ceases to be the church. When apostolic doctrine is neglected, personal opinion takes precedence over biblical truths, ethics become situational, cultural notions replace vital orthodoxy, and emotion becomes a controlling force. Sound doctrine is needed to monitor personal experience and keep believers true to scriptural orthodoxy.

To support this view, Dr. Massey kindly quotes my words. We are to remain "text anchored and Spirit enlivened."[1] The apostles' doctrine is needed to help us discern and guard against the subtle evils of our own time. One evil worrying Massey is the consumer orientation of some "megachurches" that are growing fast but neglecting "such centralities of Christian faith as who Jesus is, why Jesus came, why Jesus died, what salvation means, the problem of

---

1   Barry L. Callen, *Authentic Spirituality* (Baker Academic, 2001, revised, Emeth Press, 2006), 19.

sin, and the importance of conversion." Massey insists that doctrine should be the source of church growth.

Walking with God, in Massey's view, means a change in our very *beings* and then a resulting desire to be *sharers of God's likeness*. Theology leads to evangelism, a loving sharing of the good news. Evangelism demands the right message on the one hand and the right spirit for sharing it on the other. Having reviewed the extensive biblical background of evangelism in one entry, Massey makes clear that our confidence in God's revealed Word should drive us to share, and our humility should cause us to share gently and lovingly as Jesus did. Massey commends Pastor Kevin Earley's book because it seeks to foster in every congregational member the development of disciples who know and use their gifts instinctively to God's glory in both the church and world.

In the entry "Culturally Conscious Evangelism," Massey reports, "The gospel is God's appeal to the world to be saved, reconciled, and freed from the power of sin. Evangelism is the task and privilege of voicing that appeal and opportunity to all." Never separating theology from this evangelistic task, he names the elements of necessary theological underpinning: (1) Jesus Christ authorized the evangelical message and commanded the evangelistic mission; (2) the entire world needs to hear that message and know the opportunity it makes possible for life here and hereafter; (3) the given message must not only be shared with all, but shared in the spirit of agape love; and (4) the visible unity of believers is a must to give our going forth its greatest impact in a world that has to see before it will believe.

Massey's entire ministry and his theological heart beat on behalf of Christian unity, otherwise evangelism lacks credibility. And his heart longs to address the urgent spiritual and social needs of the present—no escapist and irresponsible theology here. He ends his entry on "My View of End Times" with this: "*Meanwhile* is the key word for us disciples caught in the remaining miseries of the present time. What should we be doing in the meantime before God makes all things new? We must go on with our holy work even while we watch in hope for what God surely will do."

18

THE ROLE OF THEOLOGY
IN CHURCH LIFE

by James Earl Massey

James Earl Massey, in Barry L. Callen, *Heart of the Matter* (Emeth Press, rev. ed. 2016), 127, 205. Used by permission.

Creeds appear to play good and bad roles in church life. On the good side, they are milestone occasions when the best of Christian thinking gets captured, preserved, and holds the church together with a proper grounding and respect for biblical revelation and church tradition. Creeds are part of that process of the church ordering its life to maintain its corporate identity.

However, there is another side. Too often creeds are grasped as ultimate wordings of wisdom and used in ways that restrict further thought and even justify sharp divisions among Christians who may hold slightly differing perspectives. That's why my own church tradition, the Church of God (Anderson), has been wary of championing creeds in any formal and restrictive way. We would rather be in the position of learning and growing than using stances from earlier times as available weapons of church division.

Granted, this theological tentativeness opens the door to possible confusion, but it also keeps available the possibilities of innovation, relevance, and progress. Not being divisively creedal surely does not exclude being strongly convictional about biblical foundations. We preach with confidence, but also with measured humility.

This tension between boldness and caution frames my general view of the role of theology in church life. I surely believe in serious theological work—after all, I was the Dean of a graduate school of theology and promoted scholarship however I could. Even so, when we have finished our theologizing, some mysteries will remain. We are all pilgrims following the pathways of knowledge and to the end we will "know in part." Regardless of that limitation, our faith in Jesus Christ can give us the *assurance* of things hoped for and the *conviction* of things not seen.

Where does that leave me? I continue to depend on a biblical perspective as I view life, experience its stages, confront its mysteries, order my ways, and make a mark in the fresh concrete of history. I use my mind to its fullest and surround it with the wisdom of a full heart nurtured by God's amazing grace.

Two systematic theologies have arisen from good friends in my particular church tradition. They each lean on the riches of divine grace and dare to also think hard while staying appropriately humble. I have had the following statements of mine placed at their requests on the covers of their fine works.

Regarding Barry L. Callen's **GOD AS LOVING GRACE** (Evangelical Publishing House, 1996, reprint Wipf & Stock, 2018).

> Focus is all-important. This book, biblical throughout, proceeds from the perspective of God's loving grace, and maintains this perspective as the whole revelation of God is unfolded in its light. The Trinity is rightfully honored as this theology interacts helpfully with many

other theological views and clarifies anew much that traditionally has been valued. This is truly fresh material that serves the church fruitfully and also speaks meaningfully to contemporary culture—exactly what good theology should do.

I also shared the following about Dr. Callen on the cover of his *A Pilgrim's Progress: The Autobiography of Barry L. Callen* (Emeth Press and Anderson University Press, 2008, rev. ed. 2013).

> The multi-phased career of Barry L. Callen is unique. His superb gifts and servant leadership have made him a valued theologian, historian, professor, author, administrator, and trusted colleague in the Church of God movement and in other church and academic circles, both in North America and around the world. This well-written life story lets us trace his inspiring path as a loyal son of the church and a courageous man of faith, learning, and service. A rich read!

Regarding Gilbert W. Stafford, ***THEOLOGY FOR DISCIPLES*** (Warner Press, 1996, rev. ed. 2012).

> The systematic considerations Dr. Stafford has offered about the life of Christian faith not only help make theology intelligible but make Christian discipleship in particular intelligible, persuasive, and a shared life. He reports with responsible bearing what he has distilled from his depth study of the Christian Scriptures, the relevant literature within his chosen field of scholarly expertise, his own long and fruitful ministry, and his

prolonged observation about the perennial needs of the church and the world.

Christian discipleship involves both a life-long learning "at the feet of Jesus" and a life-long involvement in the church, with each believer receiving from and supporting the church's "way of being and manner of doing," always with an eye toward being faithful to the churches Lord. Christianity does not need to be reinvented—as some post-moderns would assert—but thought about with due seriousness and lived out in full trust.

19

A "THEISM" THAT'S BIBLICAL

by James Earl Massey

James Earl Massey, in dialogue with theologians
John B. Cobb, Jr., and Clark H. Pinnock, in Barry L. Callen,
Heart of the Matter (Emeth Press, rev. ed. 2016), 40-43.
Used by permission.

Massey: Here's a key issue that lingers among conservative Christians. It can be summarized by the confusingly similar words "pantheism" and "panentheism." John [Cobb], you and other "process" thinkers have been accused of being at least semi-pantheists, people who virtually *equate* the world and the world process with God. You, of course, have denied this, and I think rightly so.

As to the second of these two confusing words, your teacher, Charles Hartshorne, clearly affirmed it. The reason, he says, is that panentheism suggests that, while God has a distinctive identity, the creation, and especially humans, have been freed to act as co-creators along with God. In the process, they contribute to God's life and are taken up into God's "consequent" nature, which is itself in the process of becoming. God is understood, then, as the One in whom all reality is gathering, so much so that, for "process" thinkers like yourself, John, it becomes difficult to conceive of God apart from God's relationship with the world.

I hope I'm putting no foreign words into your mouth, John. There is a clear contrast here, I think. "Open" theists like Clark Pinnock and Barry Callen separate from process thought at this point since process theology appears to eliminate an important aspect of the biblically revealed God. God is presented biblically as the *sole* creator of all that originally was, although now God is very much engaged jointly with us and the rest of creation. God can and should be conceived as both *prior to* and *separate from* us, although now actively engaged *with us* in the ongoing historical and creating process.

Many of us, John, still insist that the God who prefers loving persuasion over brute force (as you clearly affirm) should also be known as the God who is not lacking in potency to create from nothing and finally to achieve the divine will despite human sin and defiance. Persuasion is prominent, as Randy Maddox has shown was John Wesley's view, but power—understood as the potential of sheer force—also emerges on occasion as God relates to this free and fallen creation and eventually will judge it. In my humble view, the truly loving God persuades without having lost the capacity to bring about the divine will in the face of human sin. I have preached many sermons that took this for granted.

Pinnock: Let me emphasize this point of yours, James, and it's an important one. I argue this contrast you present so clearly as a key difference between "open" evangelicals and "process" theologians. The open group, myself included, affirms without qualification that God exists sovereignly apart from and in advance of this creation. We also gladly affirm that this loving God voluntarily Self-limits in order to have meaningful relationship with the creation, especially with humans to whom the freedom of choice has been granted. We think of God as existing *apart from* the creation as well as now deeply involved with us *in it*. What we don't do, as process people generally do, is reduce theism to a "panentheism" where God and the world are *necessarily* interdependent and somehow overlapping, even in some sense shared realities.

Massey: Let's do a little biblical reflecting. We humans obviously struggle with language and philosophy, and how best to speak of God in human words and in changing times. My instinct is to return to Scripture. Let me direct our attention to Psalm 19 where we learn some clear truths *about* God, even as we are inspired to respond in depth *to* God.

The psalmist reports in celebrative awe about how nature speaks a thought-enlarging word of witness about the God who fashioned it all in our interest. But nature is not our only or our best witness to God. The Scriptures are a word *from* God. The psalmist understood this divine word as one of "testimony" (*edah*) and of "law" (*torah*), granting wisdom to the simple and direction for life. God's gracious Word is filled with heart-inspiring, hope-instilling, life-sustaining promises, all given by the God who is worthy of our worship because he made us, and in love he meets our need for guidance, salvation, and a meaningful life in this world.

What is God's supreme Self-witness? It's none other than Jesus who came that we might have life and have it abundantly (Jn. 10:10b). What a wonderful and mighty God we serve! That's the heart of the matter.

20

SEMANTICS AND HOLINESS: THE FUNCTIONS OF HOLINESS TEXTS

by James Earl Massey

Originally appeared in the *Wesleyan Theological Journal*
(Spring 1975), 60-69. Used by permission.

My topic involves our language statements which deal with the subject of Christian holiness. By "our language statements" I refer both to the New Testament writers and our Wesleyan holiness emphasis. To treat this subject from the perspective of semantics is but to use another methodological approach to our perennial task of interpreting the biblical text.

Holiness is both a subject and an experience, and with respect to both of these the New Testament tradition has a lot to say. Semantics helps us see how the saying was done, the focus being upon the forms and logic of the language system used, and how these functioned to express and provide meaning.

We are familiar with the syntactical approach to biblical interpretation, an approach in which we use grammars and lexicons as our tools to dig out meanings. The science of semantics offers an additional approach and another useful set of tools by which to interpret the texts.

Christian holiness is an experience of depth and ultimacy. The New Testament writers have used a dynamic religious language system in writing about their own experience of holiness. These statements, expressions, and prescriptions used in their language system vividly reflect the experiential stance, thought-categories, and intentions of these writers with reference to that experience. When the sentence units within their language system are analyzed in terms of functions to be served, then the basic meanings within what they wrote tend to become quite clear.

Semantics has to do with this concern for clarity and understood meaning. The interrogation of sentence forms and the isolation and interpretation of sentence functions help us to discern meaning. This paper is based upon that method of approach in interpreting the function of New Testament holiness texts.

The Use of Religious Language

The science of semantics is of a comparatively recent origin, but sufficient growth and development have occurred to make it a mature and valuable member within the family of sciences. Simply put, the science of semantics deals with the logic of language and explores the conditions under which language statements become meaningful. The work of semantics is language analysis, the exploration and classifying of sentence forms and functions, and testing the empirical basis for what is said and meant.[1]

---

1 For a treatment of this process, and some statement of the history behind its uses, see: Max Black, *Language and Philosophy: Studies in Method* (Ithaca, N.Y.: Cornell University Press, 1949); S. I. Hayakawa, ed., *Language, Meaning and Maturity* (New York: Harper, 1954); Stephen Ullmann, *Language and Style: Collected Papers* (Oxford: Basil Blackwell, 1964); Donald E. Hayden and E. Paul Alworth, eds., *Classics in Semantics* (New York: The Philosophical Library, 1965). The literature is quite vast.

There are many determinants at work in the use of a language: assumptions, attitudes, culture, experiences, perceptions, etc. When these determinants are considered for what they are, it is possible to see the way that they influence what is said, and to see as well how they condition what is meant. The use of "religious language" is also deeply influenced and conditioned by many determinants, the foremost being the religious situation or experience within which the speaking person is based or to which he stands related.

The new concern among philosophers about language analysis called the attention of the world to the "meaning" and "significance" of all language uses. The new emphasis was upon a more precise "placing" of words and phrases to insure a more precise function toward clear meanings. "Religious language" has also been explored and examined against the new criteria. Many philosophers (logical positivists and others) who tested religious language for its limits and functions differed in their final assessments of its validity and value, but the encounter has not been without value to the Church.[2]

Some philosophers who were more congenial to the Christian faith recognized in the new philosophical concern an important tool by which to render theological statements more precise; they also saw its value for studying the logic at work within the unique religious statements within the Bible. At the present time there are many studies available which deal with religious language as a specialized category, and essential treatments have been offered of the assumptions, terminology, logic, locus, essence, functions, and

---

2   For a brief overview of how the more critical approach posed a distinct problem to the position of religious thought, see John Macquarrie, *Twentieth-Century Religious Thought* (New York: Harper and Row, 1963), esp. 301-17.

truthfulness (empirical placing) of such a language system.[3] This new and prolonged look into the nature and function of religious language has been shared by a sizable number of investigators, including ethnologists, anthropologists, linguists, theologians, historians of religion, and even sociologists.[4]

The Meaning of Religious Language

I have referred to the dynamic religious language system of the New Testament writers, and I somewhat passingly categorized their treatment of Christian holiness under three functions- headings: "statements," "expressions," and "prescriptions." It is in order now to treat these designations in more detail because this is crucial to the purpose of the paper.

Semanticists have pointed out that in uttering a sentence in our everyday use of language we do one or more of four things: (1) We make a statement—analytical terminology for asserting or affirming some fact; (2) We make an expression, an utterance in which emotion and impulse play a considerable role; (3) We speak prescriptives, directing that something should be done; (4) We utter performatives, saying something that creates a new state of affairs, like making a promise. (The very speaking of the promise is the act

---

3   See especially: Ian T. Ramsey, *Religious Language* (New York: Macmillan Co., paperback edition, 1963); Anders Jeffner, *The Study of Religious Language* (London: SCM Press, Ltd., 1972); an earlier work is by Frederick Ferre, *Language, Logic and God* (New York: Harper, 1961).

4   See Thomas Fawcett, *The Symbolic Language of Religion* (Minneapolis: Augsburg Publishing House, 1971), a study that draws upon the work of many scholars in various fields of research; Thorlief Boman, *Hebrew Thought Compared with Greek* (Philadelphia: Westminster Press, 1960), ET from German by Jules Moreau; James Barr, *The Semantics of Biblical Language* (London: Oxford University Press, 1961); Eugene A. Nida, *Toward a Science of Translating* (Leiden: E. J. Brill, 1964); Gerhard Ebeling, *Introduction to a Theological Theory of Language* (Philadelphia: Fortress Press, 1973), ET by R. A. Wilson from the German.

of creating the new situation, which is to say that a performative is a spoken action.) Meaning is intended through the use of any and all of these ways of speaking; performatives, however, are of a more critical nature since they have to do with speech-action in which meaning, emotion, and effect all go along hand in hand.[5]

These categories of sentence-function provide us with an interesting measure for testing the function level of New Testament holiness-texts.[6] Although I am drawing upon these descriptive categories from the current perspective of semantics, it should be mentioned that the study of sentences by function-level and intention is not a new effort at all. Aristotle categorized sentences in this way long, long ago in his *Poetics*,[7] although he outlined five categories rather than four. However ancient the categorizing might be, there is an evident history of its influence upon later cultures.[8] With the current help we have for utilizing language theories and refining language uses, we have a meaningful tool for our research into the intended meanings of the New Testament message. We also possess a relevant method to help us pass on those meanings in our preaching, teaching, and theological work.

---

5   On these categorical descriptions, see Anders Jeffner, *The Study of Religious Language*, esp. pp. 11-12, 68-104. See also J. L. Austin, *How to Do Things with Words*, ed. J. O. Urmson (New York: Oxford University Press, Galaxy Book, 1965); John Wilson, *Language and the Pursuit of Truth* (Cambridge: At the University Press, 1960), esp. 47-74.

6   By "holiness-texts" I refer to sentence units that utilize one or more of the words based upon the root HAG, and in addition occur in a context significantly related to the holiness concern (behavior, codes, experience, etc.).

7   See Aristotle, *The Poetics* xix. 7, trans. W. Hamilton Fyfe ("Loeb Classical Library") (Cambridge: Harvard University Press, 1960). See also I. Bywater, *Aristotle on the Art of Poetry* (Oxford: Clarendon Press, 1909), 258f.

8   See E. J. Revell, "Aristotle and the Accents: The Categories of Speech in Jewish and Other Authors," *Journal of Semitic Studies* 19, no. 1 (spring, 1974): 19-35.

Examples from Holiness Texts

I am impressed by the number and functional forcefulness of the many New Testament holiness texts. In terms of sentence-functions, the "statements" and "prescriptives" are the most plentiful. This is characteristic not only of the holiness texts but of other teaching and hortatory themes, particularly in the Epistles since these materials were addressed to evoke within readers a reaction-response of faith and commitment. The holiness texts are being highlighted here, however, since the whole issue of the kerygma and the experience of salvation are toward righteousness and the fulfillment of the will of God in the holiness of obedient love.

It is instructive to watch the massive dependence of the writers upon the function of prescriptives in aiding this end; their usage of the imperative keeps us mindful of how the imperative and the indicative relate in the holiness experience.[9] There are many implications to be seen in this epistolary constant for developing a theological ethic of holiness, as well as for a constructive psychology of the Christian experience of holiness.[10]

As a basic illustration of how plentiful the "statements" and "prescriptives" are within holiness texts, consider the following

---

9 There are several excellent discussions on the relation between the indicative and the imperative in the writings of Paul. See Rudolf Bultmann, *The Theology of the New Testament*, trans. Kendrick Grobel (New York: Charles Scribner's Sons, 1951), 1:332-33, 338-39; Robert C. Tannehill, *Dying and Rising with Christ: A Study in Pauline Theology* (Berlin: A. Toepelmann, 1967), esp. 77-83; Victor Paul Furnish, *Theology and Ethics in Paul* (Nashville: Abingdon Press, 1968), 153-57, 224-27.

10 As both W. Curry Mavis, *The Psychology of Christian Experience* (Grand Rapids, Mich.: Zondervan Publishing House, 1963), and Mildred Bangs Wynkoop, *A Theology of Love: The Dynamic of Wesleyanism* (Kansas City, Mo.: Beacon Hill Press of Kansas City, 1972), have certainly seen and explored, with Wesleyan emphases as their province of consideration.

instances drawn only from sentences using words based on the root *HAG*." Observe the sentence-functions with care.

1. Beginning with the 27 appearances of *hagiazō* (meaning: to sanctify, consecrate, make holy), 4 are not applicable to our concern here (Matt. 6:9; 23:17, 19; Luke 11:2); 9 are statements (1 Cor. 6:11; 7:14; Eph. 5:26; 1 Tim. 4:5; 2 Tim. 2:21; Heb. 2:11; 9:13; 10:14; 13:12); 4 are expressions (John 17:17; Rom. 15:16; 1 Cor. 1:2; 1 Thess. 5:23); 6 are of a mixed character, showing either a double function as statement-expression (John 10:36; 17:19; Acts 20:32; Heb. 10:10, 29), or statement-prescription (Acts 26:18); while 2 are plainly prescriptive (1 Pet. 3:15; Rev. 22:11).

2. Continuing with the 10 textual appearances of *hagiasmos* (meaning: holiness, consecration, sanctification); 3 uses are in statements (Rom. 6:22; 1 Cor. 1:30; 1 Thess. 4:7); 2 are expressions (2 Thess. 2:13; 1 Pet. 1:2); 1 is of a mixed character, showing a statement-expression function (1 Tim. 2:15); while 4 of the texts are clearly prescriptive (Rom. 6:19; 1 Thess. 4:3, 4; Heb. 12:14).

3. There are only two instances where the word *hagiotēs* (meaning: holiness) appears, and both instances are of a mixed character showing a blend of statement-expression functions (2 Cor. 1:12; Heb. 12:10).

4. There are three texts in which *hagiōsunē* (meaning: holiness) appears. One is a statement (Rom. 1:4);[12] one is

an expression (1 Thess. 3:13); and one is prescriptive (2 Cor. 7:1).

5. *Hagneia* (meaning: purity) appears in two places and is used both times to denote a virtue. Both uses are prescriptive (1 Tim. 4:12; 5:2).

6. *Hagnizō* (meaning: to purify) is found in seven places: four instances of use are not applicable here because they reflect a purely cultic matter (see John 11:55; Acts 21:24, 26; 24:18); one use is clearly prescriptive (Jas. 4:8); while two uses are of a mixed character, showing an expression-prescriptive function (1 Pet. 1:22; 1 John 3:3).

7. Eight holiness texts use the word *hagnos* (meaning: pure, holy). One of these texts is a statement (Jas. 3:17); one is of mixed function, statement-expression (2 Cor. 11:2); one is a clear expression (2 Cor. 7:11); and the other five uses are all prescriptive (Phil. 4:8; 1 Tim. 5:22; Titus 2:5; 1 Pet. 3:2; 1 John 3:3).

8. Only two texts employ *hagnotēs* (meaning: purity, sincerity), and in both cases we are dealing with expressions (2 Cor. 6:6; 11:3—a doubtful reading).

I do not intend to list here the many instances where the word *hagios* (meaning: holy) appears since there would be hundreds of texts for which to account and analyze. This would not better serve the point which the given listings already show, namely, that the New Testament treatment of Christian holiness involves statements, expressions, and prescriptives that clearly organize our view about the life of man in the will of God, and they evoke a deep realization of call and demand within us.

The New Testament statements about holiness make clear assertions and sponsor a claim that challenges. They show great excitement about a life to which the witnesses were committed as real, valuable, engaging, and conclusive. The New Testament prescriptives about holiness are unsparing in stress and demand, using imperatives with high warrant, strict realism, and decisive intent. Writing from the locus of a confirmed faith, and using language appropriate to the experience—as well as the understanding of their audience—the New Testament witnesses are seen to report, confess, exalt, proclaim, prescribe, invite, and challenge. The statements are often clearly doctrinal, the expressions convictional, and the prescriptives reflect both. In reading the holiness texts from such a perspective, one gains a new "feel" for the life that is being shared there.

Life in the Spirit

In speaking of "feel," there is one holiness text with a functional force and "prescriptive power" which almost guarantees it for us by the way that text excites and expands the consciousness. I refer to Paul's prescriptive sentence in Eph. 5:18: "And do not get drunk with wine, for that is debauchery; but be filled with the Spirit." [Scripture quotations are in some instances the author's personal translations.] The thrust of the picture is immediate. It opens up a conspicuously contagious psychology for the reader, inviting him to be "influenced" by God. Paul's use here of the imperative passive—*plērousthe en Pneumati*—makes his words injunctive and prescriptive, but the sentence-function also makes a promise.

Paul's choice of language opens a new situation for the reader. His prescriptive challenges an old pattern and illuminates the reader's new possibilities. There is a deep treasure of meaning in what Paul has said, and the sentence he used creates a "feel" for that meaning. His imperative is more than a demand; it is an opening for the reader into the will of God.

Historians and commentators have reminded us that in the early period of Church history life in the Spirit was understood as initiation into enlightenment and enthusiasm. The early Christians viewed life in the Spirit as entrance into a higher range of abilities and enablements, as movement into a new sphere of relations by which certain natural limitations, felt helplessness and the sense of incompleteness, could be overcome.

Rom. 8:26 certainly reflects this view. Although Paul's statement there that "the Spirit helps us in our weakness" only mentions prayer as an illustrative instance, we "sense" that his stated fact about the ready help of the Spirit applies to a wider range of human needs.[11] When scriptural reference is being made to persons "full of" or "filled with the Spirit," the contexts usually show some action being accomplished by those persons which could not have been done otherwise.

The materials in Luke-Acts are especially illustrative of this. There we are shown men and women being helped in their *astheneia*, and they are thus able to utter prophetic speech (thereby interpreting some event or predicting one) or to give a public witness (thereby creating or handling some religious situation). The Luke-Acts materials abound with the descriptive phrase "full of,"

---

11 Ernst Kaesemann sees here a use of the *oratio infusa* motif by Paul. The technical concerns to be met in interpreting this verse are many indeed. See his *Perspectives on Paul* (Philadelphia: Fortress Press, 1969), esp. 127-37. ET from the German by Margaret Kohl.

or "filled with the Spirit" (Luke 1:15, 41, 67; 4:1; and Acts 2:4; 4:8, 31; 6:3; 7:55; 9:17; 11:24; and 13:9); and in each instance of use the phrase is linked with a context where someone has been fitted by God for handling some task, speaking some needed word, or doing some strategic deed. The whole notion is that of readiness to act by the help of God. According to Luke's somewhat strict usage, being "filled with the Spirit" is a discernment-disclosure expression. It is explanatory and descriptive. It tells how some person was aided to make some action take place.

Paul also used the expression, but he widened the framework within which it was first understood and made it into a prescriptive: "Be filled with the Spirit." Luke wrote to report about events and how they occurred; thus, his statements and expressions. Paul wrote to shape an event, to make something occur; thus his are prescriptives and performatives. Understood in this way, both the adjectival use by Luke and the imperative use by Paul of the description "filled" can be viewed in a way that frees us from any notion of quantity in connection with the meaning of the term.

Paul's prescriptive word "Be filled with the Spirit" functions as a challenge to hold a conscious relationship with God. He is encouraging the believer to receive the rich help offered by the Spirit. The point of the prescriptive is practical holiness, the enhancement of experience, the fulfillment of ethical demands, and being readied for service in the arena of human need. There is small wonder, then, that Paul could risk being misunderstood when he confessed his prayer that all the Ephesian members would be "filled with all the fullness of God" (3:19), using a problematic expression with which later generations of believers and scholars still wrestle.[12]

---

12 On this, see: J. Armitage Robinson, St. Paul's Epistle to the Ephesians (London: James Clarke and Co., Ltd., n.d.), esp. pp. 87-88, 255-59; C. Leslie Mitten, The Epistle to the Ephesians (Oxford: At the Clarendon Press, 1951), esp. 95-97, 245;

There is some evidence that the question was raised in the Early Church about the extent or degree to which one could be "full of the Spirit." The question is implied in John 3:34, which states: "For he whom God has sent utters the words of God, for it is not by measure that he gives the Spirit." Scholarly opinion is still divided over whether this is a saying of Jesus, or whether it is the summarized reflection of the Evangelist regarding Jesus,[13] but the point of the statement is clear: There was no limitation of the Spirit in the life of Jesus.

Perhaps the question about degrees of Spirit-relatedness was influenced by a current rabbinic teaching that the Holy Spirit was given sparingly even to the prophets, that He only "rested" on them—and in measured fashion.[14] The New Testament writers do

---

C. F. D. Moule, "'Fullness' and 'Fill' in the New Testament," *Scottish Journal of Theology* 4, no. 1 (March, 1951): 79-86. Markus Barth has explained, "It is not impossible—though convincing evidence is still missing—that the terms 'fullness' and 'fill' contain an allusion to some religious, pagan-syncretistic vocabulary and system" (*The Broken Wall: A Study of the Epistle to the Ephesians* [Valley Forge: Judson Press, 1959], 72; see also 256-57).

13   On the question, see C. H. Dodd, *The Interpretation of the Fourth Gospel* (Cambridge: At the University Press, 1954), pp. 308-11; Raymond E. Brown, *The Gospel According to John: Introduction, Translation, and Notes, The Anchor Bible* (Garden City, N.Y.: Doubleday and Co., Inc., 1966), 1:159-60; George Johnston, *The Spirit-Paraclete in the Gospel of John* (Cambridge: At the University Press, 1970), pp. 13-14, 21; Leon Morris, *The Gospel According to John,* New International Commentary (Grand Rapids, Mich.: Wm. B. Eerdmans Publishing Co., 1971), 243.

14   So Rabbi Acha (c. 320), in comments on Leviticus (Midrash Rabbah): "The Holy Spirit, who rests on the prophets, rests [on them] only by weight (= by measure)." See Hermann L. Strack and Paul Billerbeck, *Kommentar zum Neuen Testament aus Talmud and Midrash* (Muenchen: C. H. Beck, 1956), 2:431. J. H. Bernard cites another Talmudic saying on the same point, "The Spirit of God did not dwell upon the prophets *nisi mensura quadam,*" but wondering if this form of the saying is original or reflects a Christian influence upon it. See Bernard, *A Critical and Exegetical Commentary on the Gospel According to St. John,* vol. 1, ed. A. H. McNeile, International Critical Commentary (Edinburgh: T. & T. Clark, 1928), 125. See also Brown, *Gospel According to John,* esp. pp. 158, 161-62, for additional comments on John 3:34. The wording of 3:34 could be reminiscent of Wisdom of Sirach 1:10, where the statement is made, "She [Wisdom] dwells with all flesh according to his gift," i.e., in measured quantity.

not give this question any direct treatment, but their descriptive phrase "filled with the Spirit" does witness to an understood relation with the Spirit. Using such a description, they confessed and affirmed that there is indeed a dynamic relationship between the believer and the Spirit.

Appealing again to the Gospel of John, we find there some sayings from Jesus which promise that the Holy Spirit will give the believer enlightenment (14:25; 16:13-15) and sense of divine presence (14:16-17; 16:7-11). The theology in these sayings is the same as that reflected in Luke-Acts, as we have seen. Both Luke and John describe the work of the Spirit in the life of the believer as that of enlightenment, enablement, and a shared sense of divine presence.

In our time, another question has been raised in the Church: whether the "filling" of the believer by the Spirit can be perceived by the believer as a felt experience. The way this question is answered usually marks the boundary between churches of the holiness tradition, which are "Pentecostal" by description, and those of that same tradition which are not. That boundary between the churches is mainly psycho-theological because there are very few substantial theological differences between them to block unity. The Arminian-Wesleyan tradition is the religious milieu in which both groups are rooted. The separate paths they follow are conditioned mainly by a difference of view regarding the nature, form, content, and outworking of "enthusiasm"—God-within by His Spirit.[15]

---

15   I use this term "enthusiasm" despite the extreme disrepute in which some hold it. On the varied history it has had as a word, see Susie I. Tucker, *Enthusiasm: A Study in Semantic Change* (Cambridge: At the University Press, 1972). For excellent studies regarding Pentecostals, see Gary Schwartz, *Sect Ideologies and Social Status* (Chicago: University of Chicago Press, 1970), esp. 137-81; W. J. Hollenweger, *The Pentecostals: The Charismatic Movement in the Churches* (Minneapolis: Augsburg Publishing House, 1972), trans. from the German by R. A. Wilson. See esp. 291-456.

While the world of our day continues to wrestle with the question about the existence or absence of God, the Church is in a state of unrest as many believers stand puzzled over questions about the presence and manifestations of God. All of us know that there is an intensive search on for "peak experience," that there is a widespread longing within the Church to experience that which motivates to optimism, joy, and depth belief. It is really a quest for "the touch of God,"[16] and to know that touch in a felt way. Charles R. Meyer has explained.

> By peak experience we would mean that which is particularly striking and significant. It is the type of experience that we cannot easily forget because it is so unusual or different. Peak experiences are those which bring about notable changes in behavior, changes that are profound and lasting. From a peak experience a person might well develop a whole new outlook on life, a different or more meaningful philosophy.[17]

Our Wesleyan-holiness tradition, following the witness of the New Testament, has always associated "the touch of God" with the working presence of the Holy Spirit. This interpretation is biblical and this emphasis is still needed.

The whole thrust of the New Testament witness is toward "peak experiences"—as man needs them and as God wills them. The fact is that Christian living is the result of the peak experience of conversion, and it is sustained and deepened when holiness,

---

16   See Charles R. Meyer, *The Touch of God: A Theological Analysis of Religious Experience* (Staten Island, N.Y.: Alba House, 1972).

17   Ibid., 63.

"the vision which transforms,"[18] is given freedom to fulfill itself on every level of decision and realized intent. The fact is that those who let the vision fulfill itself do learn more and more about the presence of God because, through God's Spirit within them, God is realized as "manifested Presence."

This is the explanation behind the fruit of the Spirit in Christian holiness (see Gal. 5:22- 23). Nor should it be overlooked that a felt experience is implied in connection with the realization of certain fruit: "joy" and "peace," for example, not to mention "self-control." These are by no means unrelated to our realized emotional states; they are certainly perceivable effects for which the "filling Presence" is responsible. Full commitment can have an "overflow" effect. Conscious yielding of inner consent to God can occasion passionate joy. A will reinforced by the Spirit to live out the demands of the imperatives will learn the glory of the indicative and enjoy what Richard Niebuhr called "the intimacy of believing.[19]

Openness to the Spirit releases one's moral energy and forbids that "bottled-up" self-containment that results in sin. Commitment centers the self, focuses identity, and gives a sense of being engaged. There are times when the believer might perceive a "filling" on the level of feeling. If so, then it is but the participatory work of the Holy Spirit to either ready or renew the believer. Even the body can share in some of God's manifest effects.

The expression "filled with," widely used by Luke, is found in more contexts than those which link it with the Holy Spirit. Some verses describe persons filled with wisdom (Luke 2:40), or filled with wrath (4:28), or with awe (5:26); or fury (6:11); wonder (Acts

---

18   Title of a now classic study by George Allen Turner, *The Vision Which Transforms* (Kansas City, Mo.: Beacon Hill Press, 1964).

19   Richard Niebuhr, *Experiential Religion* (New York: Harper and Row, 1972), 57.

3:10), grace and power (Acts 6:8), deceit and villainy (Acts 13:10), or joy (Acts 13:52). In most of these instances we can recognize affective states of which the person is aware while being influenced by them. The person experiences himself as struck, stirred, and shaped by the state. Being "filled with the Spirit" can also be an affective realization. Paul must have been aware of this wider possibility within his functional directive. Perhaps this is why he gave it, along with the prohibition against being drunk!

The New Testament is filled with a language that holds power to affect a situation of "discernment-commitment," to use Ian T. Ramsey's phrase.[20] For believers, the holiness texts found there are especially crucial to this end. Those texts present an organized view by which Christian experience is to be ordered, measured, and fulfilled. Those holiness texts show us an all- important "vision which transforms," and call us to an interaction with God through statements that are often "logically odd,"[21] always morally gripping, admittedly unique, and with power to unmask.

I agree with Wayne E. Oates that "the Hebrew and Greek languages are at their bases structured, psychological points of view to those who look close enough."[22] That is so; and as for the New Testament writers, their Greek usage became the vehicle for a dynamic witness concerning life in the Spirit. The syntactical approach is still basic for research study of their message. A semantical approach to the study of that witness both deepens the level of our reach and assures the gaining of results.

---

20   Ramsey, *Religious Language*, see 11-54.

21   Ibid., 106.

22   *The Psychology of Religion* (Waco, Tex.: Word Books, Publisher, 1973), 13.

21

SHARERS IN HOLINESS

by *James Earl Massey*

Originally appeared in *The Asbury Seminarian*,
vol. 26, no. 1 (January 1972), 35-47. Delivered at
Asbury Theological Seminary, Wilmore, Kentucky,
on October 27, 1971. Abbreviated because of some
duplication with entry eight in this volume.
Used by permission.

William Temple once wrote, "The most agreeable experiences in life are those which are marked by a coincidence of duty and pleasure."[1] I have that happiness as I meet with you in this experience of sharing and celebrating. The Francis Asbury Convocation Committee has done me honor in inviting me to be the Wesleyan witness concerning the experience of holiness.

We are engaged here in nothing less than a reconsideration of the nature and results of our experience of God, "the Holy One." Just what is that experience? How does one posture himself for it? What is our posture because of this experience? What are its personal aspects, and what issues from the inward level of the

---

1   *Nature, Man and God* (London: Macmillan and Co., Ltd., 1934), vii.

experience to affect the outward and social aspects of our lives? Our holiness heritage speaks pointedly to these questions. I now move on to trace that pointing, and test it all anew against scriptural categories, definitions, and insights, strongly believing that the basic framework for interpreting our life and living must be forever biblical.

The phrasing of my subject has been influenced, as you have already discerned, by two highly-suggestive New Testament verses. The first is Hebrews 12:10, the context of which calls us to reconsider our trials as agents of God's concern to shape us like himself. The analogy drawn by the writer between life under our earthly fathers and life under our heavenly Father is immediately clear. The final thrust of the comparison is razor-sharp in its theology. "For they disciplined us for a short time at their pleasure, but he disciplines us for our good, that we may share his holiness."

The second of those verses is 2 Peter 1:4. The connection of thought demands a reading of verses 3 and 4 together. "His divine power has granted to us all things that pertain to life and godliness, through the knowledge of him who called us to his own glory and excellence, by which he has granted to us his precious and very great promises, that through these you may escape from the corruption that is in the world because of passion, and become partakers of the divine nature."

These two verses draw attention to one of the most pertinent and positive claims of the early church. The texts are prophetic, admittedly technical, and unmistakably argue for a Christian mysticism. But their message is clearly put: a true knowledge of God gives the Christian believer *a share in holiness*. It is with this conspicuous fact of New Testament doctrine and experience that the Wesleyan holiness emphasis has concerned itself.

God as Holy

Every serious student of Scripture knows that the central concept of its vast teaching about God is his holiness. This descriptive word about the nature of God occurs with such frequency and emphasis that it cannot be missed or overlooked. Holiness is the basic and key concept for understanding the witness of both Testaments concerning God, both as to his nature and to his relations with humans, things, and races. As regards his nature, God is referred to, and speaks about Himself, as "the Holy One" (Job 6:10; Isa. 10:17). Another description relates God to his people as "the holy One of Israel" (2 Kgs 19:22; Ps. 71:22; Isa. 1:4, 12; Jer. 51:5; Ezek. 39:7).

As the Holy One, God is distinctly "Other." He is separated, marked off in nature from that which is ordinary, common, human. The "Otherness" of God is so distinctive and unique, so absolute in its perfection and purity, so utterly peculiar to deity, that it occasions radical awe in man when God deigns to confront him. Both Testaments supply us with multiplied instances when men recoiled upon confronting the "Mysterium Tremendum," as Rudolf Otto has aptly termed it.[2]

The holiness of God not only stirs a reaction to his presence but also invites a relationship with himself. God is not unapproachable but is unavoidable. The clearest pictures of divine action show God's concern to relate with men and *share himself with them*. That is the dominating theme of the Scriptures. But it is necessary to ask, Does God only *impute* his holiness to us, or does he actually *impart* it to us who believe? Our Wesleyan tradition makes claim upon God's holiness in more than a figurative manner because

---

2   See Rudolf Otto, *The Idea of the Holy* (London: Oxford University Press, 1923), 12-24.

holiness of life is for us more than a figure of speech. We affirm our faith that God has let us have a share in his holiness.

Jesus Christ as the Manifestation of Holiness

On the Christological level of our witness, we affirm that *God has shown us his holiness* on our human level in his Son Jesus. The sonship of Jesus is real and revelational. The character of his life was a manifestation of holiness in the flesh. This is in view in John 1:14 where the witnessing writer exclaims, "And the Word became flesh and dwelt among us, full of grace and truth; we have beheld his glory, glory as of the only Son from the Father." In Jesus Christ we have what Paul referred to as the visible "image of the invisible God" (Col. 1:15). So Jesus could rightly claim, "And he who sees me sees him who sent me" (John 12:45), and he could truthfully declare, "He who has seen me has seen the Father" (John 14:9). God has revealed his holiness on our level in the unique sonship of Jesus.

Jesus of Nazareth understood and declared himself to be the Son of God. He used the sonship designation when teaching his disciples and openly addressed God in prayer as *"Abba,"* as if it were his custom to be intimate with Him, and as if that way of addressing God possessed a deeper meaning and relationship.[3] His use of that term of endeared relation is much too intense and intimate to allow me to believe only that "the decisive feature of the title [Son] is subordination."[4] I rather believe, with the New Testament writers, that Jesus lived among us with a consciousness of unique

---

3   See Gustaf Dalman, *The Words of Jesus* (Edinburgh: T. & T. Clark, 1902), esp. 280-287. See also Joachim Jeremias, *The Prayers of Jesus* (SBT, Second Series, No. 6) (London: SCM Press, Ltd., 1967), esp. 44-57.

4   See the treatment of this view by Hans Conzelmann, *An Outline of the Theology of the New Testament* (New York and Evanston: Harper and Row, 1969), 127.

relation with God. I believe that Jesus held, and now holds, with God a unique position, a unique relation, a unique life, a unique sonship. God was Father for Jesus and in a manner we are not able to understand or explain completely. The New Testament witnesses to his life did not get side-tracked over metaphysical questions of his genesis or descent as divine Son; they rightly and wisely celebrated Jesus as saving person-giving honor to God the Father. What they saw in Jesus they began to share through his company. "And from his fullness have we all received, grace upon grace." "No one has ever seen God; the only Son, who is in the bosom of the Father, he has made him known" (John 1:16, 18).

It has been necessary to repeat these statements about Jesus as the revealing Son because what we are to share of the holiness of God is related to what we see in Jesus. As John 1:12 puts it, "But to all who received him, who believed in his name, he gave power to become children of God." As children of God we stand related to him, saved by grace and secure in his love. But there is more. As children of God we stand responsible to him—responsible to reflect his likeness and honor his name. We believers not only draw confidence from our Father's care; we must dare a full commitment to our Father's will. Jesus himself shows us the model Son. Jesus himself is the "Beloved" for whose sake we have been admitted into the family of God. Paul classic expression of this is in Ephesians 1:3-6.

The Holy God stands behind it all, working through Jesus Christ in our interest and to his honor. Here Paul speaks again: "He [God] is the source of your life in Christ Jesus, whom God made our wisdom, our righteousness and sanctification and redemption" (1 Cor. 1:30). Jesus is not only God's model Son, he is our means for sonship at its best, which means a derived holy likeness to the Father.

Christian Holiness through Christ

Ours, then, is *Christian* holiness—that holiness made possible for us in the Spirit of Christ. It is derived. It is definite. It is distinctive. It is also holiness as *imitatio de Christi* since his person, life, teachings, actions, and spirit form the visible norm for our conduct and concerns. Just as Jesus "imitated" God, doing as Son the deeds of his Father (see John 5:19-20; 8:38-47), we "imitate" Jesus, following him, keeping his commandments, and living for his interests. Jesus Christ himself conditions our share in holiness as the source of our sanctification (1 Cor. 1:30). Sanctification is that moral and ethical state that results from the commitment of our will to God's will as seen in Christ. Christian holiness involves our will in the same way that God's own original holiness necessarily involves his every act of will.

Christian holiness always involves the will. The gift of holiness is procured to the believer by the Spirit of Christ, but it develops in line with the believer's dedication and decisive openness toward God. What we have before us in Christian holiness is a qualitative life, a life that is both consequent and commitment.

[For a development of this section, see entry eight of this volume, "Proclaiming Holiness: The Divine Attribute and Christian Character." Massey there explains our share in holiness as individual, identifiable, intelligible, and instrumental.]

A Share in Holiness

It is Jesus who shows us the perfect life of holy sonship to God. It is the Holy Spirit who initiates us into that sonship life. That initiation is called *conversion*. Jesus spoke of this experience as being "born of the Spirit" (John 3:6), as being "born anew" or "born from above" (John 3:3, 7). Our human nature can originally reflect only our natural heritage of flesh, but by spiritual rebirth through conversion we can meaningfully intersect with the higher order of existence— and secure share in it as new sons.

But that initiation is anticipatory. Conversion beings us into the new life, but sanctification grants us a fuller share in it. Conversion is the divine mode of our begetting; Sanctification is the divine mode of our maturity as sons. The experience of sanctification is both existential—that is, having to do with the problem of our human nature and the possible character of our lives—and it is eschatological—that is, having to do with our future. This being so, there are aspects within the experience that are conclusive and processive. It is conclusive in that our sonship has been "sealed" (Eph. 1:13) with the Holy Spirit, tagged and authenticated as God's very own through a share in holiness; yet it is processive in that the full realization and manifestation of the sonship state increasingly takes place.

As Spirit-filled sons and daughters who have a share in holiness, we can publicly announce God as our Father. We can make that cry in witness or in prayer, and say it with overwhelming joy, with moral strength, with sure insight, with responsible emotion, and with definite assurance. It is with the possibility, necessity, excellence and availability of this experience that the Wesleyan emphasis on Christian holiness has been concerned.

The Joy of Holiness

Our celebration is not because we are "beside ourselves." We rather celebrate because we have grounds for being "enthusiasts," literally so: *God has sent the Spirit of his Son into our hearts.* God has placed his holiness at our disposal for life in this world and in the next! God has let us begin to apprehend him in his own holiness, while at the same time deepening and clarifying our own humanity. We are learning to live more and more out of God and less and less out of ourselves.

I speak honestly and without reluctance. I speak, like the writer of John 1:14, because I too have experienced the "glory." It is a vast company of believers for whom I speak in witness, a company of men and women who have known the disciplines and delights and duties of holiness. It is a company filled with men and women who eagerly affirm, with Paul, "But by the grace of God I am what I am, and his grace toward me was not in vain" (1 Cor. 15:10a).

It was to such a company that John Wesley belonged, and he could ably trace out the source and meaning of his experience. Wesley knew "holiness and happiness" through divine promises fulfilled in his own sonship. Declared he, "I now am assured that these things are so: I experience them in my own breast. What Christianity (considered as a doctrine) promised is accomplished in my soul. And Christianity, considered as an inward principle, is the completion of all those promises. It is holiness and happiness, the image of God impressed on a created spirit, a fountain of peace and love springing up into everlasting life."[5]

Francis Asbury was also of such a company. He testified, "All my desire is for the Lord, and more of his divine nature impressed on my soul. I long to be lost and swallowed up in God."[6] Such a company takes divine sonship seriously. Such a company knows the deeper ways of God with men. *Soli Deo Gloria.*

---

5   From his letter to Dr. Conyers Middleton, dated January 4, 1749. See *The Letters of the Rev. John Wesley*, ed. By John Telford (London: Epworth Press, 1931), Vol. II, 383.

6   *The Journal*, Vol. I, 178. The entry is dated Feb 12, 1776.

22

CONCERNING CHRISTIAN UNITY

by *James Earl Massey*

Originally appeared in *Concerning Christian Unity* by James
Earl Massey (Warner Press, 1979). Excerpts throughout.
Used by permission.

T he Dedication of my 1979 book reads: "To the officers
and members of the Metropolitan Church of God, who
trusted and lived out the 'spirit of relation' discussed
in this book for the twenty-four years of my leadership as their
senior pastor, and who upon my departure lovingly named me
Pastor-at-Large." What is meant by the "spirit of relation"? Let
me explain.

The Christian faith involves more than standards; it involves
a ready and sympathetic sharing with each other as well. Unity
made possible in Christian faith calls upon all who have experienced salvation through Christ to stretch themselves and touch
each other, to open their mouths and speak openly with each
other. No Christian should view his or her life singly. It is part of
God's wider group of redeemed people.

Unity is spiritual; it is a divine gift. The real experience of it is
the work of love. Agape love stirs us to be related, and when we are
not so stirred, that love mandates us to open ourselves to become

interested and stirred. Becoming open to love and staying open to its restraints is the responsibility of every Christian.

Every Christian has a legacy in every other Christian. We experience that legacy only as we receive each other and relate, moving eagerly beyond group boundaries. It is helpful for us to remember that, throughout the Bible, salvation is usually discussed not as solitariness but in the context of community.

Christian community is the bringing together of persons whose lives have been touched and changed by Christ. His life and work are the basis for the bond between believers, and his Spirit always promotes experiences of that bond in personal openness in regard for each other. The fact of denominational families and denominated forms is one of the most familiar facts in religious life. It is also one of the most questioned and problematic of contemporary religious concerns.

We know that there is something negative about institutionalism in church life. We also all know that there is something unworthy about bureaucracy and competitiveness within the church family. We should all know that there is something unnecessary about being at cross purposes because our smaller group labels and orientations to the church differ.

Strongly drawn denominational lines have encouraged separateness among believers. Although the patterns of church separateness often have strong reasons behind them, the boundaries between the separated church groups have occasioned many prevailing problems. It is for this reason among others that we must re-examine the boundaries posed by denominational differences and distinctions in the attempt to understand and live out the imperatives of Christian unity.

I had the special privilege of participating in two outstanding unity events designed to promote Christian togetherness and outreach. They were international congresses of Christians gathered from around the world convened in Berlin, Germany, in 1966, and in Lausanne, Switzerland, in 1974 (joined by my colleague and friend Barry L. Callen). These amazing events focused on needed Christian togetherness for the sake of Christian evangelism. Then in 1978 my wife and I were guest leaders for The Uniting Church in Australia where we sensed and actively promoted a spirit of interdependence and belonging among previously separated Christian fellowships.

The writer of Ephesians aptly refers to "the unity of the Spirit" (4:3). The Spirit of God specializes in helping believers experience oneness. The Spirit influences us toward togetherness and cooperation, aids our growth in love (Rom. 5:5), and establishes in disciples of Jesus the impulse that prompts relations and proper responses in dealing with each other. The result is the church in health and the church effectively on mission.

23

MY VIEW OF THE END TIMES

by James Earl Massey

Dr. James Earl Massey, in dialogue with theologian
Stanley J. Grenz and popular Bible interpreter Hal Lindsey.
Originally appeared in Barry L. Callen, *Heart of the Matter*
(Emeth Press, rev. ed. 2016), 180, 183.
Used by permission.

While I don't agree with the details of many of your biblical interpretations, Hal, I do affirm your basic evangelistic agenda. Even so, I note that, ten years after your extremely popular 1970 book *The Late, Great Planet Earth*, your focus had changed considerably. Your newer *The 1980s: Countdown to Armageddon* carries a full-blown political agenda. You blame America's ills on groups of liberal conspirators who, as you saw it, were dismantling the military and undercutting the free enterprise system. It was time to clean house in Washington.

My point is that I have seen you being carried along by the shifting winds of the times. You have made significant adjustments when what you once thought was biblical prophecy just didn't work out in fact. I fear for any of us who read the sacred pages of the Bible and move quickly to unknowingly printing and preaching our own social and political agendas.

Stan, your review of controversial subjects like the multiple millennialisms helps us consider the alternative positions held by serious Bible believers. I applaud your sensitivity to the history of biblical interpretation and your willingness to leave unclear matters in doubt, exactly where the Bible leaves them. As to these theories of future events, you properly see a key lesson to be learned from each, but without absolutizing any of the theories themselves as the biblical one. I see that as wise and biblically responsible. Such wisdom is explained at length in my friend Barry Callen's book *Faithful in the Meantime*—the biblical focus is on present responsibility and not future speculation.

I have occasionally preached a sermon titled "All things Will Be New." It's included, for instance, in my 2000 book *Sundays in the Tuskegee Chapel*. I begin with the verse in Revelation 21:5 that announces that God will indeed make all things new. John wasn't speculating on the many details of the distant future, maybe our very times. He was repeating, for world-weary saints under Roman oppression, the Old Testament prophets who kept announcing good news about the renewal of history.

A divine happening, announced the prophets and now John, would determine the future that is controlled only by God. The future we need is beyond our human shaping. But, as Paul made clear, one day the creation will be set free from its bondage to decay (Rom. 8:18-21). God promises to make all things new. In fact, aspects of this coming newness are already a present reality! Those of us privileged by grace to now be "born again" know this very well. And we know that there is much more to come. The best is yet to be!

"Meanwhile" is the key word for us disciples caught in the remaining miseries of the present time. What should we be doing in the meantime before God makes all things new? We must go on with our holy work even while we watch in hope for what God surely will do.

24

DOCTRINE AS THE SOURCE OF BIBLICAL CHURCH GROWTH

by James Earl Massey

Originally appeared in the *National Baptist Voice*, Winter 2007
(Vol. 6:1), 24-25, 27, and also in *The African American Pulpit*,
Spring 2007 (Vol. 10:2), 31-35. Used by permission.

Across many decades now, the Greek word *megas,* meaning "large, great," has been part of our common talk. Since the late 1920s "megahertz" has been used with respect to radio frequencies. Since the late 1940s, the word "megabucks" has denoted large sums of money. Since the late 1960s, "megabyte" has been a computer term and "megacity" has been used to denote a city with a population of one million or more. "Mega-corporation" is a familiar term, and so is the related term "mega-deal."

More recently, we have been speaking about "mega-churches," those large churches whose exponential growth in membership of 2,000 to 10,000 or more continues to attract attention by their styles of worship, strategies of evangelism, staffing for ministry, and whose primary focus has been to reach unchurched people, particularly those in the suburbs of large cities. What is clearly evident is that what those who lead such churches have been doing has been working.

The Unchurched Public

The unchurched public often are *secularists* who live their lives with concern focused on this world and time alone. The circumstances of their upbringing and orientation have conditioned them toward a preoccupation with human affairs to the exclusion of divine matters. George G. Hunter, III has given us an informative and compelling profile of secularists, intent to help us to understand, engage, and win them.[1]

Many among the unchurched are *consumerists:* these are persons so influenced by our sales-oriented environment and the promises of a robust capitalism that they see everything in terms of goods and services and return on investments. To them, religious life is just another commodity. The entertainment-styled worship appeals to their self-interest, and so do the messages delivered about being personally successful.

The consumerists are *choosey.* They know a lot about a lot of things, and they know what they like. They like life on their own terms, and they don't like anything that threatens the way they think or affects their chosen life-style.

Some among the unchurched claim a spirituality versus being religious. "Spirituality" is the in-word these days. The term is being used to mean high- church liturgy, New Age concerns, and even religious experimentation. As theologian Barry L. Callen has explained, "Experimentation is rampant. Spirituality, variously defined, is definitely in vogue. The atmosphere is often a supermarket of options catering to personal preferences."[2] In America,

---

1   See George Hunter, III, *How to Reach Secular People* (Abingdon Press, 1992), esp. 41-54.

2   Barry L. Callen, Authentic *Spirituality: Moving Beyond Mere Religion* (Grand Rapids: Baker Academic, 2001), 16-17.

"spirituality" often means living by certain cultural values, having an altruistic attitude toward other persons and groups, and holding a basic belief that Someone superintends the universe.

Many megachurches have succeeded in their quest to reach and attract unchurched persons, and they have even attracted and embraced many who are religiously dissatisfied or disaffected. These churches have developed strategies which appeal: they meet the unchurched and disaffected where they are, offer ministries to help them with their apparent needs, engage them in dialogue to address their questions, and give them a sense of belonging. The basic approach has been to affirm people, offering them an opportunity to relate with those who care as they seek acceptance, meaning, personal help, and the opportunity to be part of a network. The churches engaged in this kind of missioning have seized an opportunity to serve their chosen public, and many of them have been reaping quite a harvest of results, including popularity and even material gain.

Lack of a Doctrinal Base

While some of what many megachurches have been doing out of concern for unchurched and religiously disaffected persons is praiseworthy, I must call attention to a problem all too few of them have handled aptly, partly because the rationale of their approach in attracting an audience has prevented the rightful handling of the need for biblical doctrine. The problem to which I point is the lack of attention in some of the megachurches, at least in their public ministries, to an openly biblical or doctrinal base in what they publish and in what those who speak for them preach.

Having read much of the literature promoted by several megachurches, and having listened intently to many messages preached on some of their televised programs, I have been disappointed with the neglect of such centralities of Christian faith as who Jesus is , why Jesus came, why Jesus died, what salvation means, the problem of sin, or the importance of conversion. While it is generally claimed that some unchurched post-moderns are more aware of doubt than of guilt, any church that is doctrinally-informed as a Christian fellowship is also aware that the "word of God is living and active, sharper than any two-edged sword , piercing until it divides soul from spirit, joints from marrow, [and] is able to judge the thoughts and intentions of the heart" (Heb. 4: 12), and that a doctrinally-based church knows that the Spirit of God still uses God's written Word to "prove the world wrong about sin and righteousness and judgement" (John 16:8).

In speaking about "Christian doctrine," I want to be clearly understood. I am speaking about what the late Jaroslav Pelikan has aptly described as "what the church of Jesus Christ believes, teaches, and confesses on the basis of the Word of God: this is Christian doctrine."[3] Pelikan's description is both comprehensive and focused. He further stated that "the Christian church would not be the church as we know it without Christian doctrine."[4]

The teaching and preaching of doctrine in the life of the church is not an option but a necessity. Doctrine informs *and* forms by influencing thought, understanding, motives and action. As Ellen T. Charry has explained: "[When] Christian doctrines assert the truth about God, the world, and ourselves, it is a truth that seeks to influence us."[5] Doctrines help to inform and shape us for godly

---

3   See Jaroslav Pelikan, *The Christian Tradition:* A History of the Development of Doctrine, Vol. 1 (Chicago: University of Chicago Press, 1971), 1.

4   *Ibid.,* 1.

5   Ellen T. Charry, *By the Renewing of Your Minds:* The Pastoral Function of Christian Doctrine (New York: Oxford University Press, 1997), viii.

character and the service of God. In an age when many are religiously confused, socially marginalized, distrustful of authority, and affected by a consumer mentality, a faithful and loving handling of the truth is both necessary and imperative. Yes, necessary and imperative, not optional, because the basics of faith are no longer common knowledge as before.

Across the recent decades, "Something like a doctrinal defoliation has occurred."[6] And the results of that defoliation have undermined and delimited the belief-system essential for Christian being and behavior. Christian doctrine is imperative to establish a vital core-belief and to maintain a godly behavior pattern. There is a statement from Paul in Romans 6: 7 about becoming "obedient from the heart [*ek kardias*] to the form of teaching to which [one has been] entrusted." That expression "from the heart" is a Pauline construction that refers to how the response of the inner self determines one's obedience, and what stimulates that obedience. Paul credited that stimulation of the heart to a specific "form" [*tupos*] of teaching," and believers who receive godly teaching with openness and obedience to its meaning and authority become trained in godliness.

Sharing Christian Doctrine

Christian doctrine must be shared because it has a "so that" dimension; it has a functional purpose. Theologian Alister McGrath has enumerated four functions of doctrine: (1) Christian doctrine demarcates and differentiates the Church from culture; (2) Christian doctrine provides a framework by which the Church can

---

6   Robert Hughes and Robert Kysar, *Preaching Doctrine for the Twenty-First Century* (Minneapolis: Fortress Press, 1997), 1.

understand and explain itself; (3) Christian doctrine is necessary to illumine human experience; and (4) Christian doctrine offers focu sed truth-claims about God and God's relationship with us.[7] Here is yet another function that doctrine serves: Christian doctrine informs the Church for both its evangelistic witness and pastoral service.[8]

Across more than fifty years now I have been active in theological education, and five of those years were spent as dean of a theological seminary. But for twenty-four years I served as the founding pastor of what became a large and active urban congregation in Detroit. During our growth in membership, which was continuous, there was one biblical passage to which I looked as an instructive model for our congregational life. That passage was Acts 2:42-47, with verse 42 being understood as the first of several summary statements by Luke about the community life of the Jerusalem Church during its earliest years: "They devoted themselves to the apostles' teaching and fellowship, to the breaking of bread and the prayers."[9]

The wording in Acts 2:42 is clearly both descriptive and prescriptive.[10] It describes the basis on which church growth began and continued, namely apostolic teaching. "The community, the apostolic fellowship," F. F. Bruce commented, "was constituted on the basis of apostolic teaching. This teaching was authoritative

---

7   See Alister McGrath, *The Genesis of Doctrine: A Study in the Foundations of Doctrinal Criticism* (Oxford: Basil Blackwell, 1990), esp. Ch. 3, 35-80.

8   For an excellent study about the pastoral function of doctrine, see Ellen T. Charry, *By the Renewing of Your Minds.*

9   On Acts 2:42 as one of several summary statements Luke used to serve his purpose as a writer, see Henry J. Cadbury, "The Summaries in Acts," in *The Beginnings of Christianity,* Vol. V, ed. by F. J. Foakes Jackson and Henry J. Cadbury (Baker Book House, 1966), esp. 397-402.

10 See Jaroslav Pelikan, *Acts* (Brazos Press, 2005), 58.

because it was the teaching of the Lord communicated through the apostles in the power of the Spirit. For believers of later generations, the New Testament scriptures form the written deposit of the apostolic teaching. The apostolic succession is recognized most clearly in those churches which adhere most steadfastly to the apostolic teaching."[11]

Acts 2:42 is also prescriptive in that the criteria itemized there are imperative for the continuity, consistency, and centeredness of the church. Although some scholars view the Book of Acts as Luke's idealized account of church life at its beginnings, his mention of specific teachings as foundational indicates what was surely normative. If normative then, it is normative now, and perennially necessary. And apart from that authoritative teaching, the church ceases to be informed properly to be the church.

The Apostolic Doctrine

From the very beginning of the church, its members were a fellowship of believers devoted to what Jesus and his apostles taught, and they showed that devotion in their relation to God, their relationship and activities with each other, and by their life in the world.[12] Sad to say, what Acts 2:42 refers to as "the apostles' doctrine" is missing from the teaching done in some megachurches.

The apostles' doctrine did not consist of loose ideas and popular concepts from culture; they taught what Jesus himself had taught (Matt. 28:20), and those disciples related that teaching to

---

11   F. F. Bruce, *The Book of Acts* (Wm. B. Eerdmans Publishing Co., 1988 rev. ed.), 73.

12   For a suggested understanding of "the prayers" activity listed in Acts 2:42, see Joachim Jeremias, *The Eucharistic Words of Jesus* (London: SCM Press, Ltd, 1966), 118f. See Daniel K. Falk, "Jewish Prayer Literature and the Jerusalem Church in Acts," in *The Book of Acts in Its Palestinean Setting*, ed. by Richard Bauckham (Wm. B. Eerdmans Publishing Co., 1995), esp. 270-276.

life, using the Hebrew Scriptures as supporting documentation. The apostles' doctrine was teaching that needed to be known, believed, confessed, and lived. The church is a place of prescribed learning, and apart from that specific training it ceases to be the church. When apostolic doctrine is neglected, personal opinion takes precedence over biblical truths, ethics become situational, cultural notions replace vital orthodoxy, and emotion becomes a primary concern and a controlling force.

Sound doctrine is needed to monitor personal experience and keep us true to scriptural orthodoxy, helping us become and remain, in Barry Callen's words, "text anchored and Spirit enlivened."[13] The apostles' doctrine is needed to help us discern and guard against the mistakes, distortions, and subtle evils of our own time. The apostles' doctrine can help us to think biblically, believe rightly, live godly, and serve God faithfully.

The New Landscape

The landscape of American religious life has been altered. We have entered a new era in American Protestantism. Denominational lines of identity are now blurred, and mega-church leaders and networks assert themselves as the most vocal and viable spiritual models.[14] Some of these churches, with their neo-Pentecostal emphases, their high energy entertainment-mode services led by praise teams using music adopted from the pop culture, have not only deemphasized denominational affiliations, but also dismissed many doctrinal constraints.

---

13   Barry L. Callen, *op. cit.,* 19.

14   For an insightful study of one such leader and mega-church, see Shayne Lee, *T. D. Jakes: America's New Preacher* (New York: New York University Press, 2005), 158.

Several denominations have felt the strain of this changed landscape. Some members within those denominations have eagerly welcomed such changes, viewing them as "spiritually invigorating," while other members are lamenting the erosion of a more orderly worship culture and the apparent loss of a traditional congregational orientation. Whether these changes in styles of worship and congregational life are for the better and will prove spiritually fruitful remains in many places a question and an unsettling point of contention.

I wish to issue a reminder and a plea to remain faithful to gospel particulars in seeking to advance the church. We cannot neglect, overlook, deliberately ignore, or downplay the doctrinal imperative our Lord gave the church without ceasing to be the church.

25

CULTURALLY CONSCIOUS
EVANGELISM

by James Earl Massey

Originally appeared in Glenn C. Smith, ed.,
Evangelizing Blacks (Tyndale House Publishers, 1988), 187-195.
Used by permission.

The work of evangelism is best understood and discussed in connection with four basic facts: (1) the authorizing command of Jesus Christ to evangelize; (2) the universal need for what evangelism makes possible in human life here and hereafter; (3) the Christian attitude of agape sharing; and (4) the imperative to cooperate in handling this global assignment. Any proper theological statement about evangelism must involve some consideration of these four basics and it must deal with them in a scriptural context. With this in mind, let us proceed first with a look at the biblical setting of the word "evangelism" and then at the four basics germane to this assigned task from our Lord.

Evangelism Defined

The word *evangelism* is related to two New Testament words, *euangelizomia* and *euanagelizo*, both activity terms used to describe the work of announcing news that gladdens. Paul and Luke made great use of these terms when writing about the spread of the salvation message. But *euangelizomai* is not to be associated only with the New Testament writers. This verb is found several times in the Greek translation of the Old Testament (Septuagint), sometimes in the neutral sense of "to bring or announce some news," but usually with a stress upon that news as "good."

The news might be secular, as the announcement given to a man that his wife had borne him a son (Jer. 20:15), or an announcement to army headquarters that a menacing enemy has been defeated on the field of battle (1 Sam. 31:9; 2 Sam. 4:10). The news was especially good, however, when it announced a promised deed from God (Isa. 52:7) or proclaimed the fulfillment of some expected action on God's part. In these instances, the Hebrew word *bassar* ("to bring or announce good news") has been translated either by the Greek term *euangelizesthai* or *euangelizomai,* activity terms which tell about what makes the hearer(s) pleased or glad. If the news was of vital affect and import, celebration was an expected action on the part of the hearer(s).

The rather wide use of *euangelizomai* in the Old Testament is given a more restricted application in the New, where the verb is used mainly to describe the action of announcing the salvation event, the happenings and hope in which Jesus Christ is the central figure.

Before the New Testament period ended, the distinct term "evangelist" began to be used in the church to describe workers whose focus centered upon announcing the good news to those who had never heard it or not yet believed it. The term appears in Acts 21:8, Ephesians 4:11, and 2 Timothy 4:5 where *euangelistes* points (like the Hebrew *mebasser,* Isa. 40:9; 41:27; 52:7; 61:1) to the speaking "herald" as one whose message will bring blessing and joy to those who hear and receive it. Ephesians 4:11 lists being an "evangelist" as a distinctive service roll, a gifted role that is ranked and honored along with apostles, prophets, pastors, and teachers.

Evangelism was so important in the life of the early church that some persons were divinely selected to focus particularly upon that ministry. Their calling was to involve them especially with those who had never heard the gospel, sharing the salvation message as intent and concerned persuaders. But, while this was indeed the case, it was also understood by the church that evangelizing was a general service in which all believers were to share. The basis of that sharing was the authorizing command of Jesus to do it.

Christ's Authorizing Command

Evangelism is an authorized work. The risen Lord commanded the church to be engaged in this task. That command is recorded in Matthew 28:18-20, the passage usually referred to as the "Great Commission." There is a parallel passage found in Luke 24:44-49 and still another in the longer ending of Mark (16:14-19).

Bearing authority from God, Jesus had come evangelizing. His synagogue sermon in Nazareth was based upon Isaiah 61:1-4, and Jesus used that "Servant Song" to explain the focus and scope of his ministry. But, having died and risen again, Jesus met with his disciples and addressed them in his lordly role with these words: "All authority in heaven and on earth has been given to me" (Matt. 28:18). It was a preparatory statement before issuing this command: "Go therefore and make disciples of all nations, baptizing them in the name of the Father and of the Son and of the Holy Spirit, teaching them to observe all that I have commanded you" (28:19, 20a).

This was an authorizing command, authorized because of the nature of the assignment, and commanded because of the importance attached to it. In referring to his received authority, Jesus was assuring the disciples that they were being given an authorization to handle their work of announcing, sharing, convincing, baptizing, and teaching. The right to call the entire world to repentance and faith in Jesus as Savior rests upon a divine authority found in Jesus himself.

The one who first proclaimed the good news had become the central figure in what was to be proclaimed as good news. This was a God-purposed result and only God-authorized persons would have the right or understanding to talk about it in depth with anyone else. The authorizing word about who backed them allowed the disciples to do their work with confidence.

But Jesus did not only authorize the work of evangelism. He commanded it. A ministry that was to be generational in its effect, global in its dimensions, of eternal importance to all, could not be left to whim, chance, or convenience. So Jesus commanded that we evangelize. This direct command stands as a challenge, charging us to deal with any hesitation or reluctance of will that we might feel.

There is nothing quite like an authorized ministry or an assigned task. Evangelism is such an assignment. The making of disciples is no mere human task to be fulfilled by human means alone. Those who are approved and sent as trained and trusted heralds of Jesus have his authorization and bestowed authority for their work. The authorizing was part of readying the disciples for their work.

We see, therefore, that New Testament evangelism does not rest upon fleshly ambition, a "winning personality," oratorical skills, or crowd psychology. Evangelism as Jesus intended it does involve natural talents, but only as sanctified tools under the Lord's controlling Spirit. Evangelistic readiness is something more than an educated mind and an eager spirit. It is mainly the result of an authorizing experience.

Jesus pointed to that experience when he told the disciples, "I send down upon you the promise of my Father. Remain here in the city until you are clothed with power from on high" (Luke 24:49). The Lord's statement in Acts 1:8 makes the point still sharper: "You will receive power when the Holy Spirit comes down on you; then you are to be my witnesses in Jerusalem, throughout all Judea and Samaria, yes, even to the ends of the earth." The authorization to evangelize was validated as the disciples were guided in their task by the Holy Spirit who filled and worked with and through them.

According to Matthew (28:20b), Jesus had earlier promised, "I am with you always, until the end of the age." Our authorized ministry of evangelism is attended by his authoritative presence. The church has more than human means for the handling of this commanded task.

The Universal Need of the Gospel

The authorization to evangelize is related to the need of a lost world for salvation. The universal sharing of the gospel matches the universal need for Jesus. The message of the gospel is that Jesus Christ came to save sinners, that the benefits of abundant life are available in him for one and all, and that all need him.

We see the worldwide need for Jesus Christ stated throughout the New Testament. "God so loved the world that he gave his only Son, that whoever believes in him may not die but may have eternal life" (John 3:16). Paul wrote to the Corinthians, "God, in Christ, was reconciling the world to himself, not counting men's transgressions against them" (2 Cor. 5:19). Paul explained to the believers in Rome why the threat of perishing exists: "[All] are under the domination of sin" (Rom. 3:9) and "the whole world stands convicted before God" (3:19) because "all men have sinned and are deprived of the glory of God" (3:23).

The gospel is God's appeal to the world to be saved, reconciled, and freed from the power of sin. Evangelism is the task and privilege of voicing that appeal and opportunity to all. Speaking as an authorized and concerned evangelist, Paul confessed, "This makes us ambassadors for Christ, God as it were appealing through us" (2 Cor. 5:20). The scope of this appeal is the world; the focus of this appeal is upon every person in the world. Evangelism makes benefits possible and available for human life, here and hereafter.

The Unselfish Concern to Share

There is a third basis on which evangelism must be understood and done: the Christian attitude of unselfish sharing, that thoughtful concern of agape love. Those who go for Jesus must do so for his reasons and reflect his spirit of care. A caring love stirred him to die for us; a caring love must stir his people to tell others about his death that saves.

The caring must be present and powerful to sustain the witnessing Christian in an increasingly secularized and sometimes hostile world. The caring must be strong and steady when governmental demands oppose us and ideological roadblocks are faced and to be defeated. The concern for evangelism has to be strong when the witnesses are swamped again and again by heavy questioning and pressures from those who are suspicious of the enterprise, mislabeling it as a mere tool of capitalism. It takes a strong sense of caring about people to leave the familiarity of one's own cultural setting, risking the dangers of alien cultures, and not quit out of fear or yield under pressure.

Paul, who had his share of sufferings as an evangelist, explained why he could not quit nor yield: "The love of Christ impels us who have reached the conviction that since one has died for all, all died. He died for all so that those who live might live no longer for themselves but for him who for their sake died and was raised up" (2 Cor. 5:14-15).

Evangelism happens best where love controls the witnessing sharers. Evangelism certainly involves scriptural truths and eternal meanings, even the distribution of Bibles or biblical books for those who are literate. But it involves as well a caring spirit in the witness. The Great Commission involves more than authorization to speak about Jesus. It also involves caring like him. Since what he did for the world was done in love, the message about his deed must be shared in love.

It is not hard to make others hear our message if we are close enough to touch them; nor is it difficult to persuade them to believe our message if they see its effects at work in our lives. This explains why Jesus insisted that evangelism proceed only after a full surrender of the self to the Holy Spirit. The love needed to relate to people as a witness is God's gift to the personality.

As Paul explained in Galatians, "The fruit of the Spirit is love, joy, peace, patient endurance, kindness, generosity, faith, mildness, and chastity [self-control]" (5:22-23a). The Holy Spirit helps us match the message we are sent to announce and share. Evangelism demands the right message on the one hand and the right spirit for sharing it on the other.

The Worldwide Scope of Our Task

There is a fourth basic related to our task, reaching the entire world with the gospel, and doing so in unity.

Our work was expected to result in a worldwide fellowship of faith. Discipling the nations means handling the demands of language differences, cultural differences, economic differences, national distinctives, and racial polarities. The field is still the world, and our work is expected to relate to all involved in the world.

The Revelation of John pictures the extent to which the message would be carried and tells us that a great multitude would be affected, "a huge crowd which no one could count from every nation and race, people, and tongue" (7:9). The gospel is not only a saving message. It is a relational message as well. Our task must advance with our spirits freed from attitudes of exclusiveness. Both the substance and spirit of the gospel argue for a universal faith and a united people of God.

The gospel is the necessary common ground for faith and the basis for a common acceptance by God of us all. The gospel affirms us as persons and relates us as believers. It takes our need for salvation seriously and it takes seriously our need for togetherness. Given our common anthropological position and our common spiritual needs, a sense of togetherness is expected and aided.

The broad scope of our task demands readiness on our part to touch the world as it is and witness in unity to that world. "As it is" will mean facing the great consciousness of color differences and cultural diversities.

The great sin of the church across the centuries is that the biological and cultural differences in the world have been more determinative in our meeting each other than has the mandate and meaning of the gospel itself. The problem is multi-dimensional and deep-seated because color consciousness and cultural distinctives remain linked with unfortunate stereotypes used as an index for judgments about people, judgments about their worth, their intelligence, their presuppositions, their values, their potential, and their importance. How often it has happened that a color or cultural difference has been a signal to embrace one and to exclude another. The great business of evangelization will be delayed so long as the church is plagued by this besetting and unity-destroying sin.

Color and Culture Have Meaning

Make no mistake about it; color and culture have meaning. We must neither deemphasize color nor idolize it. We are wrong to deny that it has any meaning or assert that it is incidental and insignificant. While it may well be said that color in itself seems insignificant, we cannot dismiss it glibly because God must have posited some meaning in what color brings into the human picture, since every human being has some color.

Color is a tangible factor of personhood; it is related to a human being and is therefore a part of that person's total human factor. Color is not negotiable. It is a fact of nature for which no one ought to have to apologize or feel lacking. Because it is also a community property, that is, a distinctive belonging to a vast aggregate of persons, color is one of the universal factors of meaning in human life.

Cultures, however, are negotiable and arbitrary. They are localized and historically oriented, and not God-derived anthropological givens. Color is an anthropological fact, while culture is a human development. Color does not relate to salvation or sin, but a culture can either block the way of the gospel or aid in its reception.

The church at its best will break through narrow color concerns and foolish conventions of culture, acknowledging the primacy of the mission, the universal human need for our work, and the crucial link Jesus forged with everyone who would believe on him as the one who saves.

Again, the command is to "make disciples of all nations." The implied result is a worldwide, loving fellowship of faith, an obedient, biblically oriented, courageous fellowship that multiplies itself in each generation, working cooperatively and unselfishly in the unity Jesus envisioned and encouraged so that "the world may believe that you sent me" (John 17:21).

Here again are the four basics for understanding and proceeding with our task, a theological underpinning to help our assurance and onwardness: (1) Jesus Christ authorized the evangelical message and commanded the evangelistic mission; (2) the entire world needs to hear that message and know the opportunity it makes possible for life here and hereafter; (3) the given message must not only be shared with all, but shared in the spirit of agape love; and (4) the visible unity of believers is a must to give our going forth its greatest impact in a world that has to see before it will believe.

26

EVERY-MEMBER EVANGELISM

by James Earl Massey

Originally appeared as the Foreword to Kevin W. Earley,
*Every-Member Evangelism: Spiritual Gifts and God's Design for
Service* (Warner Press, 2013), ix. Used by permission.
Rev. Earley pastors the Metropolitan Church of God
in Detroit, Michigan, the urban congregation pastored
for many years by Dr. Massey.

Those who pastor have the sacred task of helping individuals deal with their personal needs, problems, and possibilities in the light of Christian faith and in the setting of congregational life. That task is both spiritual and specialized in nature, and it requires not only a divine call but a distinct conditioning and commitment to serve people.

This book, written by Kevin W. Earley, a pastor with the needed conditioning and commitment, is designed to assist others in locating their place of service in the church and in the world as representatives of Christ. The book's theme is "every-member evangelism" and each chapter sets forth insights to equip and motivate the reader to be engaged in some specific service as a believer.

Mindful that many in our time are uninformed or misinformed about how Christian ministry is understood, valued, and

demonstrated in Scripture, Dr. Earley has deftly traced this in the Old Testament narratives, as well as in the New Testament. His foundational concern has been to prod the reader to become distinctly active, serving in his or her God-gifted role without feeling inferior, envious, or independent.

This book by Dr. Earley is a timely gift to the universal church. It is an excellent and needed teaching tool from a pastor concerned to foster the development of members who know and use their gifts instinctively to God's glory in both the church and the world.

27

SALVATION IN BIBLICAL PERSPECTIVE

by James Earl Massey

Foreword to *An Inquiry into Soteriology: Salvation from a Biblical-Theological Perspective*, eds. John E. Hartley and R. Larry Shelton (Warner Press, 1981), vii-ix. Used by permission.

This volume is the first in a series to be published giving contemporary statements about theological issues from a Wesleyan perspective. This present study is a long-awaited and much-needed one that fills an obvious gap in theological studies.

The general title for the series is *Wesleyan Theological Perspectives*. The concern is practical and the spirit of the undertaking is non-divisive. The stance assumed and affirmed by those who have written for this series is in continuity with the theological heritage traditionally associated with the teachings of John Wesley (1709-1791), who stressed biblical foundations for faith and Christian experience. Wesley particularly stressed the importance for every believer's having a conscious experience of salvation from sin and a maturing fellowship with God.

This book treats the biblical statements about salvation and follows the line of focus seen in Wesley's emphasis, namely that present salvation means deliverance not only from the consequences of sin but also from sin itself. Hence, found here is the Wesleyan emphasis that the believer's life is rightly one of actual moral transformation. This study treats that theme, examining it in progressive fashion throughout the Bible. The intent has not been to set forth a party line, nor is the result provincial. This volume is a contemporary theological restatement about biblical soteriology (from the Greek *sōteria,* meaning "salvation, deliverance").

Salvation is indeed the central issue and concern of true religion. This study reexamines, organizes, and affirms the biblical concept of salvation and the range of experiences about which the concept witnesses. From John E. Hartley's "The Message of Salvation in the Old Testament," an excellent blend of exegetical and theological data, to Fred D. Layman's "Salvation in the Book of Revelation," we have here a well-organized and carefully directed set of essays.

The writers are all trained professionals and experienced scholars who have examined the biblical data afresh. These writers have reexamined the biblical terms and images and metaphors that treat the salvation theme, and they have sifted the reported experiences to which these terms and images were applied descriptively. The flow of the treatment is in keeping with the order of the biblical literature, allowing the reader to sense more fully the portrayal of salvation history and the salvation hope. This study is designed for use in college-level courses, but it can be used with great advantage also as an auxiliary text in graduate theological studies.

This book appears at a timely juncture in history. With so many texts now in use that skew biblical meanings through secularistic slants and humanistic perspectives, this study offers a timely and strategic corrective toward a right understanding of this central biblical doctrine. The concept of salvation is not reconceptualized in these essays; it is rather reexplored and restated in a contemporary theological application, and in some essays by dialogue with controversial and diverse views of our time. No attempt has been made to be innovative but to be biblical in basis, scholarly in method, and practical in emphasis.

The essays that fill this book are from mature scholars who have spent many years in study and teaching. The wealth of detail has understanding and insight as its aim. It must also be said that the most apparently simple statement found here and there in these essays is backed by a mass of technical learning and solid biblical research.

Among other volumes projected and scheduled in this series on *Wesleyan Theological Perspectives* are studies in hermeneutics and pneumatology. This first volume of the series is a landmark study, the first by a team of Wesleyan scholars on this grand theme of soteriology. John E. Hartley and R. Larry Shelton, editors for the series, are hereby commended for their planning, choice of writers, and oversight of the project. Warner Press, a highly respected evangelical publisher, is also commended for showing faith in the rightness and timeliness of what is presented here under their distinctive imprint.

SECTION IV

WISDOM FOR
RECONCILIATION & SOCIAL ACTION

EDITOR'S SECTION INTRODUCTION

by Curtiss Paul DeYoung

I sat at the table some years ago where Dr. James Earl Massey was seated as he waited to be honored by the Samuel DeWitt Proctor Conference for his excellence in preaching.[1] The Proctor Conference is primarily the domain of African-American social justice preachers, biblical scholars, and theologians. Seated at the Massey table were also noted civil rights activist Rev. Willie Barrow and union organizer Rev. Addie Wyatt.

As the night went on, several social justice activist preachers stopped by to greet and congratulate Dr. Massey, including Rev. Jesse Jackson. The visits to the table that night were not a surprise given Massey's early friendships with the foremost leader of the Civil Rights Movement, Martin Luther King, Jr., and the highly regarded mentor of the Civil Rights Movement, Howard Thurman. This was simply a visible acknowledgment of Massey's long and significant involvement in the Civil Rights Movement and his commitment to reconciliation and social action.

No compilation of the works of James Earl Massey would be complete without a section considering his wisdom for reconciliation and social action. This section is a collection of writings, a sermon, and an interview. It begins with a probing and enlightening interview conducted by Dr. Henry Mitchell, the most acclaimed

---

1   Massey was one of five honorees for the "Beautiful are Their Feet" award at the Samuel DeWitt Proctor Conference, February 8, 2012.

scholar of black preaching. Mitchell was also seated at the table that night at the Proctor Conference.[2] Mitchell's interview interrogates Massey's history and cultural background, seeking to discover how he became "multi-cultured (in) the worlds of both scholarship and churchmanship." The interview reveals the amazing multi-culturalism of Massey's home, church, education, and service.

Even Massey's preaching mentors were diverse. As a result, he would serve as both the dean of chapel at the predominately white Anderson University and at the historically black Tuskegee University. This interview enables the reader to understand the roots of Massey's wisdom for reconciliation and social action. Henry Mitchell sums up the life of James Earl Massey with, "Few have walked with such grace through a minefield of so many subtle discriminations."

The insightful biblical scholarship of James Earl Massey is on full display in the next entry, "Biblical Resources for Reconciliation Ministry." As a former professor of reconciliation studies, I am quite familiar with the literature. This is the best overview I have come across that addresses the New Testament reconciliation texts. Any teaching and preaching about the ministry of reconciliation needs to begin by consulting this resource. This entry also includes recommendations for books on the social outworking of reconciliation.

In the following two entries, "Martin Luther King, Jr., and The Dream of Community" and "Christian Theology and Social Experience," Massey discusses the importance of the Civil Rights Movement of the 1950s and 1960s in the United States. He highlights the importance of non-violence as a method of

---

2   In addition to Mitchell, Barrow, and Wyatt, Rev. Robert Smith, Jr., and Rev. Raymond Chin were at Massey's table.

social action that could produce the possibility of reconciliation. Massey illustrates how King's message and action were meant to promote community. King would refer to this as the "Beloved Community." Non-violence was a means of protest that could produce community.

Massey then applies Christian theology to social experience. While he once again focuses on the U.S. Civil Rights Movement, his analysis is meant to apply to freedom movements around the world. His insights regarding the tensions between the older and more traditional civil rights organizations and the younger freedom movements (like the Black Power advocates) are of particular interest. Similar generational tensions exist today between younger activists and their older counterparts in this season of "Black Lives Matter" movements.

James Earl Massey has had much influence among evangelicals and holiness adherents throughout his ministry. This is evident in his writings on the contributions of African Americans in these circles and in his comments on racism in the church. Illustrating this are the next two entries, "The Black Witness to White Evangelicalism" and "Race Relations and the American Holiness Movement." Massey notes that African Americans have contributed to Evangelicalism and the Holiness Movement primarily through the formation of black evangelical congregations and denominations, a unique music and worship tradition, and a witness against racism in the church.

The chapter on the Holiness Movement furthers the discussion and critiques the fact that only a small number of African Americans are found in predominately white holiness denominations. Massey's comments do not include black Pentecostal denominations like the Church of God in Christ that emerged out of the Holiness Movement. He points to the Church of God (Anderson,

IN) as an exception to the norm among the holiness churches. These entries remind us that Evangelicalism was not always seen in society as a mostly white racial reality. The increasing politicization of white evangelicals, most evident in the 2016 U.S. presidential elections, has caused many persons of color to either leave Evangelicalism or stop identifying themselves as such.

Racial reconciliation is not the limit of James Massey's social concerns. In "A Challenge to Privilege" he offers a brief analysis of class issues as found in James 2. He delineates how James addressed "the rich—poor problem" in congregations. "Justice in Tension with Patriotism" follows as a discussion of how addressing injustice in society can create a tension with one's patriotism. He juxtaposes his service in the U.S. military and his involvement in the non-violent direct action of the Civil Rights Movement. Massey notes, "I often have written and preached on reconciliation, but without for a minute ignoring injustice."

This section ends with forewords to books by two reconcilers, Samuel George Hines and Curtiss Paul DeYoung, and a sermon on reconciliation. Hines was a foremost expository preacher and exemplar of church-based reconciliation. I had the opportunity to be mentored by Dr. Hines while serving at the Third Street Church of God in Washington, D.C. where he was the senior pastor for over 25 years. As Massey writes the forewords to these books, the commitment to embracing and living out biblical reconciliation is evident. Hines often referred to reconciliation as "God's one-item agenda."

The sermon "Our Task as Reconcilers"[3] is a dramatic and engaging appeal to Christians to understand their role as reconcilers

---

3   This sermon was preached at a service in Minneapolis, MN, celebrating my completion of ten years of service as the executive director at Twin Urban Cities Reconciliation Network (TURN).

to be central to their faith expression. Massey centers reconciliation in the Cross and Resurrection of Jesus. He proclaims that "reconciliation is Cross-work!"

28

INTERVIEW: VETERAN INHABITANT OF THE DESIRED WORLD[1]

Henry H. Mitchell interviews James Earl Massey

Originally appeared in *Sharing Heaven's Music*, Barry L. Callen, ed. (Abingdon Press, 1995). Used by permission.

Mitchell: James Earl, as you have long known from some of my earlier writings, I have always wondered how on earth you have managed to move so smoothly and effectively in the multi-cultured worlds of both scholarship and churchmanship. May I start with your roots? Knowing that there have been several ministers in your family tree, may I ask how many, and who?

Massey: Six, actually. My grandfather Collins Townsend; my father, George W. Massey, Sr.; my three older brothers, George, Jr., Raymond, Melvin, and myself.

Mitchell: That fascinates me, of course, because both of my grandfathers were pastors.

Massey: Interestingly, I was the first of the sons to announce my call from God to be a preacher.

---

1   This interview was conducted in August 1994, especially for inclusion in *Sharing Heaven's Music*.

Mitchell: Is preaching the specific ministry to which you felt called originally?

Massey: Yes, it was, and so it remains.

Mitchell: What was your age at the time you experienced your call, and what was the setting within which that call happened?

Massey: I was sixteen years old, a student at Cass Technical High School in Detroit, Michigan, at the time of my call. I was in a college preparatory course, majoring in music, with plans to become a classical pianist. I was also taking piano classes at the same time at the Detroit Conservatory of Music.

The call "happened" within me one Sunday morning as I was sitting in church during worship. With my deep love for music, it was my custom to have a musical score with me at all times, so that I could use every spare moment to feed my memory bank and advance my repertoire. That morning I had an album of Chopin preludes and was busy reading through one of them. As the service moved forward, my mind left the score and became engrossed in the depth of the worship. In an almost transfixed state of mind, I heard a Voice insinuating itself in my consciousness, saying, "I want you to preach!" The Voice was strange but settling. The meaning was so forceful, and the bidding was so insistent, that I knew what I would have to do. The Voice was so clear that I have never afterward had reason to question or reinterpret that moment of high insight![2]

---

2   For an earlier published report of Massey's "call story," see "Called While Reading a Score of Chopin," an interview reported in *The Irresistible Urge to Preach: A Collection of African American "Call" Stories*, ed. William H. Myers (Atlanta: Aaron Press, 1992), 230-32. For an interpretation of this call story, see also William Myers, *God's Yes Was Louder Than My No: Rethinking the African-American Call to Ministry* (Grand Rapids: Eerdmans, 1994), esp. 30-31, 49.

I knew that I had been called, but I did wonder how my natural bent toward music making would fit into the new demand God had pressed upon my life. The period of wonderment continued across a year, or longer, but as I yielded myself to be "obedient to the heavenly vision," as Paul once put it, I discovered that music was a creative outlet for my spirit. There are times now when I play Bach chorale preludes in prayer to God. I did know a time, during that first year after being called, when I hungered more for the piano than I was eager for the pulpit. But that hunger was finally disciplined, and my interest in the pulpit became keener than my retreat into music.

Mitchell: I can understand what you are saying about your great love for music. I studied voice and violin, and still sing in choirs whenever I can. But tell me, has your music background influenced your pulpit work? If so, how?

Massey: Indeed it has! I have found so much that has been of transfer value from my years as a music student. For one thing, there is the ability to focus attention on a given text, and to search its structure and the flow of meaning it seeks to give. In addition, the discipline of memorizing has benefited from a background in music. I used to practice at the piano from five to seven hours a day; I had learned how to "stay put" at the instrument until the score was not only in my mind but in my fingers as well. I afterward used that time in Scripture study, in memorizing passages, so that I gained a firm grasp of the contents of the book from which I would be teaching and preaching. My study of the biblical languages, all three of them, came later, of course, but becoming familiar with the whole Bible at that early stage allowed me to focus attention later on interpreting and applying Scripture wisdom.

There is yet another carryover from my musical past: the importance of taking the text seriously, of being servant to the text and not manipulating it. Just as I honored the musical score as a pianist, taking the composer's work as a proper guide, so also I view the biblical text as central for receiving God's message.

Mitchell: You have referred to your study of the Biblical languages. Where did you do your seminary work?

Massey: I received my seminary training and degree from Oberlin Graduate School of Theology, with a concentration in biblical studies, but I went there after graduating with a rich background as a Bible-theology major at Detroit Bible College (later renamed William Tyndale College). With two years of Hebrew as an undergraduate, plus intensive study of New Testament Greek at Wheaton College Graduate School during the summer after I graduated, I was ready for advanced Hebrew and Aramaic and the exegetical course work that filled my schedule when I was admitted at Oberlin.

Mitchell: When and where did your studies begin in communicating that Word in preaching? Who were some of your models?

Massey: I began the serious study of speech and communicating during my last year as a student at Cass Tech, since I then knew that the ministry was to be my future. I did the same while in college, and later, after graduating from Oberlin, while in the pastorate. I did postgraduate courses in communication arts at the University of Michigan.

As for my models, there were four of them. The first was my preacher-father. He impressed me by his ready knowledge and handling of the Scriptures when he was preaching. In fact, it was his masterful memorizing of the Bible that challenged me to begin my quest to know "The Book." The second pulpit model who influenced me was Raymond S. Jackson, the pastor who nurtured me during my teenage years. I learned the power and source of pulpit courage by what he modeled.

The third model was Howard Thurman, whom I met in 1949 while in college. From Thurman I gained insight into the importance of depth for pulpit work, especially spiritual depth as a witness for God. All three persons just named, my father, Raymond S. Jackson, and Howard Thurman, were African Americans. The fourth preacher whose life and work greatly influenced me differed from them in that he was white. That preacher was George Arthur Buttrick. He impressed me by his skills in sermon development and his provocative handling of a text.

Mitchell: You have mentioned an interesting mix of persons and a rather wide array of reasons why you were impressed by them all. All of this moves me to ask just what were the cultural and socioeconomic characteristics of the home and church environment in which you were reared. Did you start out in white culture as a black person, or did you start out in a black culture and become bicultural on the way?

Massey: I was born into and grew up in a bicultural setting. Our family was lower middle class. Both my father and my mother were devout Christians, and so were my grandparents. Our family life was influenced by two churches, both from the same denominational background and doctrinal emphases. The one congregation met just four blocks from our house, while the other was located in downtown Detroit. It was the "Mother Church" to all the other African-American congregations of our group in the metropolitan area.

My grandparents, the Reverend Collins Townsend and Amanda Townsend, were two of the "pillars" in the downtown Detroit church, where he had served across many years as the associate pastor to all four distinguished preachers who had filled the pulpit. The "Mother Church," as most people called it, was now predominantly black in membership, a separate group after racial frictions blighted the unity a previously interracial congregation had enjoyed in another sector of the city.

The congregation that met in our community was still interracial, however, and it was a rather intimate circle of members. I grew up in its life as one who sensed a God-given tie with all the other members, black and white. Belonging to that fellowship helped me to understand the meaning and application of the unity theme that was so often treated from the pulpit, a theme that was explained as one of the cardinal teachings of the Reformation movement of the Church of God of which our church sought to be fully representative. From an early age I was taught, and embraced, the biblical ideal of the unity of believers, on the one hand. On the other, because the majority of our members were black, I knew the impacting quality of black spiritual vitality.

There were three white families in our church in those years, and the interaction and intimacy seemed altogether natural. Early on, I saw that what is African-American can be in essential working agreement with what is Anglo-Saxon, when both traditions are informed by agape love. I learned that what is best in both traditions always provides a creative context for spiritual vision and social learning.

I took such vision and learning with me as I went to school every day. It lasted with me through my grade school years and companioned me on into high school. In both settings, I was in daily touch with whites, always aware of my distinctive differences as a black person. But I was still secure because of a sense of worth instilled within me through informed, caring, and patient parents, teachers, neighbors, pastors, and church members.

The principal at our grade school—located just across the street from our house—was white, but he was sensible about being so, which did not make us sensitive to the fact that he was white. In addition, most of the teachers I had for classes were black, which kept a black leadership presence steadily visible.

I am thinking now of one of my grade school teachers, Mr. Coit Cook Ford. He was an able, industrious, concerned and dapper figure. He had the ease of someone at home in his work, and he gave his students a steadying assurance that we mattered to him. I shall never forget the walls of Mr. Ford's classroom, each with a wall-length blackboard. Just above the border line, he had placed photographs of important black leaders for our recognition and emulation. At strategic times during the semester, Mr. Ford called attention to one or more of those pictured leaders in order to supplement the class lesson. In this way he gave us further insight into American history by treating the life and work of blacks whose stories had not been included in the textbooks we had to use.

Mr. Ford's treatments of black success stories held me in awe, like what I knew in church or in devotionals at home when listening to passages about Bible characters. In this way I came to know about black heroes and heroines, some of whom Mr. Ford had known personally. With each mention he made concerning them, the hero or heroine stood out from the photo frame a little more, life-sized and legendary, grand models for us younger Negroes (as you well know, we were not calling ourselves "Black" or "African American" in those days.)

There is one additional detail I must report about Mr. Ford. He kept us sensible about how achievement happens. Quoting what I later learned were lines from Longfellow's "The Ladder of Saint Augustine," Mr. Ford cautioned us with this wisdom:

> The heights by great men reached and kept
> Were not attained by sudden flight;
> But they, while their companions slept,
> Were toiling upward in the night.

These lines still inspire me. They stir my spirit and prod the diligence to which they point. Small wonder, then, that the spirit to strive and strength to endure is so strong within me. The need to toil "goes with the territory" of being a preacher and living, like Paul, in readiness to preach. This was the conditioning that I underwent through the providence of God, buttressed by such grand human models, some white, some black.

Mitchell: I am impressed with what you recount about your own church group. Your story differs greatly from so many others who point to denominational failure as a cause for their disillusionment where religion and race are concerned. Tell me more about the Church of God.

Massey: Gladly! As you know, the Church of God (Anderson, Indiana)—we always add that parenthesis to distinguish our group from the many who use this biblical designation—is a religious communion predominantly white in membership. Its origins lie in the late nineteenth century, and it is one of the holiness groups that have continued the tradition of honoring experiential religion, doctrinal purity, evangelistic outreach, and the quest to unify fellow believers. It's also one of the holiness groups from which blacks have not broken away. A part of the reason for this is that black members of the Church of God (Anderson, Indiana) continue to find the unity emphasis in the church's message so appealing and life within the group sufficiently open and promising.

In 1974 there were nearly 20,000 blacks among a total North American church membership of just above 160,000. By 1980 that number had increased to almost 30,000 black members among a total membership in North America of 179,000 plus. I mention these round figures because they show a steady relationship between blacks and the larger body of Church of God members in the United States. But the figures also show an instructive growth pattern.

Unlike some other church groups whose doctrinal positions accent non-relational themes, the central theme of our communion is an openly relational one: the unity of believers. Although the social relations within our church group witnessed the same problems and strains faced by other church bodies, the challenge of our unity ideal, coupled with the demand for experiential religion, has always been present as a factor to prod us toward correction and reform.

Mitchell: So the two worlds of race have been a part of your church story as well. But I am aware of some significant strides your group's story evidences, like your appointment some years ago. And there is also your present role as dean of your denomination's graduate School of Theology (Anderson University). How long was your tenure as radio preacher? What was the response of the church to your ministry in that post?

Massey: I am going to answer these questions, but let me first say that my appointments, while significant, were not as signal, racially, within our group as was the election in 1988 of Edward L. Foggs, another black leader among us, to serve as our communion's general secretary, the highest elective office within our church body. He has since been reelected after serving his first five-year term.

I must also point out that another significant appointment preceded the radio ministry to which I was elected by the General Assembly of our church body. During the last seven years of my pastorate at Metropolitan Church of God in Detroit, Michigan, I also served concurrently as campus minister at Anderson University in Anderson, Indiana. I was the university's first campus minister. I was on campus Monday through Friday, and returned to my Detroit pulpit each weekend. A steady, trustworthy staff of local ministers handled the day-to-day needs of the church across the week. I had been pastor of that church for eighteen years before I took on the responsibilities of the campus ministry assignment. So I was blessed by a strong pastoral relationship with the people— nearly a thousand members—when I was invited by Robert H. Reardon, the university president, to join the faculty and administrative staff at Anderson.[3]

---

3   For numerous references to the ministry of Dr. Massey at Anderson University, see the published history of the university, *Guide of Soul and Mind*, by Barry L. Callen (Anderson, Ind.: Anderson University and Warner Press, 1992).

I was still serving both the campus and the congregation when the invitation was issued in 1976 for me to become the denomination's radio voice. In accepting that appointment, I resigned from both Metropolitan Church and my campus ministry post. At my leaving, after twenty-four progressive years, there was a unanimous vote by the church in response to a resolution from the church council that I be made Pastor-at-Large. This encouraged me greatly. The university also asked me to continue teaching as my new schedule would allow.

The appointment as preacher on our international radio broadcast meant that I was the radio spokesperson for our communion. The fact that a black man would thus represent a majority-white religious fellowship was not a problem to the Mass Communications Board, which presented my name for ratification to the General Assembly. However, there were a few whites to whom that board's plan for the future was sufficiently strange and unsettling that they reacted with obvious reticence or cold regard initially. The climate surrounding the vote taken on me during the assembly meeting in 1876 was carefully democratic, and some whites who were from regions where blacks were not accorded equal opportunities in relation to whites had to yield their questions, fears, and preferences when the majority of delegates approved me.

My service as speaker for the church and as a guest within churches across the land proved effective, and I continued in that post across six years. It was a fruitful and productive period for the broadcast ministry. Early in my fourth year, I decided that I would not accept another term because I wanted to go back into the classroom, and I was longing for more time to do the research and writing to which I had been accustomed. Later, after I announced that I would not be available to serve another term as our communion's radio speaker, President Reardon asked me to return full-time to the university's School of Theology as professor of New Testament and Preaching. I gladly did.

Mitchell: When and why did you leave to go to Tuskegee? Did your acceptance of a post at the predominantly black university have anything to do with race concerns?

Massey: I left Anderson and went to Tuskegee University in July, 1984. My leaving was not in response to any problems at Anderson of a racial nature. My move to Tuskegee was the result of a call from the president there inviting me to become Dean of the Chapel and University Professor of Religion and Society. I had been a guest preacher there in 1983. At that time President Payton and I had talked at length about his vision and concerns for the famed University Chapel and its historic ministry. The incumbent chaplain was about to retire, and President Payton was eager to enhance the religious tradition at the school by instituting a newly structured arrangement for campus ministry that would match the growing needs of an ever-expanding school.

I was not surprised, then, when in February 1984 he telephoned to inform me that the search committee had voted unanimously that I be asked to become dean at the retirement of the incumbent chaplain. Dr. Payton then stated his own desire that I take it. You know what I did, and that period of service was one of the most pleasurable and meaningful in my entire span of ministry.

When the news broke that I was leaving Anderson to go to Tuskegee, many ministers across the Church of God voiced their surprise. Some black pastors thought I was leaving because of some disappointment or mistreatment on the Anderson campus. I informed them that such was not the case. In all my dealings with President Robert A. Nicholson, and with former President Robert H. Reardon, I could not have had a better relationship nor had

I suffered at all in my relationship with other faculty members. Interestingly, when Reardon learned about my call to Tuskegee, he came to me and, with a gleam of pride in his eyes, commented, "Now that is a premier institution!"

Neither Reardon nor Nicholson (then college dean) asked why I was leaving. Both knew that I had always followed my inner guidance. That guidance had brought me to Anderson University in 1969. When I began service as the school's first campus minister in 1984, that guidance was taking me in another direction. I was grateful for their trust in my walk with the Lord.

I readily admit that in going to serve at Tuskegee University I knew I was being privileged to minister at a strategic educational center among historically black colleges and universities. In going there, I moved with purpose into a major center of black education and into the African-American heritage in a deeper way. More importantly, Gwendolyn, my wife, and I felt assured that God was being honored in our going there to serve.

The years that followed strongly confirmed the wisdom and timeliness of our choice. From the start I gave myself with intensity to the new role, and once fully into the new pattern I felt quite fulfilled, especially in my work as a preacher to the university. I felt that I had made my final vocational move.

Interestingly, my work at Tuskegee brought me into closer relations with white members in churches of the South! Never had I enjoyed such widened windows of opportunity among white Southerners. I was especially gladdened when many of my former students at Anderson School of Theology, now settled into their work as pastors in that region, sought me out for counsel. They opened themselves to my interest and assistance, and they opened the pulpits of their churches to me. Busy each Sunday morning in the chapel pulpit, I could not accept all of the many invitations to preach, but I was grateful that ties established earlier in Anderson were still being honored, and for deeper reasons.

When I went to Tuskegee in 1984, at least ten percent of the student body was international, representing over forty different countries. I liked the international flavor that was present in nearly every worship service. In the act of delivering a sermon, I was "going into all the world, preaching the gospel" every Sunday morning. I felt a stronger sense of mission as a preacher who, by my message, was touching so much of the known world. Situated at the center of campus life as the university minister, it was my joyful responsibility and privilege to think through and share the message and implications of the Christian faith not only for "the Chapel family" but with the larger community of churches and community leaders as well.

The area pastors and ministers looked to me as their resident theologian; some of them came to the early morning chapel service to hear me preach before rushing out to fill their own pulpits at the traditional eleven o'clock hour. I did not take my post and privilege lightly. Never have I so enjoyed preparing to preach, and then standing up to preach! It was stimulating and encouraging to watch the students, staff personnel, and faculty members experience rational, moral, and spiritual change through sound religious teaching and vital fellowship. I had the added pleasure of providing counsel for several students who experienced a call to ministry through my preaching and presence. I helped some of them in their choice of a seminary and later saw some of them graduate and enter upon their own fields of service.

Mitchel: With all of that taking place under your leadership at the Tuskegee Chapel, why on earth did you break that pace and return to Anderson?

Massey: Many persons at Tuskegee asked me that very question when the news broke that I would be leaving, and even since I have been gone some have asked that when I have returned to be guest preacher at the chapel there.

To put it plainly and quickly, my answer again involves "sensed guidance." I returned to Anderson because, after praying steadily and seriously about the request from the president and search committee for my services at the seminary, I finally sensed a "tug" upon my heart to accept that duty. I had been so sure that I was already where I needed to be—and wanted to be—until time to retire. But, as someone once put it, if you talk to God, be willing to change your mind and your plans.

The decision to return to Anderson School of Theology as its dean was perhaps the hardest decision I have ever made during my ministry, but the assurance has been mine that the move was in obedience to a higher will. Even so, in leaving the Tuskegee University Chapel scene, Gwendolyn and I both "died a little." Our sense of loss was somewhat relieved when, in June, 1989, during the General Assembly vote on the seminary deanship, I was duly and strongly ratified by a ninety—five percent majority of the delegates.

Mitchell: Having myself served as dean at Virginia Union University's School of Theology, I am tempted to ask what your full and informed opinion is of the vocation of a dean. But I am going to leave that out.

Massey: You don't have to do that. Actually, I view administrative responsibilities as a necessary work, and I feel privileged to assist faculty in their work of readying students for ministry. As you well know, Paul included "forms of leadership" (1 Cor. 12:28) or administration in his listing of the spiritual gifts.

Mitchell: Yes, I know, but so often being an administrator plac-es one in a vulnerable position, with little opportunity for being thanked or duly appreciated for what one does.

James Earl, your pulpit prowess and exemplary teaching have made you an acknowledged, well-received leader in the field, and leading seminaries have had you do major lectureships on preach-ing. I marvel that Yale has never sought you to do the Lyman Beecher Lectures on Preaching at the Divinity School. Or have you been asked?

Massey: No, I have not been invited to serve that lectureship at Yale, but I am pleased that two of our mutual friends who followed you in giving those lectures did quote from my written work about preaching while treating their themes. Kelly Miller Smith quot-ed from my *Designing the Sermon* during his Beecher Lectures in 1983.[4] In 1986, James. A. Forbes, Jr., commented at length in one of his Beecher Lectures about my concept of "anointing," on which I wrote in the last chapter of my book *The Sermon in Perspective*.[5]

Mitchell: Let me ask another question with respect to homiletics. As a competent practitioner of the African-American approach to preaching, how do you draw from that tradition while teaching homiletics to the white students who fill your classes? What do you hold forth as the major emphases within that tradition?

Massey: I'm glad that you asked this question because it allows me to point out how I apply my principle of a bicultural approach as I teach seminarians about our preaching task. In addition to course work on the general history of preaching, together with acknowledgement of

---

4   See Kelly Miller Smith, *Social Crisis Preaching: The Lyman Beecher Lectures, 1983* (Macon: Mercer University Press, 1984), esp. 82ff.

5   See James A. Forbes, Jr., *The Holy Spirit and Preaching: The Lyman Beecher Lectures, 1986* (Nashville: Abingdon Press, 1989), 53-55.

styles of delivery, I always expand the range of lectures and assigned readings to include the abundant data from the strongest preaching traditions, including the black pulpit. The inclusion of such additional data has been made standard within the discipline wherever I have taught. This has also demanded the gathering of substantial resources for use in daily classroom instruction, as well as supportive library holdings of rich materials on noted African-American preachers (i.e., autobiographical and biographical works, taped and printed sermons, and other instructive memorabilia).

As for the emphases drawn from within the black preaching tradition, I tend to stress five as essential for effectiveness in any setting, bicultural or others. (1) The first emphasis is on the functionality of the sermon—an emphasis on the end or purpose of the sermon. (2) The second is the encouragement of festivity, celebration in the worship of God. Festivity allows the sermon to be spirited instead of stilted. It offers a positive clue about being one's full self—with emotions included—as a spokesperson for God. (3) A third emphasis within our black preaching tradition is the promotion of community through the sermon. I explain to all my students that preaching must unify the gathered congregation; it must affirm and undergird each worshiper, generating vision, yes, but also sharing. (4) A fourth element is the necessity for radical proclamation—the imperative for a free and authoritative stance in the sermon as God's messenger. (5) And fifth, I stress the importance of the sermon's producing a climax of impression. It is the climax of impression that helps the hearer feel the touch of the Beyond.

Drawing thus upon the black preaching tradition, I seek to flavor my teaching of homiletics. In teaching, I am committed to a bicultural approach, always seeking a two-way acculturation as most germane for classrooms filled with persons whose horizons need to be expanded. The homiletics professor must be concerned to inculcate the principles of preaching as one aim, and to unlock the personal gifts of the preachers as the other. Unlocking the potential of any preacher demands that attention be given to that student's process, expectations, and abilities, not in strict relation to the ideals of the majority culture and its settings, but without failing to take these into account.

Our beloved Gardner C. Taylor is a grand example of a biculturally conditioned preacher. So were the late Howard Thurman and Kelly Miller Smith, Sr. Because of their bicultural approach in preaching, each one of these pulpit masters was equally at home in any pulpit. All three excelled because within their pulpit work they wedded the best from more than one preaching tradition. This is what I seek to help my homiletics students achieve.

Mitchell: I applaud that, as my own teaching approach attests, and I can see how your bicultural background has played such a role in shaping your approach and point of view. I must confess, however, that when I read your first books about preaching, I wondered whether you started out in a white cultural setting, or if you started in a black setting and became bicultural.

Massey: I recall that sense of wonderment showing itself in a review you kindly prepared of two of my preaching books for our guild's homiletic journal. I believe it was the first volume.[6] While you commended each of the two books being reviewed, *The Responsible Pulpit* (1974) and *The Sermon in Perspective* (1976), you did clearly state your hope that in any future treatments of the subject I would deal more in depth with the black preaching tradition "with which he is unashamedly familiar."

---

6   See *Homiletic: A Review of Publications in Religious Communication*, I (1976), listings 9 and 10.

Mitchell: Now, at last, I understand your motivation. So, it was a conscious decision on your part not to major in black homiletics?

Massey: Yes, it was. I also remember a published comment that appeared about me in a survey of recent studies on black preaching, which you prepared for a later issue of *Homiletic*. After making mention of one of my books, you paid me a kind of "back-handed" compliment when you suggested that my book showed "how literate and creative a Black preacher can be within the bounds of the White tradition, since he has very little to say about the black church tradition."[7]

Working as I have done "within the white tradition," as you put it, I consciously chose an approach by which our black preaching particularity could be taught, modeled, assessed, and hopefully adopted. To this end, it was wiser for me to treat our pulpit particularities within the wider context of preaching approaches. With me, it has never been a matter of living at the extreme of no recognition of my black heritage or the opposite extreme of emphasizing only the black heritage. My concern has been, rather, to honor and live out of my heritage while engaged, as a teacher, within others who bring into the circle of life and learning the best from their own heritage. As I look back on my efforts and their results across these years, I remain convinced that my bicultural approach has helped me to be reasonable, realistic, relational and effective.

Mitchell: Listening to you, after watching your life and career, I am convinced that your home background and religious ideals have added something fundamental to your being.

Massey: Indeed, they have. The insights and emphases of the Church of God (Anderson, Indiana), my "denominational home"

---

7   See *Homiletic* IV (1979), 9.

to use your expression, have been of inestimable value to me in my heart concern to be genuinely related in the problematic social settings that make up America. I have dared to trust the creative power and possibilities of agape love, and I have found that it is possible to commit to heart and mind a way of relating that promotes unity and trust rather than hate and divisiveness. This is one of several reasons why I have continued in ministry as a member of the Church of God movement.

Mitchell: Well, James Earl, I certainly want to thank you for this candid, fascinating sharing of yourself. And I am sure that I am already speaking for those who will read these words. In very truth, you have demonstrated that an African American with rare gifts and under rare circumstances and in the providence of God can live a relatively color-blind existence. Few if any of our ethnic brothers and sisters have transcended as many boundaries as you have, and with such grace. To use another metaphor, few have walked with such grace through a minefield of so many discriminations.

What you have illustrated, across the board, places in the concrete worlds of church, denomination, and the theological academy an ideal otherwise only abstract for all too many. You have mastered Euro-American culture and made so rich a contribution that your white colleagues were made at ease and forgot to consider your race. Thus, you have lived all your days in an almost raceless world that most of us have talked about and hoped for, but never have seen. An awareness of your rare experience is essential to any comprehensive understanding of race and culture in the Christian churches of the United States.

African Americans especially must know that what you have accomplished is not to be thought of as able to be replicated by human effort. Nor should anyone even try to take the same path without comparable providential preparations. The odds against such are too great; the kingdom hasn't come yet, not even in the Church of God (Anderson, Indiana). They still have an all African-American conference ground in Pennsylvania, about which I have heard, and lots of black members have had less than comparable experiences to yours at the membership base, as opposed to the top leadership. Nevertheless, it has been a marvelous experience to walk with you through these years, and all of us will be enriched and inspired by your gift of yourself. May God bless and continue to use you in your retirement years.

29

BIBLICAL RESOURCES FOR RECONCILIATION MINISTRY

by James Earl Massey

Originally appeared in Timothy George and Robert Smith, Jr., *A Mighty Long Journey: Reflections on Racial Reconciliation* (Broadman & Holman Publishers, 2001), 199-222. Abbreviated. Used by permission.

Everywhere one looks, whether at life within America or at life across our world, conflicts between persons and groups are playing themselves out, and all too few are the voices of wisdom being addressed to those involved in the fray.

I invite you to join me in re-exploring the major biblical passages regarding reconciliation, giving due attention to the terms the writers used, the contexts within which those terms were used, and the meanings to which we are heirs. I then want to trace some lines of guidance that I am confident are crucial for our lives as we return to our labors as people of God.

Reconciliation: The New Testament Teachings

The first passage for consideration is found among the ethical instructions from our Lord. It's located in Matthew's account of the

Sermon on the Mount (5:21-26). The new life under the lordship of Christ is to surpass life under the old laws of Moses, thus, "You have heard that it was said . . . but I say to you." Jesus offers instruction on how to handle anger before it blocks a relationship with God and reaches a stage of belligerency. Note that the speaking of rash, insulting words to others, all selfish speaking out of intense feelings that are full of human wrath, even if those feelings have been provoked by someone's prior selfish action, is viewed by Jesus as a selfish response to the offending person and a sinful deed in God's sight.

Hostility is an activity of the heart, and those who wish to be accepted in peace by God must be serious about remaining at peace with humans. True worship is blocked whenever and as long as hostility rages within the heart against another human. As verses 23-24 state, reconciliation between the aggrieved parties must take place before God will accept our worship.

The second passage I call to your attention is found in Acts 7. The entire chapter reports Stephen's defensive speech to the Sanhedrin as it sat in council against him and he witnessed about Jesus. He engaged in historical retrospect, seeking to show that the history of their people pointed to the very happenings to which he was witness. He recalled the life and times of Moses and how he had been readied for his role by growing up as a prince in Egypt, the place of their first and longest confinement. Then comes 7:26. "The next day he came to some of them as they were quarreling and tried to reconcile *[sunēllassen]* them." The word used for *reconcile* is *suttallassō*. The imperfect form, *sunēllassen*, of that verb is used to indicate that Moses "tried to reconcile" the two recalcitrant brawling Hebrews.

A third passage that mentions reconciliation employs a third term, *katallassō*. In the instruction Paul gives in

1 Corinthians 7:10-11, it is quite clear that he has appropriated a known teaching of the Lord and passes it on in the interest of restoring a fragmenting marriage relationship. *Katallassō* is the most used word in the New Testament for reconciliation. The basic meaning of the Greek term is "to change, or exchange; to effect a change." The image in the word shows something having been set aside or put down *[kata]:* an attitude, a grievance, a position, a deed, a distance, a result, in order to induce or bring about a change for the better. A new disposition is exhibited, a new stance is assumed, a new framework is established granting a rich togetherness where enmity and distance previously were the order. As used by Paul, the noun "reconciliation" *[katallagē]* reports something proffered to us by God (Rom. 5:8-11) and something experienced by us on the basis of the sacrificial death Jesus Christ underwent on our behalf (2 Cor. 5:17ff).

There is a fourth term used in the New Testament for reconciliation, the word *apokatallassō* found in Ephesians 2:16 and Colossians 1:20, 22. It is a part of the same theological message that the apostle Paul states regarding the meaning and effects of the death and resurrection of Jesus for those who believe on him. Let us examine 2 Corinthians 5:16-21, that classic passage regarding reconciliation. Paul is making a personal statement and an advisory claim.

Having entered upon a new life-course through his converting contact with the risen Christ, and having undergone a full change of worldview thereby, Paul here states his reasons for the ministry at which he had long been engaged: (a) He is part of a "new creation" inaugurated by being "in Christ" (inhabiting a new sphere of reality); and (b) he has received a commission to announce to all the reconciling action of God in Christ by which that newness became possible.

Paul wrote as he did because he was concerned about two things: to keep trusting believers rightly informed about his ministry; and to become reconciled with those who were his detractors. He wanted his critics to be compatriots in Christ and in right relation with him again. As he sought to inform, influence, and win them, he became poetic, and his lyrical bent comes through in the hymnic statement we find in this great passage. Viewing the whole of life and humanity now through eyes touched by the risen Christ, Paul wanted his readers to be fully oriented to a new way of viewing him and all others as well.

Paul explains that God is the reconciler; God took the initiative, while the world, i.e., humankind, is the object of God's reconciling action. Christ is God's agent of reconciliation, and through Christ alone was that reconciliation made possible. What God initiated through grace and has proffered in love, we can experience through acceptance in faith and continuing obedience.

In Ephesians 2:16 we see Paul's discussion of reconciliation as it relates to the removal of the previous division that existed between Jews and Gentiles, a division based upon not just one but several separating factors: religious difference, legal differences, cultural differences, racial and social differences. In a bold and declarative announcement, Paul states that God's reconciling deed in Christ has changed that distancing division altogether and has made the two groups one in his sight.

Then follows that grand announcement about the believing Gentiles' privileged participation, on equal footing, with believing Jew in God's "household," the church. Here we see a wider communal interest to God's reconciling deed in Christ, a wider social application of the effects of reconciliation. The God-ordained relationship between Christian believers, of whatever previous backgrounds, is not just one of harmony but a oneness where neither group is dominant nor subservient anymore. The fence that once stood between them is now down. Because believers are reconciled to God, they are also related to one another. A new set of criteria now applies for human relations in the church. A sense of oneness and equality must prevail.

The last reference test is Colossians 1:20, 22, where that fourth term for reconciliation, *apokatallassō,* is used again. The universal and cosmic significance of God's work through Christ is in view where the passage speaks about "all things" being reconciled, "whether on earth or in heaven." Reconciliation, then, will finally involve the universe as a whole and not just believing humans; the time will come when the universe will no longer be subjected to decay or dissolution but will reflect the harmony that God originally intended for all that was created.

The actual work of reconciling requires of us a distinctive frame of reference. According to the several texts we have examined, in Christ God has acted kindly toward us, proffering forgiveness for sins, restored harmony after a life of disobedience, and peaceful relations after our selfish waywardness that displeased God. Christ acted on our behalf as God's reconciling agent. Paul explains that having received reconciliation he had been given a ministry as a reconciler. This means that he had to learn to see other people as God sees them; he had to be open to relate to people with a view to their God-given worth, their human potential, and their deepest human need. This framework and focus is the basis for evangelism in depth and human community in full.

Reconciliation: Aspects of Our Task

Our reexamination of the biblical statements and terms about reconciliation has yielded at least three results: (1) It has reminded us and clarified anew what reconciliation means in the vocabulary of faith; (2) it has refreshed our understanding about God's reconciling work through Christ Jesus, thus deepening our gratitude for received grace, which in turn can stir us to worship God more attentively; and (3) it has brought into sharper focus our task as reconciling agents, a task that in the press of our times calls for greater attention and more strategic action on our part.

The first and second of these results from our study are in the vertical category of our Christian experience since God and the self are related by a personal faith. The third result involves the horizontal dimension of our Christian experience since it requires interacting with other humans. The longer we consider this, the greater the awareness becomes that personal faith in Christ—the vertical dimension—and the obedient outworking of that faith in dealing with others—the horizontal dimension—*always form a cross.* This must be remembered as we go about our work in the world because reconciliation is always a costly matter. It was by cost to Jesus Christ that we were reconciled to God, and we cannot be reconciling agents in his name without undergoing some demands that will press upon us.

For insights on the social outworking of the reconciliation concern, note especially Howard Thurman's 1963 *Disciplines of the Spirit* and Curtiss Paul DeYoung's 1997 *Reconciliation: Our Greatest Challenge-Our Only Hope.* Thurman offers his wise counsel about how to become and develop as a reconciling person. His discussion about the discipline that *agape*-love provides in the life of someone who *wills* and *works* for reconciliation in the best I have ever read.

Curtiss Paul DeYoung is white, a former student of mine, and presently serves as a catalyst for reconciliation and social justice in Minneapolis and St. Paul, Minnesota. He is one of those voices of goodwill speaking out to offer guidance and give help to persons and cities experiencing social conflict. This book is his attempt to share a wisdom that is biblical and tested in his own life struggles. He offers counsel on the process one must understand and follow in developing a reconciliation mind-set, entering into meaningful relationships, and taking responsibility for the polarization that exists in order to take action to shape the necessary and God-willed harmony.

There is a discipline demanded of those who would work as agents of reconciliation. It is a discipline that demands realism in the face of divisive walls, hostility, and hate; a discipline that refuses to cower before the barriers that block harmony; a discipline that properly and steadily informs, encourages, and energizes one to engage in the divine process of reconciliation, that readies one to take responsibility and, understanding the necessity for forgiveness, seeks to effect it by touching the soul, repairing the wrong that injured, and establishing the needed relationship. This discipline demands an active love, a healthy self-image, the willingness to risk oneself, and a sense of being companioned in the task by God.

Our Lord's mandate that we evangelize (Matt. 28:18-20) is at one with our assignment to be reconcilers (2 Cor. 5:19-20). Both service roles have been entrusted to us, and both are strategically related in two ways: first, the same message that brings salvation is the basis for reconciliation not only with God but with other persons; and second, the same *agape-love* that motivates us to evangelize also motivates us to be reconciling agents. These two ministries might well be described as two sides of one coin since they are so closely conjoined for believers.

Let us be reminded of Paul's declaration about how he handled his prior conditioning as a Hebrew as he dealt with the wider world of differing groups in the Roman Empire; it is a declaration about the principle that disciplined his preferences and kept him open as a relational and reconciling person: That declaration is found in 1 Corinthians 9:19-23. Paul explains that he kept his preferences ordered and informed by the higher principle of the relational imperative of *agape-love*. This kind of caring-sharing love does not concern itself with social expediency but with spiritual necessity and the best human future.

30

MARTIN LUTHER KING, JR., AND THE DREAM OF COMMUNITY

by James Earl Massey

Originally appeared in *The Princeton Seminary Bulletin* (IX:3),
211-215. Used by permission.

Most Americans are familiar with the story of Dr. Martin Luther King, Jr., and even those who vehemently opposed him cannot erase from their memory the depth of the impression his presence and proclamations made on audiences everywhere.

King's speech during the celebrated March on Washington in 1963 is still being quoted.[1] He ascended that platform at the base of the Lincoln Memorial like a man accustomed to vast throngs, and he was. He spoke to the gathered multitude of 200,000 like a man who had something important to say, and he did. His words flashed a stirring dream across the screen of every mind, a dream that he was concerned enough to tell and courageous enough to live.

He stood there giving so much, but he would be sharing much more in time. He stood there deeply rooted in the black church

---

1   The imagery of this famous King speech was the inspiration for the title of this present volume.

tradition of picturesque rhetoric, but he used it creatively to help persons of diverse traditions share a universal insight. The need was clear. The time had come. He spoke his word, shared his dream, and made history. Howard Thurman rightly commented afterward: "Never again would the boundaries be as established as they were before his coming."[2]

2   Howard Thurman, *The Search of Common Ground: An Inquiry into the Basis of Man's Experience of Community* (New York: Harper and Row, 1971), 95.

The Theme of Community

If one would search for the leading theme among King's many speeches, lectures, addresses, and sermons; if one would probe for that one central motif among his many essays, articles, and books; if one sought to isolate the very heart-throb in his deeds, one would find it in his concern for *community*. Again and again King tried to help us understand the nature of community, the need for community, and the concern of God that we work at being open to experience community.

He was forever reminding us about the importance of persons, and talking about the effects of relationships and social process in shaping the development and destiny of persons. From the time of his first pastorate in Montgomery, Alabama, to his untimely death in Memphis, Tennessee, fourteen years later, Martin Luther King, Jr., worked rigorously to sensitize our concern for each other and acknowledge our ties with each other—ties admittedly circumstantial but definitely providential.

Like other reformers, King prodded us to invest our life histories in the historical moment that was upon us, and to do so not only in our own interest but in the interest of all who will follow us here. He warned the nation again and again that we should not define ourselves by our past but by our ideals, and that we should not test ourselves by grand opportunities but by our responses to them. He put the "identity crisis" of American whites and Afro-American blacks in social, ethical, and spiritual perspective. As a minister, he offered pastoral care to individuals in search of a soul, and he sounded a prophetic challenge to an erring racist nation that was damning its soul.

Martin Luther King, Jr., was constantly saying that this nation can find itself only as its people live communally. He was right.

The fulfillment of all who live here *is* tied up with the dynamics and deeds of all who interact here. This is why he often quoted John Donne's words, "No man is an island, entire of itself," and it is why he often repeated his own words:

> In a real sense, all life is interrelated. All men are caught in an inescapable network of mutuality, tied in a single garment of destiny. Whatever affects one directly affects all indirectly. I can never be what I ought to be until you are what you ought to be, and you can never be what you ought to be until I am what I ought to be. This is the interrelated structure of reality.[3]

No man or woman is an island—nor should any man or woman be uncaringly set apart to die in an unfriendly ocean of isolation, suspicion, and neglect. King called on all to be caring persons, and he confronted the nation with its need to show care and concern for all who comprise its people. Again and again he sounded the trumpet of conscience and pierced the air with a stern word about our responsibilities under God, and a caring word about our possibilities because of God.

Times of Collective Catharsis

Let us never forget the high purpose behind King's much-criticized methods of ethical confrontation and direct-action nonviolence. His ministry was filled with "showdown situations," but his motive

---

3   From his sermon "The Man Who Was a Fool," in Martin Luther King, Jr., *The Strength to Love* (New York: Harper and Row, 1963). The quote was influenced by Howard Thurman's thought from "Finding God," a chapter in *Religion on the Campus*, ed. Francis P. Miller (New York: Association Press), 49ff.

was not divisive. Although it is true that his public marches often stirred opposition out of which violence sometimes resulted, his way of confronting the submerged evils was to make them publicly known *for the sake of needed change*. He forced these face-to-face meetings because that method made available a time for personal and collective catharsis, a time for reflection, forgiveness, and social renewal.

Martin Luther King, Jr., sought to challenge this nation's identity confusion and moral compromise; he knew that the widespread strife and social trauma among its citizens were generated by negative identity, a compromise with evil, and a racist rationale—thus his confrontational moral witness. He witnessed with concern to give help and promote healing.

This nation still needs help and healing. The diagnosis King made in assessing the national sickness is still valid for present conditions in the United States: "Overwhelmingly America is still struggling with irresolution and contradictions. It has been sincere and even ardent in welcoming some changes. But too quickly apathy and disinterest rise to the surface when the next logical steps are to be taken."[4]

Challenging that apathy and lack of interest, King spoke and acted from a base of ethical claims and with a positive attitude concerning human need and our social potential. He spoke and acted with care. He spoke and acted with an interest in community. He spoke and acted in obedience to that awesome "vertical pressure" of his call from God to help this nation where it was hurting.

King knew what it is to experience hurt and need healing. How well he knew that it is the black man in this land, with the

---

4   Martin Luther King, Jr., *Where Do We Go from Here: Chaos or Community?* (Harper and Row, 1967), 5.

much-heralded theme of "liberty and justice for all," who has been severely compromised. He knew that the values and principles formulated in the Bill of Rights promise a worthy social experience, but he was deeply hurt when he saw that the status of black people was frozen, and that our lot was to be victims of the system rather than full participants in it—thus his reacting stance to change those conditions of disadvantage.

Because he was concerned about a Christian handling of the crisis, King committed himself to be relational as well as reactional. To quote his own words, he would be satisfied with nothing less than a "morally and practically sound method open to oppressed people in their struggle for freedom."[5] The hurt was deep. The quest for a reasoned Christian approach to the problem was long and costly, and following it proved costly indeed.

So costly was his path that again and again King fell to his knees seeking reinforcement from his God. He needed to handle threats that harassed his family, and he had to deal with fears that hounded his own soul. To mention but one incident, there was that awesome night in Montgomery in January, 1956, when he felt too burdened by fears to continue as social leader. He felt a sickening pressure from the work of desperate and violent opposers. Since he could not fall asleep, King rose from bed and began to pace the floor. He finally went to the kitchen, heated a pot of coffee, and poured a cup for himself, but he was too preoccupied in thought and feelings to drink the coffee, trying hard "to think of a way to move out of the picture without appearing a coward."[6] He later wrote:

ᵣr King, Jr., *Stride toward Freedom: The Montgomery Story* (New ᵣs, 1958), 97.

In this state of exhaustion, when my courage had all but gone, I decided to take my problem to God. With my head in my hands, I bowed over the kitchen table and prayed aloud . . . . At that moment I experienced the presence of the Divine as I had never experienced Him before . . . . Almost at once my fears began to go. My uncertainty disappeared. I was ready to face anything.[7]

Caring and Daring

We must not let this nation misunderstand, overlook, or forget what Martin Luther King, Jr., was seeking to do. And we must ourselves remember the concern behind his deeds and daring. Just what was that concern? To help our nation (and all of us who are part of it) face the need to be *persons in relation*. His concern was to help us become open enough to meet each other, seek to understand each other, and grow to love and help each other.

Behind King's deeds and daring were a communal attitude and caring spirit. King *dared* to do because he *cared* to do. Like a true physician, he worked to overcome those things that distress, disease, and destroy. Like a true reformer, he strove to arrest damage done by faulty thought and errant behavior. Like a true counselor, he offered insight, intent to help the nation with problem solving. Like a concerned parent, he extended his hand to effect reconciliation through renewed trust and the will to be one. He had a caring spirit. He did what he did and said what he said because he had a dream about community, an interest in persons in relation.

Martin Luther King, Jr., was not ordinary—but saying this is only to state what is obvious. He had the highest training, a broad

---

7   Ibid., 134-135.

understanding, a keen perception, some deep convictions, a cooperative attitude, and a caring heart. Trained as a systematic theologian, King set himself to give that theology a human shape and
guarantee that it would serve a noble human end. He determined
that with God's help he would relate to life as it is in order to know
life as it is and shape it as it ought to be.

King believed and taught that the life and teachings of Jesus
are not just radical but relevant and redemptive. He was convinced
that life at its source and center is personal, and that every person
has inherent worth, so he dedicated himself to serve the needs of
persons, and to do that service in the spirit of trust and love—thus
his prolonged and persistent push for needed social change, and
for just laws to replace the unjust strictures by which black life had
been shackled.[8]

He called for integrated living, the practice of agape love, and
the reconciliation of the races. The need for and importance of
community were never far from his thought and planning. King
knew that the dream of community had been a prime concern at
the inception of this democratic system heralded as "of the people,
by the people, and for the people."

Dream of the "Beloved Community"

Most Americans are familiar with the *story* of Dr. Martin Luther
King, J r., and that is good. But our need today is to affirm and
assume the *stance* of Dr. King, whose passion was the realization of
mmunity." This was the dream in his heart. This

---

nt assessments of King's views and actions as a personalist
mith and Ira G. Zepp, Jr., *Search for the Beloved Community: The
tin Luther King, Jr.* (Valley Forge: Judson Press, 1974), esp. 99-
. Ansbro, *Martin Luther King, Jr.: The Making of a Mind* (Maryknoll,
ks, 1982), esp. 71-109.

was the quest of his life. This was the organizing principle for his thought and deeds.

I close with King's own convictional statement about the dream that stirred his soul and urged him on: "At the heart of all civilization has meant and developed is 'community'—the mutually cooperative and voluntary venture of man to assume a semblance of responsibility for his brother."[9]

---

9   Martin Luther King, J r., "The Ethical Demands of Integration," *Religion and Labor* (May 1963), 7.

31

CHRISTIAN THEOLOGY AND SOCIAL EXPERIENCE

by James Earl Massey

Originally appeared in *The Covenant Quarterly* (vol. 27, no. 3, August, 1969), 26-36. Used by permission.

T he Freedom Movement in America is one of the most interesting, persistent, instructive, publicized, disturbing, productive, and problematic social facts of our time. But the concern of the Negro American for full freedom is not merely of our time; it is as old as the introduction of human slavery in this New World. Several factors now operate, however, to give that movement for freedom increased reason, strength, vigor, and urgency. One factor is the rise of non-white nations around entire world, the breaking of the bondage of colonization. A second factor is an increased self-consciousness on the part of the United States, brought about particularly through an awareness that the rest of the world watches our society and is quick to criticize as well as commend us.

It has been obvious to the world that our much-heralded tradition of "liberty and justice for all" was severely compromised with respect to the Negro American, and it is with considerable interest and concern that others watch our American society and system. By way of illustration, Howard Thurman was lecturing at the University of Ibadan in Nigeria, West Africa, when the news about the assassination of President John Kennedy arrived. Thurman took special note of the impact of that dread happening upon the people of that nation; he sensed deeply the extent to which Kennedy had been viewed by the Nigerians as a symbol of hope, courage, change, and progress. The decisive actions of that leader in the realm of human rights made the conscience of America articulate to them.[1]

Carl F. H. Henry was also traveling abroad when the assassination occurred. A young Bantu sought to converse with Henry and his wife one evening as they walked along a street in Johannesburg, South Africa. Some early radio reports that day had caused the young man to believe that Mr. Kennedy had been killed because of his strong stand for civil rights. He asked, with extreme feeling, "Well, what hope remains for us if *that* can happen in your country?"[2] A young man in his mid-twenties was speaking for millions of South African black men, all living under subjection, and all had envisioned a new day of racial freedom through the decisive influence of a young, concerned, and informed American president. That young man's sense of despair was possible only because of his sense of identification with the American dream.

There should be no question why a freedom movement has been necessary. There has been a need to affect an improvement of the status of the Negro American in the land. The abolition of slavery did not fully free the Negro in America. His status remained frozen after slavery, and his lot was predetermined by subjectivity

---

1   Howard Thurman, *The Luminous Darkness: A Personal Interpretation of the Anatomy of Segregation and the Ground of Hope* (Harper and Row, 1965), 52-3.

2   Carl F. H. Henry, *The God That Shows Himself* (Words Books, 1966), 35.

along political, social, educational, and economic lines. Full freedom could only occur through an open attack upon the segregation that followed slavery, against laws written into the system to preserve and perpetuate racism as a rationale, against social and political patterns that excluded and ignored the interests and needs of Negroes.

Segregational serfdom followed the abolition of slavery. The freedom movement has been a necessary corrective phenomenon. It has been necessary in order to interpret the history behind the evident imbalances. It has been necessary to isolate and identify the sad consequences of inequality in the American system. The freedom movement has been necessary to remind the nation of legal and moral obligations to the Negro American and of unfulfilled promises clearly stated in the federal constitution. The goal has been full freedom for the Negro American.

I speak of freedom. Let us understand that term to mean the state or condition of not being bound by the will and restrictions of another, or others, imposed from without. Let us also understand the term to mean the liberty to direct one's own life and affairs without subjection to despotic or arbitrary rule, either direct or indirect. Freedom involves the power and liberty of self-determination. Rightly understood, freedom implies a structured social arrangement between consenting and agreeing partners.

A free society is one in which no man is a victim but all are members of value. It is this kind of freedom that is promised in the federal constitution for every American citizen. It is this kind of freedom that the Negro American has been seeking to experience. Full freedom for the Negro in America means that he is included in the society and system as a sharer, a consenting sharer of value, and no longer as a victim along any line—legal, social, economic, or educational. Inclusion has always been the proof of freedom in

SELECT WRITINGS OF JAMES EARL MASSEY

America, and the chief component of that freedom has always been participation in the control of resources, government, and patterns of the society.

The Freedom Movement and Its Organizations

The Freedom Movement has been variously labeled. Some refer to it as the civil rights movement; some view it as a protest movement. Some refer to it as the integration movement. More recently the movement has been dubbed as the Negro revolution. However named, the basic concern within the freedom movement has been to effect experienced freedom for the Negro American.

A wide assortment of agencies, individuals, and organizations have been working together toward such an end. Some of these agencies and organizations are comparatively new on the national scene while others are older and time-tested. Among the older organizations are the National Association for the Advancement of Colored People and the National Urban League. Founded in 1909, the NAACP was interracial in origin and operation. The leaders sought to build upon the work of the earlier frontiersmen of freedom, the abolitionists, and therefore addressed themselves in particular to legislation and litigation in the interest of the Negro American.

The National Urban League was founded in 1910; it was also interracial in origin and operation and had the specific goal of negotiating between Negroes attempting to adjust to city living and white employers who were willing to train and use them. The work of these two older organizations has been comprehensive and of large-scale. Both organizations pioneered in social reform. Both have been conservative but crusading, democratic but decisive, flexible in action but fixed as to basic stance.

Both the NAACP and the National Urban League operated from the start from a base of trust in legal and moral process in the American system. Both took the American concept of democracy seriously, trusting that proper returns were sure to result. The program of each organization depended upon open trust, hope, and optimism. This persisted across many weary years, despite vigorous opposition from many sectors of society in which passionate racism and prejudice were openly at work.

Actually, it is because such stringent opposition continued against the older organizations that new groups emerged to prod more militant action and to protest more vigorously against the false promises of the nation to the Negro community. The Congress on Racial Equality, popularly known as CORE, was founded in 1942. The Southern Christian Leadership Conference, otherwise known as SCLC, began in 1957. The Student Non-Violent Coordinating Committee, SNCC, began in 1960.

These three major new organizations sought some formula by which a more rapid social change in the Negro's interest could be effected. All three initially developed to solve local problems, but the logic of their rationale and the apparent successes of their local efforts suggested that their work could be of compelling importance on a wider scale in the nation.

It is important that the differences between these older and newer agencies and organizations be noted. The similarities are evident, set as they are upon effecting full freedom for the Negro American. The differences have to do not only with historical background but with ideology, methodology, disciplines, tactics, machinery, dynamics, leadership, spirit, and appeal. Some of these organizations within the wider freedom movement are conservative and work within prescribed limits, utilizing approaches and techniques made perfect through previous use.

Other of these organizations are more assertive, dogged, direct, and demanding.

Indeed, CORE and SNCC have more recently demonstrated in order to disrupt as well as protest and insist. As each group moved out from its original sphere of work, the anticipated success did not always follow and the previous purism of non-violence was altered to allow for other plans of direct action which would permit pressures other than mere moral suasion. It should be evident, then, that some of the newer organizations do not operate by any faith in the American way. Some no longer consider negotiation and conciliation as practical in the struggle for civil rights and race concerns.

The older organizations like NAACP and the National Urban League, however, have maintained loyalty to their professed ideals and have kept the structure for their operation somewhat separate from the personal charisma of any leader. The character of the freedom movement has come under threat because of the multi-dimensional differences between the older and newer organizations which comprise it. One central question that is now under debate among the organizations is whether trust in the American system is at all reasonable in the light of the nation's history and present objections against the Negro American.

The Negro community in America continues to confess frustration over the lack of openness and integrity on the part of white society in dealing with its needs and concerns. It's true that new legal orders have been achieved and that legal breakthroughs have been evident. The popular attitude in America is that the barriers are all down, but the Negro community knows that many of the written mandates are not being implemented or enforced and that national conscience and national leaders lack concern to implement and enforce the new mandates. The tempo of change remains in low gear while white backlash to legal changes in the interest of the Negro is an ever-present reminder that those changes, although historically important, will all too slowly affect the American scene.

The comparatively recent cry of "Black Power" has taken root in that soil of disillusionment. That cry has both positive and negative poles of concern. As for the positive elements, that cry encourages the Negro American in a new role and spirit of increased dignity. It is a hope slogan. It is a call to assemble the black uniqueness and experience into strong and united programs for race achievement. "Black Power," positively understood, is a call for self-organization, group solidarity, distinctive black identity, tactical strength, and active confrontation with white America toward the end of changing a faulty pattern in the social arrangement here. It is a psychological call to manhood, a conscious rejection of the deep psychological indoctrination used by slave masters and segregationists to make the black man comply with unreasonable and racist conditions.

The "Black Power" slogan also has inherent dangers, some negative aspects. The slogan tends to exalt color, defensive separatism, and a polemic of militancy rooted in unhealthy disregard of all that is white. This reaction against all things white was largely responsible for the riots and overt violence in the inner cities across the nation during recent years. In such instances "Black Power" was aggressively active on the scene not as black *value* but as black *vengeance*.

The meaning and implications of the struggle have been well articulated by several writers, one of the most noteworthy being the late Dr. Martin Luther King, Jr., whose book *Where Do We Go from Here: Chaos* or *Community?*[3] provides a polemic

---

3   Published by Harper and Row, 1967. 209 pp.

of reasoned Christian response to the crisis. King has offered a worthy philosophy and broadly-outlined program of courageous concern to solve America's longstanding and deep-seated problem of racial polarity and distance. The book is more than urgent rhetoric. It reflects the concern of that late leader to keep essential issues and claims clear in the light of the Christian ethic as well as national ideals.

Christian Theology and the Social Crisis

Christian theology speaks loudly to us in the midst of such a social situation. Theology has always been a vital voice to the church. We need hardly remind ourselves that theology is basically God-talk, our talk about God and such implications that follow for our living from what allows us to so talk (divine revelation, historical events, the incarnation, salvific experiences, Scripture). Our nature, environment, experiences, and destiny are a concern of God. Our theology can help us to apprehend, understand, interpret, categorize, and speak of all of life with reference to divine ends.

Our theology, being Christian, deals with all of life in the light of God *in Christ.* We hold in our heritage of beliefs an immense deposit drawn from the Old Testament and Judaism, but our Christian theology involves more than that heritage; indeed, it involves much, much more. We confess to certain extensions of thought beyond the Old Testament teachings. We affirm certain distinctively new revelations, unique experiences, fulfilled hopes, shifts in emphasis, and projections for the future. Our resources for viewing life are uniquely abundant. The present social crisis is also clarified by Christian theology, and so is our responsibility within that crisis.

1. *Christian theology underscores the dignity of human freedom.* The biblical doctrine of free will has many distinctive implications. That doctrine reminds us that a free will is a condition of essential humanity. It also reminds us that a free will is an essential component for moral and social responsibility.

The writers of the Bible assert in several instances—and with important shifts in figurative and literal emphasis—that the very meaning and depth of human experience lie in realized freedom. One major theme of the apostle Paul was spiritual liberty, but even he wrote explicitly about human bondage as a natural and historical situation, a situation that a slave should seek to surmount if he found it possible. According to 1 Corinthians 7:21, Paul said: "Were you a slave when called? Never mind. But if you can gain your freedom, avail yourself of the opportunity."

Although Paul's letters make no condemnation of human slavery but condone it as a part of the system of his day, that verse—together with the specific tone of the letter to Philemon about his converted slave Onesimus—lets us see that even Paul believed that a man's subjection to another as a slave is not something divinely ordered but a circumstance that is to be brought to an end whenever possible.

Christian theology recognizes the legitimacy of human freedom and promotes the dignity of every man as equal and responsible before God. Freedom is a just claim and a proper goal. Our theology presses us to ratify any man's attempt to be responsibly free and have something to say on his own in society as well as before God.

2. *Our Christian theology cautions us against giving social systems an ultimate position as ends in themselves.* Christian theology must always judge any system, testing it as a means and rejecting it as an end. Groups, parties, societies, movements, governments are means; they are not ends. It is for this reason that the spirit and philosophy of any such group or system must remain under scrutiny.

Every spirit and philosophy that glorifies one racial group and rejects and undermines another must be labeled as evil. Any form of racism is an idolatry of color or condition. It overly stresses a natural condition, undermines human dignity, and makes race the standard of belief, loyalty, and behavior. Our theology forbids that we should espouse any cause that elevates the genetic features of a man and his race to an ultimate position. We must therefore reject and condemn the pejorative judgments of white extremists, on the one hand, and the vengeful concerns of certain black militants on tire other.

It is instructive to compare the ethno-centrism of ancient Israel with that reflected in the history of neighboring nations, especially as this had to do with race concerns. In the midst of countries and cultures that made distinctions between men and stratified men on the basis of race, custom, background, and religion, Judaism dared to differ. Pride of race and feelings of superiority were not countenanced. Israel rejected the notions of inherent superiority or inferiority of persons and peoples. This is not to say that Judaism did not recognize differences between men and nations; those differences were all too evident. But it is to say that the Hebrew religion did not allow for distinctions between men in their essential humanity.

No rationale was structured against non-Hebrews on racial grounds. Fear of admixture with other peoples was primarily a thought based on religious concerns and not on racial differences. A basic law of social regard appears in several settings in the Pentateuch: "There shall be one law for the native and for the stranger who sojourns among you" (Ex. 12:49). The *ger* was the one who was strange, different, foreign-not originally part of the group;

but he was to be treated with respect and without discrimination, even when he had to assume a role of dependence. The *ger* was to have equal justice. He was not to be treated as an inferior.

Even the Genesis story of human origins is a polemic that stresses the common origin of men at the hands of God. Acts 17:26 echoes that same theology, saying "And [God] made from one every nation of men to live on all the face of the earth . . . . Paul used such a statement to undercut Athenian pride in a claimed a distinct origin for themselves. He thereby underscored the unity of the human race as God's creation. Race pride, prejudice, and notions of superiority all stand rebuked in such a verse as ill-founded, unbiblical, and morally unjustifiable. Christian theology requires us to test our communities and our nation with respect to these.

The American experiment of democracy has not yet proved itself on all levels. Christian theology helps us to relate strategically to the furtherance of this social experiment. It helps us make a careful exposition of what community means. It fits us with objective and biblical criteria to help our nation match its process with its goal, to find right means to a right end, using attitudes and premises that are morally and theologically consistent.

Meanwhile, Christian theology reminds us that social process and group demands can only effect results and that no human action, system, movement, or even revolution can bring in the kingdom of God. Our theology informs us rather on how to guide men in turning in the direction of God, to whom that kingdom belongs and from whom that kingdom is promised to fully come.

3. *Christian theology insists that the fully human and responsibly free life needs Jesus Christ for its order and progress.* The support of natural law and mere human concern does not carry the matter quite far enough. Both natural law and moral law are required for effective interdependence between persons. A truly responsible freedom demands ethics and morals for order and progress.

Freedom requires interdependence between consenting sharers. If equality is to persist in that willed relationship, and if individual adequacy is to remain, then there must be positive resources as well as stable reasons to undergird that sharing. A salvific experience with Jesus Christ uniquely blesses relationships between persons. The kinds of choices demanded in living responsibly with others require a God-referent and a criterion for true sharing. The experience of redemption carries such plus elements for disposing one person toward another in good will and love.

Social dynamics are influenced by scientific thought, philosophical notions, and group and personal concerns, but persons can only remain in true oneness with each other when they are able to abnegate selfish concerns and prefer each other in a higher love. Christian theology rightly insists that the shared love of Jesus Christ is the ground of responsible community. Love will grant safeguards when secular projects and knotty problems produce disagreement. The love of Christ undermines divisiveness and opens the soul to trust and confidence. It seeks to reconcile where there have been hurts and hindrances.

No life is fully human that is not lived in love. No life is responsibly free that lacks relation with God and others. Our Christian theology holds this forever in view before us as we live and work in such a world. And that theology bids us to live by its claims, entering into social crises to work there as Christians.

32

THE BLACK WITNESS TO WHITE EVANGELICALISM

by James Earl Massey

Originally appeared in *Evangelicalism: Surviving Its Success*,
vol. 2, The Evangelical Roundtable Conference,
ed. David A. Fraser (Princeton University Press, 1987), 50-58.
Used by permission.

T he evangelical faith has meant much to Black Americans. At this time when evangelicalism has re-emerged as a potent presence in American life, I am pleased to discuss what Black Americans have contributed to this mosaic-like spiritual grouping and movement.

It has not been difficult to trace these contributions. Almost since the beginning of their presence in this land, Blacks have been receiving a biblically based message, testing and proving the viability of that message, sharing their spiritual experiences, and passing on the evangelical heritage with concern, creativity, and gusto.

The Development of Black Evangelical Churches

Foremost among the many contributions Blacks have made to evangelicalism is the development of Black evangelical churches.

In speaking about "black evangelical churches," I am referring to those congregations and denominations which took their rise in history under the evangelical witness and work of alert and intent black preachers. More often than not, these were servants of the Lord who found no full welcome in white churches because of racist barriers against fellowship.

Black religious separatism was not initially something that evangelical blacks desired. Historian Albert J. Raboteau, assessing the black experience in American evangelicalism during and after slavery, commented: "The opportunity for black religious separatism was due to the egalitarian character of evangelical Protestantism; its necessity was due, in part, to the racism of white Evangelicals."[1]

Something more must be said, however. The separateness forced upon black evangelicals did become a vehicle for the full assertion of black independence and pride. The very fact that blacks became and remained Christian in the face of racist barriers against them was proof that the essence of Christianity was not the creation or property of whites. When black believers designated their groupings as "African Methodist" or "African Baptist," it was their way of affirming themselves while staking their claim in a distinctive system of spiritual life. The existence of black churches allowed blacks a spiritual home, a meaningful social setting, and a political base from which to engage the forces of a racist society.[2]

It must be reported that the majority of black churches across our nation are rooted in the evangelical faith. There are some

---

1   "The Black Experience in American Evangelicalism: The Meaning of Slavery,"in Leonard I. Sweet, ed., *The Evangelical Tradition in America* (Macon: Mercer University Press, 1984), 183.

2   On these benefits, see Gayraud S. Wilmore, *Black Religion and Black Radicalism* (Anchor Press, Doubleday, Inc., 1973), esp. Chapter IV, 103-135.

critics who seek to dispute this fact.[3] The fact remains, however, that a strong commitment to the gospel message still pervades the majority of black church groups. The black churches still insist on a biblically-based faith, still teach that the revelation of God is in Jesus, and that Scripture is the Word of God for all of life. There is still strong concern among black believers to accent the savior-hood, lordship, and "onliness" of Jesus Christ. Black evangelicals are not deficient in their theology, even though they often differ with white evangelicals over what should be understood as the so-cial implications of the faith.

A Musical Tradition

A second contribution blacks have made to evangelicalism is a mu-sical tradition that encourages self-expression in worship. It is a tradition that not only honors biblical faith but personal experi-ences of life as well. This musical tradition allows the whole self to be expressive in the public worship of God.

This tradition of personal expressiveness in worship dates back as early as the slavery era when black slaves created such "spiritu-als" as "Nobody Knows De Trouble I Seen," "Steal Away to Jesus," and "Were You There When They Crucified My Lord?".[4] But it became increasingly evident to others through the traditional gospel music that developed and flourished in the black urban churches. The many compositions of Rev. Charles Albert Tindley

3   See the early criticisms from James M. Washington, *Black Religion* (Beacon Press, 1964). In his 1967 *Politics of God*, Washington altered a few of his initial criticisms of the black churches, and also in his even more recent "The Peculiar Peril and Promise of Black Folk Religion," in *Varieties of Southern Evangelicalism*, ed. by David E. Harrell, Jr. (Mercer University Press, 1981), 59-69.

4   See Eileen Southern, *The Music of Black Americans: A History* (W. W. Norton & Co., 1983), esp. 172-177, 197-200.

(1851?-1933) fall into this category. Tindley was a famous black United Methodist preacher and songwriter, and his soul-stirring musical works became widely known and used. Tindley's style and focus on personal experience heavily influenced the later development of such composers as Thomas A. Dorsey (b. 1899), the "Father of Gospel Music."

This later style was characterized by a piano (or Organ) improvising on the melody and harmonics of a song while the singer(s) improvised on the words.[5] Tindley's work also influenced Lucie Campbell (1885-1963). Campbell wrote "I Need Thee Every Hour" and "He'll Understand, and Say 'Well Done!'" "Still further development in the Gospel Music tradition took place under Sallie Martin (b. 1896), who wrote "Just A Closer Walk With Thee," and W. Herbert Brewster, Sr. (b. 1899), who wrote "Surely, God Is Able."

Charles A. Tindley's songs have been incorporated into white denominational hymnals and songbooks. It is not unusual to find white evangelical soloists singing such songs as "Nothing Between," and white choirs doing "Beams of Heaven." Interestingly, both of these songs illustrate the ever-present focus in black Christian worship upon Jesus as religious subject, on the one hand, and as religious object of faith on the other, with concern on the part of the singer to be companioned and assisted by Jesus in life's struggles. The refrain in "Beams of Heaven" affirms this:

I do not know how long 'twill be,
Nor what the future holds for me.
But this I know, if Jesus leads me,
I shall get home some day.

---

5   Ibid., see 451-453.

Statue of John Wesley on the campus of Asbury Theological Seminary. Dr. Massey, Life Trustee of this institution and like Wesley, proclaimed the Word of God from this tradition to all the world.

The acknowledged contagion of this expressiveness stands documented in the continuing popularity black singers and gospel choirs enjoy in inter-racial gatherings. But far more important than such popularity, it must be said that the present sacred concert culture within which Bill and Gloria Gaither, Sandi Patti, and other whites shine like stars owes more than a little to the black musical tradition. This is so at the level of the free vocal style, the lively instrumental accompaniment, and the devotional focus on Jesus. The evangelical world would be musically poorer apart from the rich and engaging musical contribution from Black Americans.

A Witness Against Racism

A third major contribution Black Americans have made to evangelicalism is an active witness against racism in the church and an insistent call for white believers to become more socially responsible and active. In 1973, historian Earle E. Cairns wrote: "Contemporary Evangelicals, who for a time ignored their responsibility as Christians in society, are becoming increasingly aware that . . . they have a responsibility to put the principles of Christ into action . . . in the social order in which they live."[6]

To be sure, some change in evangelical social views was stimulated by Carl F. H. Henry's writings in *Christianity Today* magazine and in strategic books such as his *Aspects of Christian Social Ethics.*[7] Sherwood Wirt also called attention to several clear issues for response in his *The Social Conscience of the Evangelical.*[8] But we must not overlook the fact that both Henry and Wirt wrote after much sensitizing about the American social scene had been initiated by socially active black leaders.

It might be helpful for me to mention a few of the more noted evangelical black leaders who have helped to promote change in race relations within evangelicalism.

1. **Howard O. Jones**, associated evangelist with the Billy Graham Evangelistic Association since 1958. To understand the responsible level at which Jones has helped in the struggle, one need only read his book *White Questions to a Black Christian.*[9] The questions Jones treated in that book were those asked him on the "race question" during evangelistic crusades, at Bible conferences, during missionary conventions, college and seminary engagements, and those sent to him in response to his radio ministry. The motive behind the writing was to provide "a bridge of communication between

---

6   Earle E. Cairns, *The Christian in Society* (Moody Press, 1973), 162.

7   Carl F. H. Henry, *Aspects of Christian Social Ethics* (Wm. B. Eerdmans Publishing Co., 1964).

8   Sherwood Wirt, *The Social Conscience of the Evangelical* (Harper & Row, 1968).

9   *White Questions to a Black Christian* (Zondervan Publishing House, 1975).

the races." The book gained a wide hearing and went into several editions.

2. **Tom Skinner**, national evangelist, whose book *Black and Free* chronicled his movement from a street gang leader in Harlem to a converted spokesman for Jesus across the nation and into other parts of the world.[10] When several hundred black evangelical young people were attending the 1970 Inter-Varsity Missionary Convention at Urbana, Illinois, it was Tom Skinner who used his scheduled address to interpret their militancy and the need for the rest of the church to understand it in a positive light.

3. **William E. Pannell**, an activist-interpreter-evangelist, whose book *My Friend, the Enemy* vividly set forth his personal story of how the Civil Rights Movement helped him understand how his membership in a majority white church group culture obscured the meaning of his black heritage.[11] Pannell is now Professor of Evangelism and Director of Black Church Studies at Fuller Theological Seminary in California.

4. **John Perkins**, whose Voice of Calvary Ministries in Mississippi, and whose books *Let Justice Roll Down*[12] and *With Justice For All*[13] have marked him as a master

---

10   *Black and Free* (Zondervan Publishing House, 1968).

11   *My Friend, the Enemy* (Word Books, Inc., 1968).

12   *Let Justice Roll Down* (Regal Books).

13   *With Justice For All* (Regal Books, 1982).

planner for racial betterment and church witness. Will Norton, Jr.'s, featured cover story on Perkins in the January 1, 1982, issue of *Christianity Today* was aptly done and properly titled "John Perkins, The Stature of a Servant."[14]

5. **William H. Bentley**, a Chicago based minister-theologian who has given steady leadership to the National Black Evangelical Association (founded in Los Angeles, California, in 1963), and has actively sought to promote a distinctly biblical, theological, and social framework of study within which the black perspective. During his presidency of the Association, Bentley has stirred the members toward theologizing about social action. In his 1979 history of the Association, Bentley explained the origins and focus of the organization: "The point made is that we cannot allow the *determination* of who we are to be placed into, or remain as the case may be, outside ourselves and in the hands of others, no matter who they are."[15] The concern has been to understand blackness as a God-given distinctive, gaining a proper self-understanding out of which to serve and relate with dignity. "Fellowship and Ministry—these are the poles around which the Association revolves."[16]

William H. Bentley's theological leadership among black evangelicals has been recognized by the wider

---

14   *Christianity Today*, January 1, 1982, 18-22, with his picture featured on the cover.

15   William H. Bentley, *National Black Evangelical Association Reflections on the Evolution of a Concept of Ministry* (Chicago: 1979), 67.

16   *Ibid.*, 10.

evangelical world. It was he who accepted the assignment to write the chapter on "Black Believers in the Black Community" for the book *The Evangelicals,* which was edited by David F. Wells and John D. Woodbridge.[17] In that chapter, Bentley correctly explained black evangelicalism as a very distinct phenomenon originally rooted in the theology and cultus of the Bible school movement which had trained many of the black evangelicals. The chapter goes on to explain why blacks had dared to differ with white evangelicals over social matters, and why blacks found it necessary to re-define the issues for which white definitions were inadequate.

There is more which should be surveyed, e.g., the impact on the evangelical pulpits of the black preaching tradition,[18] insights from black urban churches about ministering in the city, to cite two more.

---

17 (Abingdon Press, 1975).

18 The three preaching textbooks by black author James Earl Massey have had wide use in evangelical theological seminaries: *The Responsible Pulpit* (Anderson: Warner Press, 1974); *The Sermon in Perspective: A Study of Communication and Charisma* (Grand Rapids: Baker Book House, 1976); *Designing the Sermon: Order and Movement in Preaching* (Nashville: Abingdon Press, 1980).

33

RACE RELATIONS AND THE AMERICAN HOLINESS MOVEMENT

by James Earl Massey

Originally appeared in the *Wesleyan Theological Journal*
(Spring 1975), 60-69. Used by permission.

S ome years ago I was privileged to take part in a special conference of Evangelicals. They were assigned to report about the
contributions of African Americans to Evangelicalism—that
perennially interesting and mosaic-like spiritual movement among
contemporary Christians. It was not difficult to trace and comment
on those contributions because, quite early in the history of their
presence in this land, Blacks received the gospel of Christ with openness. They rigorously tested and proved its viability, and began passing on the evangelical witness with concern, creativity, and gusto.

As an African-American Christian, I felt an understandable
pride as I handled my assignment.[1] The pride had to do with the
three particular contributions I sought to highlight at the time.
One was the widespread development of Evangelical churches within the African-American grouping; a second was the continuing

---

1   For a published report, see James Earl Massey, "The Black Contribution to
    Evangelicalism," in *Evangelicalism: Surviving Its Success*, edited by David A.
    Fraser (Princeton: Princeton University Press, 1987), 50-58.

influence on the Evangelical music scene of the Black church tradition of celebrative and self-expressive worship music; and the third contribution was the courageously prophetic witness African-American believers have steadily made in calling White believers to become more socially responsible in their concern to evangelize.

The 1970s had just ended, a pregnant period of years during which Evangelical Christianity had grown faster in America than any other religious movement, with a grouping that then numbered more than forty million. Yes, I felt a distinct pride in reporting about how African-American believers had responded to the gospel, and had eagerly busied themselves in passing on the Evangelical heritage with ready faith, steady creativity, and acknowledged contagion.

Sensitizing Evangelicals

Among the more than forty million reported at that time as comprising Evangelical Christianity in America were many African-American believers. The membership of most of these was in Black evangelical churches which gave them a spiritual home, a meaningful social setting, and a political base from which to engage the contrary forces and patterns of a racist society. Their history of organized separateness from White churches in groupings designated as "African Methodist" or "African Baptist," etc., was due in the main to the problematic course of Evangelical Protestantism under the influence of those contrary forces and patterns in a racially partitioned society.[2]

---

2   Among the myriad of studies about this, see Albert J. Raboteau, "The Black Experience in American Evangelicalism: The Meaning of Slavery," in Leonard I. Sweet, editor, *The Evangelical Tradition in America* (Macon: Mercer University Press, 1984); Gayraud S. Wilmore, *Black Religion and Black Radicalism* (Garden City: Anchor Press, Doubleday, Inc., 1973).

Efforts to sensitize the Evangelical conscience about racism and social implications of the faith have been as prolonged, persistent, and necessary as those to stimulate the national conscience. It is a matter of fact, and a matter for shame, that major changes regarding race relations and social action began taking place earlier on the social scene in America than they did within the churches of Evangelical Protestantism. To be sure, some change in Evangelical social views was stimulated by Carl F. H. Henry since 1956 through his editorial writings in *Christianity Today* magazine and in 1964 through his pacesetting book *Aspects of Christian Social Ethics*. Also in 1968, Sherwood Wirt called attention in his *The Social Conscience of the Evangelical* to several issues needing a decisively Christian response from Evangelicals.[3]

But one must not overlook the fact that Carl Henry and Sherwood Wirt, among others, were writing and publishing their views to the church during the era of the Civil Rights Movement of the 1950s and 1960s. Those were the strategic and stressful decades when the American social scene was being impacted by the charismatic presence of vocal and socially active African-American leaders who unrelentingly kept calling the nation to make its "liberty and justice for all" motto a lived reality for all its citizens.

As for efforts to sensitize Evangelical believers for greater social and racial openness, I am reminded of something that happened during the first World Congress on Evangelism, a convention that brought evangelical leaders from around the world to Berlin, Germany, for a ten-day gathering in November, 1966. During the convention, those of us who were delegates heard many position papers which treated aspects of the Congress theme, "One Race,

---

3   See Carl F. H. Henry, *Aspects of Christian Social Ethics* (Grand Rapids: Wm. B. Eerdmans Publishing Co., 1964); Sherwood Wirt, *The Social Conscience of the Evangelical* (New York: Harper & Row, Publishers, 1968).

One Gospel, One Task." But, as the Congress continued across those ten days, some of us who were African-American noticed that no attention had been devoted in any of the position papers to the first part of the theme, "One Race." Nor had any paper on that aspect been distributed to us for a private reading, as had some topics related to other aspects of the general theme.

The Congress delegates had been drawn together from across the world, literally, and the vast assemblage represented the largest ecumenical and evangelical gathering of the Church since Pentecost in A.D. 33. Even though it reflected a great diversity of nationalities, geographical locations, and color distinctions, no major statement about the oneness of the human race had been given in any plenary session!

A few of us African-American delegates discussed this omission among ourselves and finally gained audience with Carl F. H. Henry, Congress Chair, to voice to him our question about this evident gap in planning. Interestingly, we later learned that some delegates from India, Africa, and South America had also noticed the omission. Henry listened to us with openness, and soon acknowledged to us that the planning committee had taken the "One Race" aspect of the general theme as a given, and therefore had not assigned anyone to treat it.

Aware now of the problem as we had voiced it, he apologized on behalf of the planning committee and asked if we would be willing to work at developing a summary statement about "One Race" which could be included in the final report scheduled to be distributed to the world press as an outcome of the Congress. Although it was rather late in the day for anything like a major paper on the matter, six of us agreed to help develop such a statement.

Jimmy McDonald, Howard O. Jones, Bob Harrison, Ralph Bell, Louis Johnson, and I worked into the late hours of that night.

We managed to finish a clearly focused statement on race. Our statement underscored human equality as a biblical principle rooted in the oneness of the human family under God as Creator. We stressed the imperative of *agape* love in our dealings with all humans, and the need to reject racial and national barriers which forbid full fellowship and cooperative ministry in the Church. *[See the full text of this statement at the conclusion of this article.]*

As it turned out, the section the six of us prepared about the world-wide problem of racism was undoubtedly the strongest statement evangelicals had ever made on the subject until that time.[4] It was a basic statement that declared our biblically informed understanding about racism as an unjust attitude, a social evil, and a barrier to cooperative ministry as believers. Within another decade, by 1977, Evangelical Christianity in America would comprise a mosaic-like grouping of more than forty million members,[5] but its influence as a leader in fostering racial understanding and social harmony in the land would, sad to say, still remain negligible.

Relations Within the American Holiness Movement

The story has not been very different with the churches which comprise what I refer to here as the American Holiness Movement. This movement is comprised of those church groups with a history of an emphasis on Christian holiness and with some historical

---

4   The full text of the Congress Statement was published in *One Race, One Gospel, One Task*, Volume I, edited by Carl F. H. Henry and Stanley Mooneyham (Minneapolis: World Wide Publications, 1967), 5-7. Personal reports about the Congress were published in books written by two persons from among the six who prepared the statement about race. See Bob Harrison, with Jim Montgomery, *When God Was Black* (Grand Rapids: Zondervan Publishing House, 1971), 145-146; James Earl Massey, *Concerning Christian Unity* (Anderson: Warner Press, 1979), 121-126.

5   See the feature story in *Time* Magazine, December 26, 1977, 52-58.

relation to the transmission of this tradition through holiness associations and conventions. In fact, in tracing the patterned story of the Holiness Movement in America, one will discover that the number of Blacks involved in its life and witness has been even more disturbingly meager than the number of Blacks in the Evangelical Movement.

A significant number of Black evangelical leaders have had ministries which involved them steadily in both Black and White settings throughout Evangelicalism. They comprise a very distinct group whose spiritual concerns and emphases are rooted in the theology and cultus of the Bible school and biblical seminary movement which trained them. Although they have often differed with White evangelicals over how to answer certain social questions, and found it necessary to identify and sometimes redefine the issues for which White definitions were judged inadequate, they nevertheless have been respected and continued to serve as bridge-builders between the races.[6] The number of such leaders within the American Holiness Movement is considerably smaller. Let me trace the reason or reasons why I believe this has been, and continues to be so.

In my judgment, the Black presence in the American Holiness Movement has been comparatively slight because this movement's major concerns have not seemed as appealing or germane to Black

---

6   On this, see William H. Bentley, "Black Believers in the Black Community," in *The Evangelicals*, edited by David F. Wells and John D. Woodbridge (Nashville: Abingdon Press, 1975); William H. Bentley, *National Black Evangelical Association: Reflections on the Evolution of a Concept of Ministry* (Chicago: 1979). See also Tom Skinner, *Black and Free* (Grand Rapids: Zondervan Publishing House, 1968); William E. Pannell, *My Friend, the Enemy* (Waco, TX: Word Books, Inc., 1968); William E. Pannell, *The Coming Race Wars? A Cry for Reconciliation* (Grand Rapids: Zondervan Publishing House, 1993); Howard O. Jones, *White Questions to a Black Christian* (Grand Rapids: Zondervan Publishing House, 1975); Samuel G. Hines, with Joe Allison, *Experience the Power* (Anderson: Warner Press, 1996).

believers as has the basic salvation emphasis articulated by the Evangelical Movement. Although it is clear that the Scriptures call for a dedicated life that honors God and the divine will— a call that is indeed known and heralded in the Black churches, African Americans have been "grabbed" by other currents of truth and meaning in the Scriptures. One in particular is that strong and steady current in Old Testament thought that accents the importance of social regard and race uplift. When African-American Christians think and witness about renewal and restoration, or about Christian unity, they also envision what these should mean for those who have been victimized by a racist system. In addition, they reason that any personal quest for spiritual depth or closeness to God must inevitably include some concern for bettering the social process in America.

Given America's racist environment, one of the predominant issues with which African-American believers and their churches have been concerned is social survival. Along with the biblical message about salvation through faith in Jesus, they have been encouraged by the clarifying anthropology taught in the Scriptures, that validating message about all humans being children of God. Given our set of social circumstances in the chequered course of American history, the concern of Black believers has been for salvation and survival, with the social implications of the faith being viewed as far more germane than an emphasis on a strictly personal, pietistic inwardness. This is not to say that a concern for the deeper life is neglected; it is rather to say that the social and the spiritual are viewed in a more related fashion by Black believers than by most proponents of the Holiness tradition.[7]

---

7   This criticism does not apply to those proponents of Holiness who showed such social concern as to seek societal reform during the mid-nineteenth

The concern for freedom, social equality, and general race up-lift has so absorbed the energies of Black church leaders in particular and Black churches in general that sometimes little energy has remained for much else. To sense the extent to which this has been the case, one need only explore the various histories of the Black denominations, on the one hand, and the studies which report about Black membership in predominately White denominations, on the other.[8]

By and large, African-American believers tend to honor and promote what Peter J. Paris has aptly described as "the black Christian tradition." As Paris explains it:

> The tradition that has always been normative for the black churches and the black community is not the so-called Western Christian tradition per se, although this tradition is an important source for blacks. More accurately, the normative tradition for blacks is that tradition governed by the principle of non-racism which we call the black Christian tradition. The fundamental principle of the black Christian tradition is depicted most adequately in the biblical doctrine of the parent-hood of God and the kinship of all peoples—which is a version of the traditional sexist

---

century. On this, see Timothy L. Smith, *Revivalism and Social Reform in Mid-Nineteenth Century America* (Nashville: Abingdon Press, 1957).

8   For examples, see the rather broad treatment of the major Black Baptist groups in Leroy Fitts, *A History of Black Baptists* (Nashville: Broadman Press, 1985), esp. ch. 2, 41-106, in which he details how the socio-political needs of Blacks spawned the various conventions which reflect and promote the Black Baptist tradition. See also James Melvin Washington, *Frustrated Fellowship: The Black Baptist Quest for Social Power* (Macon: Mercer University Press, 1986).

expression "the fatherhood of God and the brother-hood of men."[9]

In contrast with the emphases highlighted in the Evangelical and Holiness traditions, *this* is the emphatic tradition that became in-stitutionalized in the African-American churches.

To be sure, African-American interest in revivalistic religion and a depth relationship with God has not been lacking, as those who have experienced a Black worship service can readily testify. Nevertheless, Blacks have never accented personal piety at the expense of a needed accent on the social meaning of a religious experience. The develop-ment of higher Christian graces, or a "closer walk with God" as it is popularly termed, continues as a concern and advisement among Black evangelicals; but the perfectionist emphasis that prevailed in holiness circles in the nineteenth century did not gain as wide an ap-peal among Blacks as among Whites. For one thing, Christian per-fectionism seemed "too Methodist-like" to those who were Baptist by orientation. For another, it seemed too unattainable to those who did not hear a clear enough explanation about the doctrine.

African-American believers always have insisted that true religion is essentially experiential. It has not been as necessary to Blacks that there be a refined doctrinal system to expound this belief. Blacks were in tune with American revivalism at an early point in its development, and benefited greatly from its impacting influences, but they did not get as involved as Whites in that wing of the American Holiness Movement which blended Pietism and Wesleyan perfectionism.[10]

---

9   Peter Paris, *The Social Teaching of the Black Churches* (Philadelphia: Fortress Press, 1985), 10.

10   On this blending of Pietism, revivalism, and Wesleyan perfectionism, see Melvin E. Dieter, *The Holiness Revival of the Nineteenth Century* (Metuchen, NJ: Scarecrow Press, Inc., 1980), esp. 3-10, 18-63.

The Church of God Movement (Anderson)

The following are holiness-teaching denominations which have had primary and extended contact with African Americans in the course of their history and witnessing in America: The Christian and Missionary Alliance Church, The Church of the Nazarene, The Pilgrim Holiness Church, The Holiness Christian Church, The Salvation Army, and the Church of God (Anderson, IN.). These groups are also among the larger Holiness bodies registered in the nation. Although the separate history of each of these groups has not always reflected the best social arrangement with the Blacks who became members in them, it is of interest to report that their Black members did not break away from these groups to form independent organizations, as did those who experienced segregation in the Methodist Church, for example.[11] Perhaps among the reasons for their not breaking away might be the fact that most of the named groups have had so few Black members in comparison with their White majorities.

A word is in order regarding the history of some of these groups in relating to African Americans. The Church of the Nazarene put forth well-planned and organized efforts during the 1940s to promote holiness evangelism among African Americans, but those efforts yielded rather meager results. In fact, during the total history of this group's contact with African Americans from the late

---

11   The experience of segregation within the Methodist Church led to the formation by Blacks of the African Methodist Episcopal Church and the African Methodist Episcopal Zion Church. On the origins of the A.M.E. Church, see Harry V. Richardson, *Dark Salvation*: The Story of Methodism as It Developed Among Blacks in America (Garden City, NY: Anchor Press/ Doubleday, 1976), esp. 76-116. On the origins of the A.M.E.Z. Church, see Richardson, 117-147, and William J. Walls, *The African Methodist Episcopal Zion Church* (Charlotte: A.M.E. Zion Publishing House, 1974).

nineteenth century to the early 1980s, there were never more than twelve Black ministers associated with it.[12]

The Salvation Army has not fared much better in attempts to promote the holiness theme among African Americans. Booker T. Washington, the noted Tuskegee educator and national race leader, was so impressed by the rich history of The Salvation Army in social outreach and group openness that in 1896 he wrote: "I have always had the greatest respect for the work of the Salvation Army, especially because I had noted that it draws no color line in religion."[13] And yet, despite such an endorsement from a leading Black educator and race statesman, The Salvation Army never experienced widespread success in gaining African-American members or in holding them.

Among those holiness-teaching groups that have had a rather prolonged contact with African Americans, the one that has been the most fruitful is the Church of God (Anderson, IN). In 1968 there was in this body a Black membership of 16,703 within a total United States member- ship listing of 144,243. By 1974 the number of African-American members had increased to nearly 20,000 among a total reported membership of 160,198. In 1980 the Church of God (Anderson) listed 472 predominantly Black congregations, with 27,628 Black members among a total membership in the United

---

12   See W. T. Purkiser, *Called Unto Holiness*, Vol. 2, *The Second Twenty-Five Years, 1933-58* (Kansas City, MO: Nazarene Publishing House, 1983), esp. 197-200. For two additional and earlier reports regarding efforts by The Church of the Nazarene to evangelize Blacks, see Raymond W. Hurn, *Mission Possible: A Study of the Mission of the Church of the Nazarene* (Kansas City, MO: Nazarene Publishing House, 1973), esp. 84-85. See also Roger Eugene Bowman, *Color Us Christian: The Story of the Church of the Nazarene Among America's Blacks* (Kansas City, MO: Nazarene Publishing House, 1975).

13   Quoted by Edward H. McKinley in his book, *Marching to Glory: The History of the Salvation Army in the United States of America, 1880-1980* (San Francisco: Harper & Row, 1980), see 53, note 41. For the story of Salvation Army efforts to win Blacks, see 50-53, 150-151, 183-184, and 196-201.

States of 179,137. These figures show a pattern of steady relationship between African Americans and the larger body of Church of God members in the United States, and an instructive growth pattern among African Americans associated with the Church of God.

It is most enlightening to compare the race membership percentage in this holiness-teaching group with those percentages reflected within the mainline majority-white denominations, especially during the late 1970s when American Baptists reported a 12% Black membership, the Episcopal Church 5%, the United Church of Christ 4.3%, the Disciples of Christ 3.8%, the United Methodist Church 3.5%, the United Presbyterian Church 2.7%, the Lutheran Church in America 1.7%, and the Southern Baptists a meager 1.0%.

African Americans are by far the largest ethnic minority within the Church of God (Anderson). In 1989, of 199,786 members listed for the Church of God in the United States, 37,435 were African Americans. The reason for this significant percentage is historical, theological, and social. It is due in no small measure to the appealing and promising unity ideal that is at the heart of the Church of God message; it is an ideal that has from this movement's beginning in 1880 been allied in the church's message and practices with the call to scriptural holiness. As church historian John W. V. Smith has explained it: "Many church groups avoided making a strong interracial stance. The Church of God reformation's message of unity of all believers, however, made a very strong interracial position inherent in the message itself."[14]

The message voiced by the Church of God about the unity of believers appealed strongly to African Americans who were otherwise restricted and segregated in a racist society. The message

---

14   John W. V. Smith, *The Quest for Holiness and Unity: A Centennial History of the Church of God* (Anderson: Warner Press, 1980), 162.

of unity provided promise for a needed affirmation of self-worth, on the one hand, and for needed social togetherness, on the other. Unlike other church groups whose doctrinal positions accented non-relational themes, the central theme of the Church of God was, and remains, a relational one: believers belong together, united by love.

Although social relations within the Church of God have witnessed the same problems and stresses all other church bodies have faced, the challenge of the biblical insistence on unity has always been present in the group's heritage and message as a prodding factor toward freeing its life from racist concerns in the national environment and toward reform of its life as people of God called to practice holiness. To be sure, evidences that some persons within its congregations have yielded to prevailing social patterns of race distancing and polarization can be documented in the history of the Church of God, just as in the history of other church groups in America. Nevertheless, the unity ideal central to its heritage and reason for being has never allowed such lapses from the ideal to stand unchallenged.[15]

The two worlds of race have not yet disappeared from the Church of God, but some significant strides have been made in recent years which show an increased openness and intent to fulfill this movement's unity ideal. Among the many available evidences of this, the following will sufficiently illustrate this openness and intentionality.

Since the early 1970s, several African Americans have served in full-time posts as staff persons for the major boards and general

---

15   For more about the history of race relations in the Church of God, see John W. V. Smith, *op. cit.*, esp. 161-169, 385, 389, and 403-406; *Red & Yellow, Black & White & Brown*: Home Missions in the Church of God (Anderson: Warner Press, 1981), esp. 42-53. See also James Earl Massey, *African Americans and the Church of God: Aspects of A Social History* (Anderson University Press, 2005).

agencies of the Church of God. In 1988, an African American was elected by the General Assembly of the Church to serve as the body's executive secretary, a post that is the highest elective office within the church. Reelected following his first term, this leader continues to serve with distinction and wide regard. In June, 1989, the General Assembly of the church ratified an African-American educator, a former pastor within the group, to be dean of the church's graduate School of Theology. For many years in the recent past, the chair of the Board of Trustees of Anderson University, this movement's largest school, was a gifted Black pastor and campus alumnus.

Like other church communions with a history within the American Holiness Movement, the Church of God (Anderson) is not yet perfected. It stands, along with these and multitudinous other religious bodies in America, between the alternatives of advance and decay, fulfillment and failure, witness and waywardness, significance and selfishness. The twin concerns of holiness and unity beckon us to full openness and obedience to our reason for being. If our obedience is full, and if our experience of holiness is thoroughgoing, then renewal will be the result—and our continuing witness may yet prove convincing to many others. May it be so, to the good of all whose lives we touch, to the good of this socially fractured nation, to a divided Christendom that needs our witnessing presence, and to the greater glory of God.

Editor's Note

Here is the full text of the statement prepared by Dr. James Earl Massey and three of his colleagues at the World Congress on Evangelism in Berlin, Germany, in 1966. The wording is as it appeared in *One Race, One Gospel, One Task* (Worldwide Publications, 1967), 5.

One Race

We recognize the failure of many of us in the recent past to speak with sufficient clarity and force upon the biblical unity of the human race

All men are one in the humanity created by God himself. All men are one in their common need of divine redemption, and all are offered salvation in Jesus Christ. All men stand under the same divine condemnation and all must find justification before God in the same way, by faith in Christ, Lord of all and Savior of all who put their trust in him.

All who are "in Christ" henceforth can recognize no distinctions based on race or color, and no limitations arising out of human pride or prejudice, whether in the fellowship of those who have come to faith in Christ or in the proclamation of the good news of Jesus Christ to men everywhere.

We reject the notion that men are unequal because of distinction of race or color. In the name of Scripture and of Jesus Christ, we condemn racialism wherever it appears. We ask forgiveness for our past sins in refusing to recognize the clear command of God to love our fellowmen with a love that transcends every human barrier and prejudice. We seek by God's grace to eradicate from our lives and from our witness whatever is displeasing to him in our common relations with one another. We extend our hands to reach others in love, and those same hands reach out to men everywhere with the prayer that the Prince of Peace may soon unite our sorely divided world.

34

A CHALLENGE TO PRIVILEGE

by James Earl Massey

Originally appeared in Beth A. Richardson, compiler, *Seasons of Peace* (The Upper Room, 1986), 64-65. Used by permission.

A man with gold rings comes into your assembly, and a man in
shabby clothing also comes in, and you pay attention to the one
who wears fine clothing and say, "Have a seat here, please,"
while you say to the poor man, "Stand there," or "Sit at my feet,"
have you not made distinctions among yourselves,
and become judges with evil thoughts? —James 2:2-4

The writer of this passage in James was a teacher concerned with helping believers adhere fully to Christian faith and practice. In promoting a thoroughgoing commitment, the writer supplies admonitions and pastoral encouragement for living by "the rules."

The passage before us addresses attitudes toward wealth. Having already advised the poor against seeking wealth as an ultimate good, and the rich against hoarding wealth as an everlasting boon, the writer now offers advice against being partial and seeking or giving privileged treatment as a result of social standing as displayed by possessions.

This word about divisive distinctions between social classes reminds us of our ties to one another through a basic humanity under God. We are reminded that class lines should not affect the way we relate to each other—whether during the times of gathering for worship or after such times. The Christian faith levels all believers; it allows no authoritative pride of place by the rich over the poor. The passage rebukes such selfishness and unwarranted distinctions.

The rich—poor problem is treated several places in James. Some of these passages give a radical criticism of wealth and influence, but largely because arrogance seems to follow pride of possessing, and social privilege is often expected when one enjoys economic advantage. The fact is that wealth can lead one astray, seducing one by a false sense of self-importance, unless one lives by a higher attitude of regard and recognized relationship. The crucial messages in our passage are that Christian faith demands a heart and that love gives proof of itself in unselfish and impartial deeds. A common faith and an open fellowship go together. True love will eagerly seek to reduce the problems and ills that people suffer; it will never increase them.

Our passage addresses the great issue of how we will regard each other and our motives for doing so. It is a clear call to live by a higher attitude than partiality represents. It is a word against arrogance, pride, and unwarranted class lines.

> The Lord said, "Say 'We'," but I shook my head, hid my hands tight behind my back, and said, stubbornly, "I."
>
> The Lord said, "Say 'We'," but I looked upon them, grimy and all awry. Myself in all those twisted shapes?

Ah, no! Distastefully I turned my head away, persisting, "They."

The Lord said, "Say 'We',"; And I, at last, richer by a hoard of years and tears, looked in their eyes and found the heavy word that bent my neck and bowed my head: Like a shamed schoolboy then I mumbled low, "We, Lord."[1]

Prayer: O God, help me to read the truth about myself and others with open, regarding eyes. Keep me back from the sin of being partial. Let me not judge, except between good and evil. Let me not fail to love and relate in keeping with the spirit of Jesus, my Lord. In his name I pray. Amen.

---

1 Karle Wilson Baker, "Pronouns," in *Worship Resources for the Christian Year*, ed. Charles L. Wallis (Harper & Bros., 1954), 401.

35

JUSTICE IN TENSION
WITH PATRIOTISM

by James Earl Massey

Originally appeared in Barry L. Callen,
Heart of the Matter (Emeth Press, rev. ed., 2016), 112, 134-154.
Used by permission.

I n April of 1963 I was on the planning committee that organized the "Freedom Walk" in Detroit when Martin Luther
King, Jr., used much of the same speech that he would use in
Washington, D.C., that summer. Some 200,000 people massed to
hear King flash a stirring dream across the screen of every mind,
a dream that he was concerned enough to tell and courageous
enough to live.

That dream had much to do with the church. It was about
community, constructive, person-affirming, God-inspired community. King was so aware of the effects of relationships and social
processes on the shaping of the identity and destiny of persons and
their groupings. We all are caught in a network of some mutuality,
and King was haunted by the negative social network strangling so
many African-Americans of that time.

I had several personal contacts with Martin Luther King, Jr.,
someone impressed with Gandhi of India. Now that some time

has passed, I think it's clear that their deep devotion to God and to God's peaceful ways of confronting social evil were effective. King often said that everyone can serve as Christ's compassionate agents of reconciliation. No ordination to ministry or college degree is required, only a heart full of God's grace and a soul motivated by Christ's love.

King's methods of addressing the problems of injustice and disunity were daring, controversial, and quite effective, but they never were intended to be *divisive*. God's concern always has been to birth a church, a united church, a redeemed and reconciling church. We who are part of it by divine grace are to be open to the God-expected experience of building a redemptive community that frees, enlightens, and reconciles. The tension of loyal church membership and loyalty to one's country came to me early in life.

At the height of the Cold War in the early 1950s, I was drafted into military service. I made up my mind to avoid complaining, believing that God would help me handle the experience wisely. I had heard General Douglas MacArthur give a dramatic radio speech galvanizing the national will to resist Communist aggression. It affected me deeply and I was ready to serve my country. Soon I was sent to Austria, became a chaplain's assistant, and had opportunity to visit Dachau and the former concentration camp there. I cringed at the pictures of that past horror and wrote in my diary, "I hereby pledge myself to the utmost defense of the personal freedom of those for whose protection I am currently engaged."

Being in the very place where the blood of Nazi victims still cries out from the ground to be avenged, I felt what I vowed. Although valuing the primacy of human life, I have never been a conscientious objector but, standing there in that place of previous torture, if there had been any residue of an unqualified pacifism left in me, the visit to Dachau destroyed it."

Here's where the obvious tension comes in. No human government is fully righteous and just. As a member of God's church, I must not be a subtle slave to any human governments. My ultimate citizenship is always in the kingdom of God. I acknowledge the tension, however. My later involvement in the American Civil Rights movement, and certainly my friendship with Martin Luther King, Jr., and our deep commitment to non-violence in actively addressing injustice, placed us in awkward relationship with our beloved nation. I often have written and preached on reconciliation, but without for a minute ignoring injustice.

Jesus tells us that God's kingdom is not promoted by human violence, that peace-making is the way to shape the best future, and that those who do this work of effecting reconciliation are God's true children." Absolutely. Even so, there seem to be limits to "unqualified" pacifism when an evil like Jew-exterminating Nazism is on the loose in this fallen world!

The New Testament gives us a dramatically mixed view of human governments. The Book of Revelation concludes the library of biblical materials by combining carefully the apocalyptic and prophetic traditions found sporadically throughout the Bible. Joined there is a sober realism about the roots of power, the fruits of idolatry, and a stern call for Christians to be keenly aware and ethically responsible.

Human history is indeed the arena of evil, the place of persecution; it also is the arena in which God has worked out human salvation, and where God's people are called to live redemptive lives. The "how" of living redemptive lives, especially in cases of extreme injustice, is not spelled out in detail and in advance by the Bible.

Justice and liberation certainly lie at the heart of the biblical revelation. And when it comes to patriotism, Christian loyalty to country finds it limits when a whole nation operates counter to the love and justice of God.

36
___

EXPERIENCE GOD'S POWER

by James Earl Massey

Foreword to *Experience the Power* by Samuel G. Hines,
with Joe Allison (Warner Press, 1993, revised 1995), vii-ix.
Used by permission.

This book treats a theme that its author knew was personal, pertinent, and programmatic. The theme is personal because its central message reports how a Christian believer can experience a sense of belonging to God at such an inward depth that the whole self is introduced to and sustained by an inward harmony, an awareness of wholeness through being loved.

The theme of the book is pertinent because the settings in which we must live out our Christian commitment will test our sense of who we are in God's gracious plan for our lives. The theme is also programmatic in that the author not only isolates, identifies, and illustrates the means by which such an experience of God is gained, but shows how that experience is to be shared. Central is the treatment of reconciliation. Students of the Scriptures will recognize the many passages to which the author refers and whose meanings he honestly and helpfully expounds in explaining the import and impact of reconciliation.

The author, now deceased, was one of this century's ablest exponents of the reconciliation theme. He was a primary example of how to engage in the ministry of reconciling—how to end isolation between persons and groups, how to remove alienation, grant acceptance, forgive, and engage in caring as God cares. As his close friend and ministerial colleague across more than forty years, I can report about a contagion that characterized Samuel G. Hines as he went about his ministry here and abroad.

When Brother Hines so often declared that "God's agenda is unity—the bringing together of all things in Jesus Christ," the statement was more than a slogan being repeated. When he writes here that "the greatest thing you can do to deliver someone from evil is to give them assurance of forgiveness," it's not to make a mere rhetorical suggestion. Samuel Hines lived, spoke, and wrote from within such a depth of relationship with God in Christ. Having experienced God's reconciling love, he lived it out. That is part of his living legacy to us.

Howard Thurman, another exponent of reconciliation, has suggested that some persons seem to have a talent for reconciliation, that they are so assured in themselves by a sense being cared for by God that they can penetrate deeply into the life of others in a manner that tames each wilderness found and introduces harmony where discord is found. Thurman further explained that such persons are but expressing a part of their praise to God for the harmony they know by sharing that sense of inward peace with others.

Samuel G. Hines was such a person. His "talent" for being a reconciler was disciplined always by an openness to God and others—all others. He kept that discipline focused and rooted in an active sense of God's agenda as the Apostle Paul expressed it in that classic passage in 2 Corinthians 5:17-20. This book highlights that agenda. It's the message of reconciliation held steadily before us, along with the divine mandate to give ourselves fully to it.

Thus, the mood that pervades this book is a call for all of us to work with others to change the shattered relationships and conflicts with which our world is laden. Many levels of estrangement mar our society, churches, and families, but these can be addressed and altered in the name and spirit of divine love. The central result of being loved by God—fully forgiven, fully received—grants an opening in the self through which that love will spill out toward others. This book propels us toward a loving mission of reconciliation.

37

RECONCILIATION:
CHALLENGE AND HOPE

by James Earl Massey

Originally appeared as the "Foreword" to
Curtiss Paul DeYoung, *Reconciliation: Our Greatest Challenge—
Our Only Hope* (Judson Press, 1997), ix-xi.
Used by permission.

This book appears at a crucial time in the life of America and the affairs of our world. Everywhere one looks, conflicts between persons and groups are playing themselves out. Conflict holds center stage and voices of wisdom addressed to those involved are all too few.

Curtiss Paul DeYoung is one of those voices, and this book is his attempt to share wisdom, a biblical wisdom tested in his own life struggles. Addressing himself courageously to our hearts as well as our heads, DeYoung honestly treats reconciliation as the costly action that it is, and he explains the need for relational bridge building at the many levels of our social interaction. One of his most strategic sentences is this: "What has cost God much cannot be cheap for us. Costly reconciliation is the Incarnation of God."

This book is a logical and planned sequel to the author's previous book, *Coming Together: The Bible's Message in an Age of Diversity*

323

which treated the Bible as a record of a culturally diverse people seeking God's will, and how the person Jesus—"an Afro-Asiatic Galilean Jew"—became a universal Christ who liberates, shapes a new and inclusive community, and empowers his followers to be agents of reconciliation. The present book was written to unpack the meaning and scope of reconciliation, the call for which ended *Coming Together.*

The strength of this book is in the systematic considerations DeYoung has offered about how the shared life of "the community of the reconciled" contributes to the work of justice issues, the greater visible unity of believers, and a positive social change. Christian faith is seen not only as intelligible but as productive and persuasive.

This is a book for which its author can be proudly accountable. There are places in it where he calls attention to how he came to know what he reports, and he reports it with a responsible bearing. What is distilled from his depth study of the Christian Scriptures is also highlighted, with necessary mention of the relevant literature within the field of his topic. One values this holistic approach, the careful exposition of insights from his prolonged observation of the perennial needs of the church in the world.

Some of the formulations voiced herein have been reshaped across the years, corrected or confirmed by interaction with other minds and lives, but the accent DeYoung places on the imperative for courage to work at reconciliation—"taking responsibility, seeking forgiveness, repairing the wrong, healing the soul, and creating a new day of relating"—is from a wisdom generated by his own serious faith and dedicated walk as a believing, teaching, active practitioner of *agape* love.

Due reflection on what he has written here should lead not only to an informed understanding of what reconciliation means, but also to commitment of oneself to the risks involved and the responsible action it demands. This book was not narrowly conceived nor is it selfishly motivated. Knowing Curtiss Paul DeYoung as I do (from across his college and seminary years and on into his service in ministry), I know this book reflects the honesty and hope that characterizes his spirit.

If read in the light of the author's intentions for it, namely, to clarify our human possibilities and enhance our lives through the spirit and work of reconciling love, this book not only offers a necessary and timely statement but alert guidance by which to work at the most challenging and necessary task in our time, reconciliation. Here is guidance, based in a vital Christian faith, that is never past tense but is contemporary, focused, and creative.

38

SERMON: OUR TASK AS RECONCILERS

by *James Earl Massey*

Delivered at the Park Avenue United Methodist Church,
Minneapolis, Minnesota, November 4, 2001, as part of an
event of the Twin Cities Urban Reconciliation Network

*From now on, therefore, we regard no one from a human point of
view; even though we once knew Christ from a human point of view,
we know him no longer in that way. So if anyone is in Christ, there is
a new creation: everything old has passed away; see, everything has
become new! All this is from God, who reconciled us to himself through
Christ, and has given us the ministry of reconciliation; that is, in Christ
God was reconciling the world to himself, not counting their trespasses
against them, and entrusting the message of reconciliation to us. So we
are ambassadors for Christ since God is making his appeal through us;
we entreat you on behalf of Christ, be reconciled to God. For our sake
he made him to be sin who knew no sin, so that in him we might
become the righteousness of God.* —2 Corinthians 5:16-21 (NRSV)

T he work of reconciling people is strategic, necessary, and always timely because everywhere one looks, whether at life
in America or across our world, deadly conflicts between
persons and groups are playing themselves out. Struggles continue

unabated between individuals, people-groups, and nations over differences in values, ethics, religious views, land claims, territorial rights, political ends, and a host of other fractious debates. The emotions connected with all these struggles have been deepened by selfish use and abuse of power.

Conflict holds center stage and voices of wisdom addressed to those involved in the fray are all too few. How glad I am to be part of this worship assembly filled with persons committed to help quell conflict, persons who deeply respect what the Christian Scriptures have to say on the subject of reconciliation, and who intentionally walk their path with concern to help others deal with the conflicts that occur when people meet. I invite you to join me in re-exploring our necessary ministry of reconciliation.

The theme of reconciliation is writ large across the pages of the New Testament. You are familiar with our Lord's ethical instruction in the Sermon on the Mount (Matt. 5:21-26) that deals with anger, that strong human feeling of displeasure which at a belligerently wrathful stage can stir a person to murder someone. Jesus instructed us, his followers, to deal forthrightly with anger, urging us to "be reconciled" rather than remain at odds, to take the initiative to remove whatever blocks a right relation with someone else so as to restore harmony and live at peace with each other.

You are also familiar with the many expansive treatments the Apostle Paul gave regarding reconciliation. For instance, in 1 Corinthians 7:10-11, Paul addressed believers struggling with a problem-threatened relationship with a spouse; he instructed the couple to remain together or, if already separated, to "be reconciled." The word he used, *katallassō*, is from a family of images that picture a changed relationship. The image in this word shows something having been set aside [*kata*]: an attitude, a grievance, a position, a deed, a distance, a result, in order to bring about a change for the better. In this way, a new disposition is exhibited, a new stance assumed, a new framework established to allow a difference where enmity and distance had been the order.

But it is in 2 Corinthians 5:16-21, our textual passage, that we find the Apostle's richest statement regarding reconciliation. Here Paul made a personal statement and offered an advisory claim. Because of his conversion Paul had entered a new life-course and his worldview had undergone a full change. He confessed that he was now part of a "new creation" that Christ had inaugurated, and that he felt commissioned to witness to others about the reconciling deed by which God made this newness possible in his life.

Says Paul: "In Christ God was reconciling the world to himself" (5:19). In light of this amazing fact, he was eager to have others experience what God proffered in love to him because that love had been demonstrated in the interest of all the world. "So we are ambassadors for Christ," Paul explains, "since God is making his appeal through us" (5:20).

In Ephesians 2:13-16 Paul discusses reconciliation as it relates to the removal of the previous division that existed between Jews and Gentiles. This division was based on several separating factors: religious differences as well as legal, cultural, racial and social differences. In a bold and declarative announcement, Paul states that God's reconciling deed in Christ Jesus has changed that distancing division altogether and has made the two groups one in his sight.

Then follows that grand announcement about the privileged participation that believing Gentiles now have, on equal footing, with believing Jews in God's "household," the church. Here we see a wider social application of the spiritual effects of reconciliation with God: the fence that once stood between people groups is no longer valid.

The expected relationship between God's people, whatever their previous backgrounds, now demands oneness and equality with persons of both groups. They become fully related. No previous group is dominant or subservient anymore. Social distance must no longer be the order, and a sense of oneness and equality must prevail when the previously-honored differences seek to intrude themselves. All of this is surely in view in 2 Corinthians 5:16 where Paul states that he could no longer "regard [anyone] from a [merely] human point of view."

All in all, our task as reconcilers requires on our part this same distinct focus and frame of reference: the distinct focus is on every other person as someone of value, whatever the facts that make that person different or difficult or distant, and the distinct frame of reference is an attitude of forgiveness and inclusiveness that can claim every person for restored relation and closeness to God and ourselves.

> They drew a circle that left me out,
> Heretic, rebel, a thing to flout.
> But love and I had the wit to win.
> We drew a circle and took him in.[1]

Paul explains that having become reconciled to God, he had been given a ministry as a reconciler. This means that Paul had to learn to see other people as God sees them; he had to be open to relate to persons with a view to their God-given worth; he had to have an interest in their deepest human need and believe in their

---

1   From the poem "Outwitted" by Edwin Markham.

potential through divine grace. This focus and framework forms the basis for human community in full. I like the way Howard Thurman once voiced it: "One person, standing in his [or her] own place, penetrates deeply into the life of another in a manner that makes possible an ingathering within that other life, and thus the wildness is gentled out of a personality at war with itself."[2]

We too can develop this ability, this way of relating to another, provided there is, first, a deep gratitude to God for having reconciled us to himself through his Son, Jesus Christ, and provided there is, second, an intentional concern to be a reconciling person. God has been open to us, despite our previous distance from him and the difficulties we placed in his path toward us. Our own gratitude for having been reconciled to God must inform our work as God makes his appeal to others through us.

There is for each of us a vertical dimension in our experience as a Christian, whereby God and the self are related by a personal faith. And there is for each of us a horizontal dimension to our Christian experience since we must interact with other humans. The greater our awareness that personal faith in Christ— that vertical dimension—and the obedient outworking of that faith in dealing with others—that horizontal dimension—*always form a cross.*

This must be remembered as we go about our work in the world because reconciling people is always a costly service. It cost Jesus his life to reconcile us to God, and we cannot be reconciling agents without undergoing some demands which will make us feel the press of a cross upon our lives. Reconciliation is Cross-work! It was perhaps with this in mind that Howard Thurman explained,

---

2   Howard Thurman, *Disciplines of the Spirit* (Harper & Row, Publishers, 1963), 108.

"The discipline of reconciliation for the religious [person] cannot be separated from the discipline of religious experience."[3]

Our task as reconcilers does demand discipline. It demands discipline informed by hope and inspired by love; discipline that is courageous in facing divisive walls, hostility, and hate; discipline that refuses to cower before the barriers that block human harmony; discipline that properly and steadily informs, encourages, and energizes the self to engage others, that readies one to take the initiative to touch another life, deal with injurious wrongs, and establish a needed relation. Such discipline demands an active love, a healthy self-image, the willingness to risk oneself, and a sense of being companioned in the task by God.

Our Lord's mandate that we evangelize (Matt. 28:18-20) is at one with our assignment to be reconcilers (2 Cor. 5:19-20). Both service roles have been entrusted to us, and both are strategically related. All of us will readily agree that the church has not only a mandated role to bring people together but the potential to do so. We are doing our proper work when we help people experience forgiveness and learn how to forgive. Such is our task. And we should be mindful of our Lord's encouraging pronouncement: "Blessed are the peacemakers, for they will be called children of God" (Matt. 5:9).

This beatitude, preserved only in Matthew's account of the Sermon on the Mount, seems to be addressed to those who have a heart for helping others to become reconciled. In the setting of that day, it could well have been a word of caution from Jesus to those in the listening crowd who were of zealotic bent, those listeners who were sympathetic to militaristic attempts to remove the yoke of Roman rule from the Jewish nation's neck.

3   Ibid., 121.

Was this beatitude from Jesus a warning word that the only *holy* crusades are crusades for peace? The beatitude reminds us that God's kingdom is not promoted by violence, that peacemaking is the only way to shape the best future, and that those who work at reconciling people are God's true children.

May God's guidance abound as we patiently pursue His agenda as reconcilers to bring people to himself and to each other, drawn by the bands of authentic love.

SECTION V

WISDOM FROM THE GREATS CROSSING MASSEY'S PATH

EDITOR'S SECTION INTRODUCTION

by Edward L. Foggs,

General Director Emeritus,
Church of God Ministries (Anderson)

While a person of high achievement and accomplishment must engage in disciplined effort and dedication to achieve desired goals, no person can authentically claim to be singularly "self-made." All persons who excel in their fields of endeavor have somewhere along the way been mentored, influenced, inspired, and encouraged by others. Wise is the person who recognizes and acknowledges others who have helped to shape and inform their journey. Dr. James Earl Massey has graciously and insightfully identified many persons who have touched his life. In turn, his influence has touched many of their lives.

Dr. Massey not only acknowledges many such persons, but identifies specific impacts they have had on his life and the variety of interactions he has had with them. As I read his reflections, I was impressed by the diversity and broad scope of their influence. Some were senior to him in age; some were contemporaries; others were of oncoming generations. One of Dr. Massey's gifts is his ability to relate to persons across generations, cultures, disciplines, and ethnicities.

Massey writes of Howard Thurman as a Black pulpit master who inspired him by his keen insight as he proclaimed God's message.

He and Thurman were kindred spirits in their probing style and clarity of presentation. Raymond S. Jackson was Dr. Massey's chief pastoral influencer. Under whose tutelage he developed as a young ministerial aspirant. Jackson helped to instill a passionate concern for race relations within the Church of God movement (Anderson) in keeping with this church's message of Christian unity. Likewise, Jackson modeled with dignity and distinction the power of the pulpit for prophetic preaching and opened doors of ministry opportunity for Dr. Massey.

The association and friendship of Dr. Massey with Martin Luther King, Jr., was particularly significant given the era in which King lived. Not all leaders and preachers—White or Black—were eager to be identified with Dr. King, partly because he was considered highly controversial by many who were less inclined to the non-violent philosophy he advocated. Massey was one of the voices that spoke for non-violence, hope, and reconciliation in the face of Dr. King's assassination. He and Dr. King were privileged to visit and interact personally in the formative years of the civil rights movement.

Another giant preacher, Gardner C. Taylor, was greatly admired by Dr. Massey. He describes Taylor as having a legendary ministry and expresses admiration for his pulpit gifts and the way he treated biblical texts. Massey provided opportunity for several of his seminary students in Anderson to experience the ministry of Gardner Taylor in New York City.

In a stellar tribute to Robert Smith, Jr., Massey expresses high esteem for one who was a generational junior. Smith had been one of Massey's former students into whose life he had sown and who, in turn, inspired Dr. Massey by the development of his gifted leadership. Smith is further referenced in Dr. Massey's "Foreword" to one of Smith's books.

Dr. Massey deemed it a special honor to succeed Andrew L. Johnson as Dean of the Chapel of Tuskegee University. They had met in earlier years while both served in the military. Massey felt that Johnson had modeled a quality of leadership and friendship that enriched his own life.

As a gifted and prolific writer, Dr. Massey credits Harold Phillips with discovering, developing, and nurturing his gifts as an author. He facilitated the publication of some of his sermons and articles in the *Gospel Trumpet/Vital Christianity*. From these early promptings, Massey went on to write for a broad range of editors and publishers.

The partnerships and relationships that Massey established over the years include significant engagement with William Pannell. Their paths have intersected in a variety of mutually edifying and enriching ventures. Their work was international and ecumenical in scope. They spoke into issues in religious circles that might have been neglected had they not jointly raised their voices.

Those who know Dr. Massey well have recognized mystical qualities to his ministry. It comes as no surprise, therefore, that he wrote the "Foreword" to Thomas S. Kepler's *An Anthology of Devotional Literature*. Massey found creativity, inspiration, and motivation in his quest for enriching the inner spiritual life. He has written several volumes bearing upon the subject.

As one who has been intimately engaged in the training and mentoring of theological students for pastoring and other aspects of ministry, Dr. Massey finds high appreciation for the efforts of others who provide guidance and wisdom for the task. Thus, of no surprise is his commendation of David Markle as editor of *First Steps to Ministry*.

Dr. Massey and one of his colleagues, Dr. Gustav Jeeninga, pioneered team teaching in Bible courses and religious studies at

Anderson University. Always eager to explore new ways of learning, Massey was open to venture with others in the search for venues for enriching the educational experience in ways that make it inspirational and enjoyable as well as highly informative.

It was my honor to have Dr. Massey write the "Foreword" to *Christ Compels Us!*, a volume I authored for the annual International Convention of the Church of God. As he so ably does, Massey added stature to my labor of love. There is neither time nor space here to share our many interactions across the years. He has enriched my life immeasurably.

There are a couple of verses from *A Psalm of Life* by Henry Wadsworth Longfellow that seem an appropriate conclusion to this section introduction.

> Lives of great men all remind us
> We can make our lives sublime,
> And departing leave behind us
> Footprints on the sands of time.
>
> Footprints that perhaps another,
> Sailing o'er life's solemn main,
> A forlorn and shipwrecked brother,
> Seeing, shall take heart again.

Even as Dr. Massey found footprints in the sands of time as he journeyed, his own footprints will be seen far beyond his lifetime, and surely they will bless generations yet unborn.

Tributes to Honored Leaders

The
Burdensome

Joy

of
Preaching

James Earl Massey

39

HOWARD THURMAN

by James Earl Massey

Originally appeared in James Earl Massey's Aspects of My
Pilgrimage (Anderson University Press, 2002), 64-66. Used
by permission.

I first heard Dr. Howard Thurman preach in Detroit in the Spring of 1949. He had come to preach for three days during the annual Lenten services sponsored by the Metropolitan Detroit Council of Churches. The contents of the three sermons delivered by Dr. Thurman are still vivid in my memory. I quickly understood why he was renowned as a black pulpit master.

I was moved by his preaching, very deeply moved, partly because what he said was so insightful, partly because hearing it all validated my own spiritual quest and findings in a way that no other preacher's words or pulpit approach had ever done, and partly because of the realization of divine presence I experienced in connection with his witness.

As I listened, understood his witness, and experienced God in my spirit, I experienced then and there that Dr. Howard Thurman and I were inwardly kin. I knew that I had found a preacher whose insights spoke to the depths of my own spirit and yearning after God. Listening to Dr. Thurmond preach across those three days reinforced my thought that preaching must give a hearer access to God. I was privileged to meet with Howard Thurman on many other occasions in the years which followed. By a sure providence, he and I developed a deep and enriching friendship that affected my life and ministry at crucial levels of importance.

Howard Thurman did not preach like most of the African-American preachers I had heard. There was no stormy struggle in his manner, no loud blaring of his words. His was rather softly spoken, assured and assuring witness, a statement that seemed to be more like an "inside word" about some treasure truth and not an outside attempt to break into the truth. His style seemed so uniquely at one with his subject.

Thurman helped me experience spoken truth more vividly than any preacher I have ever heard before. I took note of this as something other than the effects of a mere pulpit manner or an oratorical prowess. His message and manner made me sense again that wholeness of being which since a child I had come to believe belongs to the experience of hearing the Word of God!

During the spring of 1949, inspired by Howard Thurman, I sensed at a deeper level that a message and its medium should be in strict relation, and I decided that I would seek the best means possible to give a clear, God-honoring, and worship-inspiring witness about the truth entrusted to me as a preacher.

40

RAYMOND S. JACKSON

by James Earl Massey

Originally appeared in *Vital Christianity* (February 1989), 18-19,
with excerpts from James Earl Massey, *Raymond S. Jackson:
A Portrait* (Warner Press, 1967). Used by permission.

I t is not too much to say that, as regards the matter of race relations within the Church of God (Anderson), the influence of Raymond S. Jackson was in many respects greater than that of any other Black prior to his time. His position as chairperson of the Ministerial Assembly of the National Association of the Church of God was largely responsible for this result. The Ministerial Assembly held the guidance and direction of the Association's work. Jackson chaired the Assembly from 1940 to 1955.

Although he began his ministry officially in the Church of God in 1920, when he was twenty-eight, Jackson had known earlier that the prompting call of the Lord was upon him for the work of preaching. His first preaching took place in Vandalia, Michigan, the same town where he grew up. Jackson stayed in that area of Michigan for three years and worked between Vandalia and Three Rivers.

He was ordained in 1922 in Kalamazoo, Michigan. Using Kalamazoo as his base of operations as well as a pastorate, Jackson moved in and out of Michigan on call, serving churches here and there across the nation, and serving with distinction. By experience and faithful work, he was in increasing demand as a preacher. Jackson's combined background, talents, and skills fitted him for several other roles across the years of his ministry. In terms of leadership offices, Jackson's greatest distinction was gained as longtime chairperson of the National Ministerial Assembly.

The National Association represents a creative venture on the part of Black churches to cooperate in advancing the work of the Church of God among the Black community in America in particular. Through the camp meeting, which it sponsors annually in West Middlesex, Pennsylvania, the National Association provides a time for togetherness and planning for those who support it, a time for sharing, preaching, education, and consultation. The National Association has been a means for the development of both leaders and churches. Its program has helped to condition the leadership and life of the predominantly Black churches within the Church of God (Anderson), especially those churches situated in the North.

It is true that the development of the National Association has proceeded along racial lines. It is true that such a line of development has both directly and indirectly kept the questions of integration in the background. It is also true that strained relations between the blacks and whites in the Church of God during 1913-1918 influenced the later growth of the National Association.

But *it is not true* that the National Association *began* as a reaction against racial problems. The beginnings of that work were rooted in religious, not racial, concerns. Originally known and chartered as "The Western Pennsylvania Industrial Camp-Grounds of the Church of God," the concern was first for camp meeting work. Later circumstances, however, influenced many of those who began to support the Association to use the organization along racial lines.

By the time he became chairperson of the Ministerial Assembly of the National Association in 1940, Jackson had not only determined his own approach to the matter of race relations in the Church of God, he had made his views and convictions known within the churches across the nation. The Black community of churches did have particular problems, but he was determined to work out solutions for them with the rest of the church and not in isolation or separation from the church.

Jackson had come to see and understand that the prevailing patterns would be bettered only by proper handling by brothers and sisters in unity. He knew that race lines had been too highly regarded—by all. He saw the practicality of the West Middlesex Camp Meeting. He saw how strained relations within the church had made the development patterns of the National Association so largely racial. He knew the problems, but he was also intent to help provide direction in the light of the Church of God theme of unity.

That Jackson became chairperson of the Association's Ministerial Assembly had more than passing significance. He was involved, organizationally, in both the work handled at Anderson and that handled at West Middlesex. His influence extended in both directions, and he used it in both directions.

Jackson knew the dangers that lurk in divided interests and divisive planning. But he also knew the powers inherent within group loyalty and ready militancy on the part of the Blacks for claiming better conditions. Jackson thus spoke for the Black leaders in presenting a case before the leaders at Anderson; as spokesperson for the majority of the Black churches and leaders in the North, his influence was considerable indeed.

During his years as chairperson, Jackson guided the National Association—through its Ministerial Assembly—in the expansion of its influence across the nation. He was responsible for the bylaws adopted in 1947, under which the Assembly governed itself for many years. He discouraged the attitude of the National Association being a work for Blacks only. He insisted that the spirit and intent for unity should be observed and obeyed. He advised that the National Association should show the way of toward unity.

Jackson did, on occasion, guide the Ministerial Assembly in several protest actions in order to let the leaders of boards and agencies at Anderson know the mind of the Black leaders on various matters. One case was a long-term protest against the use of markings in the *Yearbook* of the Church of God to designate a minister or a church as "colored."

Raymond S. Jackson had come a long way on that road to which God directed him when he was converted. He had disadvantages but faced them. He made mistakes, but he also made history. As Jackson himself often remarked, quoting an old proverb: "He who never made a mistake never made anything else." He died in January, 1983, after some fifty-five years in the ministry. During those years he nurtured me in his congregation and then mentored me as his ministerial assistant. From his example I learned much about preaching.

There were varied elements in Jackson's pulpit power. He knew the importance and eloquence of the Christian experience. He felt the joy of a divine call to preach. He sensed the preaching values in the texts he used. He brought to bear upon his work a creative imagination and a rich background of human experience. He did not subdue the emotional factors involved in handling the Word of God when addressing an audience. He knew the power and use of an illustration. He knew what to do while in his "study-workshop." He knew the integrity and urgency of the preaching ministry. He dared to preach adventurously, not avoiding what is unpopular and controversial.

41

MARTIN LUTHER KING, JR.

by James Earl Massey

Originally appeared in James Earl Massey's *Aspects of My Pilgrimage* (Anderson University Press, 2002), 173, 246-250. Used by permission.

I t was through Rev. Allen A. Banks that I first met Martin Luther King, Jr. A friend of the King family, and as pastor of Second Baptist Church of Detroit, Banks was a staunch supporter of King's leadership during the Montgomery Bus Boycott, and earlier had hosted him as a guest preacher in his Detroit pulpit while King was a doctoral student at Boston University School of Theology. It was Banks and others who helped to arrange King's first engagement as a speaker for the Detroit Council of Churches' Noon Lenten Services, and it was during King's visit for those services in 1958 that I got to meet and converse with him for the first time. Afterward, whenever King came to Detroit, Gwendolyn and I were usually invited to attend the service or function for which he came, and joined him and our mutual friends for an after—service time at one of their homes.

In April, 1963, I was part of the planning committee and welcome party that met Dr. King at the airport when he came to speak at Cobo Hall at the end of a "Freedom Walk" down Woodward

Avenue. There also was the time when I was asked to fill in for King when he could not get to Detroit in time to preach during a Lenten service engagement at Central Methodist Church.

I will never forget that fateful Thursday evening in April, 1968, when the news that Martin Luther King, Jr., had been shot filled the airways. Rage, looting, arson, and rioting swamped Detroit and other great cities across the land. On that fateful evening, I was busy in the studio of WWJ-TV preparing for a video-taping session with our senior choir for a telecast scheduled for Sunday, April 7. The choir was taking a break and I was taking a last look at my sermon manuscript when the studio director interrupted me.

"Pardon me, Pastor," he whispered, "but there is some news that I just received over the wire service. We have not announced it to the public yet, so you are perhaps the first preacher in Detroit to know this. We have just been told that Dr. Martin Luther King, Jr., has been shot in Memphis. I thought you would want to know this before going on the air."

The news stunned me. I did not panic but my pulse increased. Knowing about the tragedy definitely affected the tone of my sermon. Interestingly, my sermon title was "God Still Loves the World" based on John 3:16. I felt sifted as I prayed for composure before the red light went on in the studio. Afterward, when I broke the news to the choir about the shooting, the singers recoiled in shock, horrified over the happening. Everyone was eager to get home, fearful of what might happen on the streets of Detroit once the news filled the city.

Later that night I received a call at home from the Executive Director of the Detroit Council of Churches. He asked if I would join in a memorial service in King's memory the next day and bring a brief address. I agreed. My tribute to King, prepared late that Thursday night, was delivered to a packed congregation of worshipers in the sanctuary of downtown Detroit's Central Methodist Church. Then, on the morning of the day of King's funeral, I was interviewed on a talk show aired on one of the Detroit news stations. The host asked questions about my relationship with the late Dr. King and sought my reactions to having lost him as leader and friend. He also invited call-in questions.

I answered the questions openly but with diplomacy, aware that not everyone understood and appreciated the tactic of non-violent civil disobedience and non-cooperation as a means for social change. I avoided any offending advocacy as I answered the questions put to me. Someone asked why it was that violence occurred so often when King led marches. I explained the concept of non-violent protest as a way to bring to public view some unfair treatment or discriminatory law or social problem, and how a march calculated to project reasonable and public-minded citizens to take action towards correcting an injustice can also offend persons who resist the changes being sought. The questioner voiced the question with civility and a tone of respectful inquiry and I answered it sensitively and constructively.

I had been invited to attend the funeral of Dr. King in Atlanta, with a seat reserved for me in Ebenezer Church, but I declined going, reasoning that I could best honor King's memory by serving elsewhere that week where I had earlier committed myself and where racial troubles had mounted.

42

GARDNER C. TAYLOR

by *James Earl Massey*

Originally appeared in *Our Sufficiency is of God:
Essays on Preaching in Honor of Gardner C. Taylor*, eds.
James Earl Massey, Timothy George, Robert Smith, Jr.
(Mercer University Press, 2010), 1-3.

When I graduated from Oberlin Graduate School of Theology, I felt a large measure of pride in knowing that, twenty-four years earlier, Doctor Gardner C. Taylor had graduated from there. He and I did not know each other then, but his graduation had a lot to do with mine.

I vividly recall a visit he made to Oberlin seminary during my student days there. I was looking out of a first-floor classroom window, pondering a statement the professor had just made. I noticed Dr. Walter Marshall Horton standing on the walkway beside one of the colonnades. He was talking to someone I recognized. It was Dr. Taylor. The two of them stopped briefly at several capitals along the colonnade and Dr. Horton was talking as he successively pointed upward to the limestone facial likenesses of graduate school faculty peering down above the two of them. The newest likeness was that of Leonard Stidley, one of Dr. Taylor's teachers.[1] I watched as Dr. Taylor listened attentively and looked up appreciatively and admiringly.

Dr. Taylor might or might not recall that visit and that happening, but I clearly do. Watching it all gave me a sense of the regard Dr. Taylor's teachers held for him, and I took note of their respect. That watching also allowed me a brief reprieve from wrestling with the intricacies of some difficult coursework and from thinking about the burden I then carried as the founding pastor of a steadily growing church. Seeing Dr. Taylor there at that time, and aware of his already legendary ministry, I remembered that he had once "sat" where I was then sitting. His visit was for me a providential happening. It quickened my faith, encouraged my hope, and strengthened my diligence. I thanked God and took courage.

Dr. Taylor became a figure of encouragement for me at that difficult time in my life, and his prior graduation from Oberlin in 1940 had a lot to do, twenty-four years later, with mine. Interestingly, it was during an Oberlin alumni gathering that we later met formally, and that tie has been one of the many factors that has blessed the bond between us across more than thirty years. He led and nurtured numerous congregations through his ministry and inspired generations of preachers both by what he has said and by what he represented every time he stepped into a pulpit. I have always admired his avid preparation to preach and how he balanced a focused word with a sense of space for the hearer.

Unlike many, he never drowned hearers in a roiling sea of words. Through apt imagery, he rather supplied rafts of meaning to keep people afloat during the storms in their lives. His mastery of descriptive language continues to tutor multitudes of ministers

---

1   For a story about the stone likenesses adorning the Boswell Quadrangle colonnades, see John Kearney, "Carved in Stone," *Oberlin Alumni Magazine* 92/2 (Spring 1996), 14-17.

about how to speak meaningfully to common experience. He has used strict forms in his sermonizing, and yet his preaching has remained dramatically flexible and accommodating as to timing, approach, voice levels, and styles of utterance. The evolution of his craftsmanship has been duly studied and rightly honored in academic treatments, especially in the more recent treatments by Gerald Lamont Thomas (2004) and L. Susan Bond (2003).

Dr. Taylor has shown a gift for prioritizing what matters most in treating a text: respect, trust, centeredness, clarity, conviction, and readiness to climax the message with a Christ-honoring call to faith and hope. His sermons have never been self-regarding. Nothing ever seems to say, "Well, here I am!" His has been a voice dedicated to spreading the gospel and helping people know the assuring benediction of God's grace.

My final years as Dean of Anderson School of Theology coincided with Dr. Taylor's final years as pastor of Concord Baptist Church of Christ in Brooklyn, and there were occasions when some of our students traveled there to see and hear him before he retired. They all returned confessing their joy at having experienced the integrity of his preaching, the nobility of his craftsmanship, and the graciousness of his hospitality. I wanted those seminarians to experience the radiance and contagion that attends "a worker who has no need to be ashamed, rightly explaining the word of truth" (2 Tim. 2:15). He truly is a *Titan*, standing tall and strong after great struggles and exemplary service across many years.

43

ANDREW L. JOHNSON

by James Earl Massey

Originally appeared in *The Chapel Bulletin*, September 1983, after James Massey, as Dean of the Chapel at Tuskegee University, introduced his honored predecessor in that prestigious role. Used by permission.

The year was 1952. The place was Salzburg, Austria. Chaplain Weldon H. Barnett, post chaplain at Camp Saslfelden, and I, his assistant and driver, were at Camp Roeder. He was to give a character guidance lecture to one of our engineer companies stationed there. After the lecture, I accompanied Chaplain Barnett to the office of the post chaplain of Camp Roeder where we were treated to afternoon tea.

How delightfully surprised and proud I was to discover that the post chaplain there was a black man—a spry, well-groomed, intelligent-looking black Major! The name-plate on this desk read "Andrew L. Johnson." I was duly impressed. Sometime later, while reading the 1952 *Negro Yearbook*, I observed that Chaplain (Major) Andrew L. Johnson was one of ninety-one black chaplains on active duty at that time, that he was one of twenty with the rank of major, and that he was an African Methodist Episcopal minister.

My memory of that first meeting with Chaplain Johnson was stirred in full in August 1983, thirty-one years later as I answered his long-distance call inviting me to the Tuskegee Chapel to preach in October. Upon hearing his name, my memory was triggered. I asked him, "Have you ever served as an Army chaplain?" "Yes," he replied. "Were you ever stationed in Austria?" I questioned. Again, he answered, "Yes." I then said, "Sir, I believe I know you." A time of reminiscence followed and a meaningful trip to Tuskegee University where Chaplain Johnson had been serving as campus minister of nearly nineteen years.

How privileged I continue to feel as the ministerial successor here at Tuskegee to such a noble servant of the Lord. Dr. Andrew Lincoln Johnson has been a friend and more. His nineteen years of exemplary ministry as University Chaplain at Tuskegee surely merited him the honor he now holds as the first *Chaplain Emeritus* here. Today we are all privileged to hear him preach again from the pulpit he graced with dignity and dramatic impact across so many years.

44

ROBERT SMITH, JR.

by James Earl Massey

"Mentored to Minister: Sermonic Tribute to
Robert Smith, Jr." Delivered during the
E. K. Bailey Expository Preaching Conference at the
Concord Baptist Church, Dallas, Texas, on the occasion of
the E. K. and V. M. Bailey "Living Legend" Award, July 13, 2017

Text: Philippians 2:19-23

My feelings run deep and rise high as I stand here today, stirred by the obvious correspondence between Timothy's experiences under the masterful mentoring of the Apostle Paul and our honoree's experiences while "sitting under" his now sainted mentors. My feelings are also from recollections from my own treasured time of learning ministry, more than seventy years ago now, under the tutelage of two pastoral giants, Dr. Raymond Samuel Jackson (1892-1983) and Dr. Howard Washington Thurman (1899-1981).

"Sitting under" them was my fortunate privilege, and I shudder even to question what my life would have been like had I not been blessed by the practice of an apprenticeship which has been germane to the training of ministers within the Black Church tradition.[1] I am confident that many of you remember your time of on-the-job training when you were supervised by an experienced minister, that time of watching them, learning from them about how to minister, and you are now grateful, as was Timothy, for "those from whom you learned" (2 Tim. 3:14) how to preach and minister.

Timothy and Paul

Timothy and his mother Eunice were probably converted during Paul's first ministry in Lystra (Acts 14:6-20), a small but significant Roman colony in south-central Asia Minor. When Paul returned there about two years later, he was impressed by reports about how young Timothy had developed in faith, and also by his standing within the fellowship. Thus impressed, Paul invited the young man to accompany him in ministry (Act 16:3). Timothy had learned the Scriptures as a lad at the feet of his mother Eunice, a Jewess, and his spiritual growth and giftedness had readied him to learn the duties and disciplines of ministry, and he did, admirably, as he worked in tandem with the Apostle.

Paul led; Timothy assisted, and learned to lead. They worked together in Thessalonica (1 Thess. 3:5), Corinth (1 Cor. 4:17), in Philippi, Troas, Miletus, as well as during Paul's lengthy and traumatic ministry in Ephesus. Working with Paul, his mentor, Timothy developed skills and faithfully managed ministry assignments. Paul even referred to Timothy as a "co-worker" (Rom. 16:21), an evident description of honor. Thus, those deeply affectionate

---

1   For an insightful treatment of how pulpit legend Gardner Calvin Taylor (1918-2015) learned to preach so well, see Jared E. Alcantara's praise for the Black Church tradition of mentoring preachers, *Learning from a Legend: What Gardner C. Taylor Can Teach Us about Preaching* (Cascade Books, 2016), esp. 68-83.

words of greeting we see in Paul's first letter to his younger but highly trusted colleague: "To Timothy, my true child in the faith" (1 Tim. 1:2).[2]

Mentored to minister, Timothy had disported himself so well that he was sometimes sent to "stand in" for the Apostle, as we learn from 1 Thess. 3:1-5, and 1 Cor. 4:17; 16:10, 11. Paul was informing the congregation at Philippi that, God permitting, he was sending Timothy to meet with them, to serve them in his absence, and to bring back word on how the church there was faring.

Confined in prison as he was writing, Paul was solicitous about how the young congregation he had founded in Philippi was faring, about how the believers there were developing in the faith. Paul knew what every seasoned pastor knows, that believers live in daily contact with threatening evils, that believers need to be assured as they face those evils, that they need to see their leader and feel the leader's caring presence. They need to hear a timely, focused, biblically-based word of faith that can arm them to effectively deal with evil.

Paul knew that Timothy was prepared for such a ministry, so he was planning to dispatch him to Philippi, and he wrote to inform the congregation there to expect Timothy and to ready themselves for his visit. Mentored by Paul for ministry, Timothy would not just "stand in" for him, but more importantly he would distinctively and courageously stand up, speak up, and lovingly serve those believers under the anointing of their Servant Lord.

Note, then, not only how Paul expressed confidence in Timothy, but also how Paul went on to commend Timothy, referring to him

---

2   For more on Paul's relationship with Timothy, Titus, and others he
    mentored, see F. F. Bruce, *The Pauline Circle* (Wm. B. Eerdmans Publishing Co.,
    1985), esp. 29-34. See also James Earl Massey, *1 & 2 Timothy, Titus, Philemon*
    [Immersion Bible Studies] (Abingdon Press, 2012).

as "likeminded," meaning, as the Greek term (*isopsuchos*) suggests, that Timothy was an "equal soul." Paul was commending Timothy as one whose feelings and concerns were the same as his, and presumably about the believers in Philippi because Timothy was with Paul when the congregation there was established through the Apostle's ministry.[3]

Paul *knew* Timothy. Timothy had proved himself. Thus came that additional comment of Paul about him: "But Timothy's worth you know, how like a son with a father he has served with me in the work of the gospel" (Phil. 2:22). Mentored for ministry, Timothy was also ready to mentor others, and he did so later as pastor in the teeming and tempestuous idol-worshipping city of Ephesus.

Timothy and Robert

What I have been reporting from our text about Timothy, his character, his relationship with a trusted mentor, and his subsequent readiness and resourcefulness for ministry, I can report about our honoree, Dr. Robert Smith, Jr. Converted in 1956, Robert sat regularly and attentively under the ministry of Dr. Elijah Lee Alexander at the Rose Chapel Missionary Baptist Church in Cincinnati, Ohio, and next under Dr. Robert Franklin Hamilton, Jr., who succeeded Dr. Alexander.

Sensing and accepting a call to the ministry, Robert preached his first sermon at Rose Chapel. Beginning in 1968, he took membership and served as a local minister at New Mission Missionary Baptist Church, and was further mentored there by pastor Dr. George Quincy Brown. Like Paul, who was impressed by Timothy's

---

3   See Peter T. O'Brien, *Commentary on Philippians. A Commentary on the Greek Text* [New International Greek Testament Commentary series] (Wm. B. Eerdmans Publishing Co., 1991), 315.

spiritual growth and evident gifts, Dr. Brown was impressed by Robert Smith, and Brown chose Robert to serve as his assistant. Following Dr. Brown, Robert became senior pastor and faithfully served there from 1976 to 1995.

Mentored for ministry by his pastors, Robert was additionally blessed by formal degree studies at God's Bible School (1970), Cincinnati Bible College (1984), and Southern Baptist Theological Seminary (M.Div., 1988; Ph.D., 1993). His wisdom and insights from first-hand ministry responsibilities during a long-term urban pastorate at New Mission Missionary Baptist Church in Cincinnati have blessed his many and regular engagements as a guest preacher in North America, Australia, and elsewhere; his services at denominational and ecumenical gatherings, and his signal academic appointments, first as the Carl E. Bates Professor of Preaching at Southern Baptist Theological Seminary and next as the Charles T. Carter Baptist Professor of Preaching at Beeson Divinity School of Samford University in Birmingham, Alabama.

James and Robert

Like Paul knew Timothy *I know Robert Smith, Jr.* We met in 1992. He was working toward his doctorate at the time at Southern Theological Seminary, and Dr. James W. Cox, a senior Professor of Preaching there, was guiding his studies, Dr. Cox and I were friends and had worked across several years team-teaching homiletics and critiquing the sermons of working pastors who came to a Preaching Clinic hosted each year at a resourceful church in Dayton, Ohio, pastored by our mutual friend David Grubbs.

It was through the good graces of Dr. Cox that I was the E. Y. Mullins Lecturer at Southern Seminary in 1981. At a later time when I spoke there at Southern, Robert Smith, Jr. was in the audience and afterward asked Dr. Cox about the feasibility of discussing with me aspects of his intended dissertation. Dr. Cox encouraged him to seek my judgment and counsel. Robert did and soon I knew that I was in touch with a person who was serious about life and living, particularly about life in Christ and living out one's calling. Later Robert enrolled in a preaching course I was teaching at Anderson School of Theology.

Robert impressed me by his focus, his stamina, his work ethic, his punctuality, his persistence, and his sense of mission. Early on, it was evident to me that he had what it would take to become a teacher of preaching. He completed his dissertation and received his doctoral degree. His aptness and readiness for the teaching profession was validated by Southern Theological Seminary when the administrators chose him to teach there as the Carl E. Bates Professor of Preaching. I watched as his teaching ministry gained deserved notice, and I was greatly delighted when in 1997 he accepted the call from Beeson Divinity School to teach there.

His teaching ministry at Beeson has been so well-received and regarded that in 2015 the Samford University Board of Trustees elected him to be the first incumbent to hold the recently-endowed Charles T. Carter Baptist Chair of Divinity in Preaching. That endowed chair is named after Baptist pastor Charles T. Carter, a long-time Samford trustee.

The appointment of Robert Smith, Jr., to hold that newly-endowed chair in preaching at Samford University's Beeson Divinity School was in every respect a significant action, and it demanded an academic celebration. The celebration took form as a community worship service in the divinity school's ornate chapel on September 22, 2015. Mindful of our relationship, Dean Timothy George asked me to share in the service of installation, and I led the gathered assembly in a prayer of dedication as the Beeson faculty and staff laid hands on Dr. Smith and his wife Dr. Wanda Taylor Smith.[4]

Dr. Robert Smith, Jr. not only occupies an endowed chair, but he is one of the few African Americans who occupy endowed chairs in the nation's leading colleges and universities, and he is the first African American to hold an endowed chair in Alabama, the key state within the Deep South. He was mentored for ministry and now mentors others.

---

4   For a report about the installation service, see Kristen R. Padilla, "Long in the Making," *Beeson Magazine* 2016, 24-25.

45

HAROLD L. PHILLIPS

by James Earl Massey

Originally appeared in *Vital Christianity*, July 31, 1977, 17. Used
by permission.

Among the many professional and personal contacts a writer is apt to make in life's pilgrimage, none is more crucial than one's relationship with an editor. One of the great moments of my life came thirty years ago when I gained the favor of Harold L. Phillips, who then was book editor of Gospel Trumpet Company (now Warner Press, Inc.). I had preached at a neighboring congregation, and the pastor, J. Willard Chitty, liked the sermon so well that he asked me to let him send the manuscript to Anderson for possible use in the *Gospel Trumpet*. I gave him the sermon, never suspecting that his suggestion was opening to me a contact of immense promise and fulfillment. But that is how I began my now long-term friendship with Dr. Harold L. Phillips.

Across these years I have learned to appreciate Dr. Phillips' management style as an Editor of Warner Press. He has been filled with appropriate suggestions and forward enough to provide steady undergirding for assignments accepted. His ministry as editor has had a pastoral flavor. He has helped to nurture gifts and encourage possibilities within many writers. I have been impressed by the manner in which he has shared responsibilities with his editorial staff, as well as his eagerness and ability to find, use, and develop an ever-wider cadre of writers to speak for the Lord to the church and world through our publications in the Church of God. As one among that list of writers he discovered and helped to develop, I gladly register my deep gratitude for his ministry as editor across these many years.

Dr. Phillips is to be lauded as well for his editorial perspectives. After searching out writers, he has helped to steer each one into specific areas of their own interest, abilities, and promise. Honoring four functions he outlined as guideposts for policy— evangelizing, indoctrination, publicizing, and undergirding (see May 29, 1977 *Vital Christianity*, p. 5)—Dr. Phillips has blessed the church by linking writers with appropriate areas of interest, insight, and competence.

The success of this venture on his part can be seen quite clearly as one examines the long list of persons (about 100) who became contributing and/or feature writers for *Gospel Trumpet/Vital Christianity* during his years as editor-in-chief (see June 12, 1977, *VC*, p. 24). And when one adds the names of those who became published authors of books under his editorship, the list is considerably lengthened. I am honored to be one of them.

The editorial balance Dr. Phillips achieved has become a standard, a model. Editor Phillips has given to the church a balanced diet of doctrine, prophetic moral concern, social insights, evangelical thrusts, a world perspective, and solid respect for the complex traditions of the church across the ages. A theologian in his own right, Editor Phillips has presided wisely over the range of writers he gathered to his side, and he always sought to maintain a balanced and representative climate for the ministry our publications have been planned to fulfill.

During his editorial ministry of more than twenty-six years, Dr. Phillips has stood up well in "fair weather and foul." He has handled successes with humility and disagreeing readers with a Christian openness and charitable aplomb. It has not been easy to maintain broadness and balance, and he did not have the approval of all when dealing with complex theological issues or crucial ethical and social questions such as we faced during the 1950s and 1960s. But Dr. Phillips kept courageously at it, with a stance both respectful and responsible, and he had a Christian temperament to match any criticisms.

Across many years now, Dr. Phillips has extended to many writers and to me the hospitality of the columns of our publications, and thereby the privilege of being read. I speak for them all in voicing this appreciation for his editorial ministry as this friend retires from his work, turning it over trustfully to other ready hands.

46

WILLIAM E. PANNELL

by James Earl Massey

The keynote address by James Earl Massey,
January 27, 2015, at Fuller Theological Seminary.
The occasion was the fortieth anniversary of the school's
African-American Studies Center which was being renamed
the "William E. Pannell Center of African American Studies."

A perceptive writer made a statement I will borrow as I stand to speak about my friend William E. Pannell. "I am only half of myself; my friends are the other half." William Pannell has long been one such friend in my life.

It didn't hurt that he and I both were born in Michigan. Nor does it hurt that, before he went to graduate school, we both had the experience of completing undergraduate degrees from Bible colleges, he from Fort Wayne Bible College and I from Detroit Bible College. Interestingly, it was his pastor and mentor, Dr. B. M. Nottage, who delivered the commencement address at my graduation. These factors helped us in understanding each other when we first met and conversed more than sixty years ago, and in the years since that blessed time our relationship has only deepened.

I have long admired and appreciated Bill's pioneering spirit. This spirit has been evidenced in many pursuits: his pioneering work with Youth for Christ, InterVarsity Christian Fellowship, the Tom Skinner Evangelistic Enterprise, the National Black Evangelical Association and most notably among other ventures his long-term tenure here at Fuller Theological Seminary, beginning with his service as the Board's first black member, and then as one of the seminary's most distinguished and longest serving faculty members.

But Bill was never actively pioneering in his own interest. His purpose-driven motive was Christian at its core, ever courageous and outgoing. He has opened windows in the church and academy to let in fresh air and increased light from the gospel, and he has opened the doors of service for many others. It was Bill who brought my name to the attention of the InterVarsity Fellowship which led to my membership on the InterVarsity Corporation for some yers. Many others here could give a good report how he helped them in one or more ways, particularly former students and working pastors who needed a listening ear, helping hand, and a well-placed word.

In November, 1966, Bill and I were in Berlin, Germany, two among about one thousand delegates from around the world who were attending the World Congress on Evangelism. Bill was there not only to attend but to deliver a major position paper to the delegates. The Congress theme was "One Race, One Gospel, One Task." Problematically, as we sat in sessions and listened to speeches for ten days, some of us noticed that no attention had been devoted in any position paper to the first part of the Congress theme, "one race," nor had any official paper about race been distributed for private reading.

I remember being part of a group of African-Americans who discussed this omission among ourselves and sought an audience with Carl F. H. Henry, the Congress chairman. Dr. Henry apologized on behalf of the planning committee and stated that the "one race" aspect of the Congress theme had been taken for granted, and therefore no one had been assigned to treat it publicly. Aware that the planning committee had blundered, Henry asked if we would be willing to work at developing a summary statement which could be included in the final report that would be distributed to the world press as an outcome of the Congress. We did, producing what at the time was considered the strongest statement evangelicals had ever made on the subject of race. It did appear in the final publication, *One Race, One Gospel, One Task* (1967).

William Pennell has been at the forefront, stimulating the church to rediscover and promote the biblical anthropology, engage itself in needed social action, and promote better race relations within American evangelicalism and the American society. His provocative 1968 book *My Friend, the Enemy* vividly narrates some of the sad experiences he had as a black Christian because of the inadequate anthropology of the white church culture in which he was reared, and yet remained open to regard the value and meaning of his diversity and that of others. He has courageously helped to redefine the issues for which majority culture definitions and approaches have proven inadequate, and he has led in working toward a more inclusive church life and witness.

William Pennell embraced Evangelicalism and his life and services have helped to advance it. In the mid-1970s, evangelical Christianity was growing faster in America than any other "brand" or religious movement active here, and it numbered more than forty million adherents at the time. Despite that growth, evangelicalism was not influencing the social level of American life to any measurable extent. Mindful of Evangelicalism's need to do so, William Pennell was not only prepared and positioned to assist in increasing that influence, but actively and ably worked to do so, and gently goaded and guided others to do so.

I stand proudly to honor him is my Christian brother, my valued friend, and a courageous Christian pioneer.

Select Book "Forewords"
by James Earl Massey

47

DOCTRINE THAT DANCES

by James Earl Massey

Dr. Massey's "Foreword" to Robert Smith, Jr.,
*Doctrine that Dances: Bringing Doctrinal Preaching and Teaching
to Life* (B & H Publishing Group, 2008), xiii-xiv.
Used by permission.

B ooks which treat the theme and craft of preaching steadily appear, answering the need among preachers for insight, inspiration, and encouragement to handle their perennial task, but books about how to sermonize Christian doctrine are comparatively few and far between.

There is a considerable span of years between Henry Sloan Coffin's *What to Preach* (1926) and Andrew W. Blackwood's *Doctrinal Preaching for Today* (1946), or between Merrill R. Abbey's *Living Doctrine in a Vital Pulpit* (1965) to Ronald J. Allen's *The Teaching Minister* (1991), all of them works prepared by seasoned and respected practitioners. Now Dr. Robert Smith, Jr., himself a seasoned and respected preacher, joins the ranks of those concerned to treat the preaching of doctrine. The insights he has shared here have been gathered from firsthand pulpit responsibilities in a long-term urban pastorate, many engagements as a guest preacher in denominational and ecumenical pulpits, and years of study and reflection and service teaching preaching in a respected divinity school.

Given his background and experience, Dr. Smith has offered something more than theory here, and he has shown both wisdom and warmth in handling his subject so expressively by letting his preaching style both dictate and dominate his expression. No overview of his treatment is necessary in this Foreword, but it must be stated that the foundational issue that binds these chapters is the importance of preaching doctrine, and to do so in a loving and lively treatment so that it is experienced as an expression of faith and a means to faith.

This book now takes its place among a steadily growing number of resources for those who preach, and rightfully so because the guidance and encouragement it offers can help preachers and their hearers to experience the benefits of which essential doctrines embody and make available.

In the introduction to one of his books about preaching, Charles Haddon Spurgeon (1834-1892), the celebrated Baptist preacher, commented thankfully about the warm reception his first book on the subject had received. He wrote: "It is comforting to know that you have aimed at usefulness, pleasant to believe that you have succeeded, and most of all encouraging to have been assured of it by the persons benefited."

Robert Smith, Jr., has written and released this present book with usefulness to preachers as its aim, and I commend it as timely, theologically apt, and readily beneficial. I have benefited and am glad to assure Dr. Smith that I have.

48

ANTHOLOGY OF DEVOTIONAL LITERATURE

by James Earl Massey

Originally appeared as the Foreword to
Thomas S. Kepler, *An Anthology of Devotional Literature*
(Evangel/Jordan Publishing, 2001), xvii-xviii.
Used by permission.

Reading materials which stimulate thought, stretch the mind, aid learning, spur creativity, and deepen our devotion to God are to be prized. When we read such works, touching other minds and hearts which have been stirred by devotion to God, when we react positively to their work, we reach up beyond ourselves and see deeper into ourselves while being steered into the new terrain of demanding truths and fresh paths for a richer life of faith.

This anthology, originally published a half-century ago by Thomas S. Kepler and now newly released in a fresh and enlarged format, is filled with such devotional materials. These are solid writings from persons whose lives exemplified the wide, deep, and multi-layered life of devotion to God. Some extracts are from those who betray a high level of emotion about their spiritual experiences, and they report eagerly what they found on their faith journey. Some others seek to spell out how the spiritual realms can be entered and fruitfully explored. Penetrating expressions fill this anthology with moral, intellectual and spiritual elements all intertwined, boldly addressed to the reader's mind and will, the head and heart.

The writings carry the open reader beyond formalism; they induce the reader to pray. John Wesley, in his *Journal* [1910 Curnock edition, Vol. 1, 467], confessed how he went beyond religious formalism after finding and reading William Law's *A Practical Treatise upon Christian Perfection,* and also Law's *A Serious Call to a Devout and Holy Life* (a selection from which appears in this anthology). Wesley's previous spiritual experience had been one of morbid sensitivity, constant introspection and search for counsel, and an extreme asceticism, but after contact with these books by William Law in 1727, Wesley experienced what he perceived as a direct touch of the hand of God upon his soul. Sound, experiential devotional materials made a difference in Wesley's spiritual life.

An incalculable gain awaits those who give themselves to prolonged involvement with the writings in this anthology. One gain is an enhanced understanding and disciplined use of devotional methods, and another is a heightened awareness of the long and rich tradition of devotional literature in Christian history. Throughout these pages both the common language and the common hungers of the soul are made clear, and an understanding is given about how serious believers can become "saints" in their time.

In the Preface prepared for the first edition of this anthology, editor Thomas S. Kepler mentioned ten ways in which the life of a Christian saint is conditioned through vital contact with God: (1) an intense love results that aids living with others; (2) an inner freedom is maintained through a trusting dependence upon God; (3) the will is strengthened to emulate Christ; (4) the desire deepens to assist others with their human journey and struggles; (5) a concern is established by which the practical side of things wins out over the theoretical; (6) an interest deepens for God's rule within and over one's life; (7) a continuous humility steadies the believer; (8) an eye is gained to see the potential of every person one encounters; (9) wisdom results by which to keep worship and social activity in proper relation; and (10) the believer's personal life becomes a channel of the light of the One who is The Light of the World.

Kepler set forth these as chief characteristics of the "saints" from whose writings he culled the selections chosen to fill his anthology. He viewed such persons as a "saving remnant" in the history of each age, but explained that these were but ordinary men and women whose spiritual capacities were conditioned at a high level because they were open to the will of God in their time and place.

Thomas Samuel Kepler (1897-1963) was himself a saintly person, and he deserves to be listed within "the fellowship of the saints." While it was out of his own reading that the anthology came into being, we must take into account Kepler's own deep interest in the devotional life as a believer if we are to begin to understand his choice of selections from its many notable representatives as he compiled materials for the first edition. Kepler's choices reflect not only the rich influence of spiritual writings upon his thought but also the deep current of spiritual life that fed his own soul.

I knew Thomas Kepler. He was my New Testament professor at Oberlin Graduate School of Theology and a mentor whose encouragement helped to sustain me during a time of stress in my life. Dr. Kepler was more than a man of the study, a scholar surrounded by learned volumes reflecting several languages mastered and several areas of knowledge explored. He was a patient teacher and an openhearted Christian believer whose office, home, and heart were all retreat places for those who knew him.

I read his anthology on *The Fellowship of the Saints* after meeting Dr. Kepler, stirred to do so because of what I sensed in him as he taught. I was challenged by his insights as an interpreter of classic religious experience, and his expertise in this area of mutual interest encouraged me to submit devotional materials of my own to his perusal before I submitted them for publication. His comments were always wise, apt, and timely, which helped me in my quest to write aptly in the devotional style.

Dr. Kepler died in the Spring of 1963 when I was in the middle of preparing a thesis under his guidance in the New Testament area. I had noticed his exceptionally slow pace as he walked up and down the stairs at the Graduate School Quadrangle, and now and again I had noticed him wincing when he shifted his sitting position at his classroom teacher's desk. I was sickeningly saddened by the news on campus one day that Dr. Kepler was in the hospital and had been diagnosed as terminally ill from cancer. I was one of three of his graduate students entrusted by Roger Hazelton, our Dean, to prepare and present the class lectures for his courses as Dr. Kepler lingered in the hospital.

His death shook us all. Interestingly, the final book from Dr. Kepler's pen was *The Meaning and Mystery of the Resurrection*, a work whose materials he had shared with us in one of his classes. The book was a fitting statement of his faith, and his life was a fitting tribute to his Lord. The present anthology, newly revised and enlarged by one of my own former students, Joe Allison, is a continuing witness through which Thomas Samuel Kepler points the way, with other notable saints, to a vital faith and a steadier step in this world.

49

FIRST STEPS TO MINISTRY

by James Earl Massey

Originally appeared as the Foreword to David Markle, ed.,
First Steps to Ministry: A Primer on a Life in Ministry
(Warner Press, 2001), v-vi. Used by permission.

T he form, focus, and substance of this book are rightly described as a "primer." The dictionary defines a primer as a book about elementary principles that underlie a subject, area of enquiry, a skill, or service-role. The word *underlie* is crucial because the principles which govern a meaningful ministry to people in matters that pertain to God must be known and honored if needed services are to be effective and sustained.

Christian ministry is indeed based upon, or rooted in, a heart that honors God, a mind nurtured by Christ, an ear opened to God's voice, a disciplined self, a gift-based role, a sense of accountability, and a spirit to serve. This book, addressed to persons taking the first steps to ministry, deals with such matters, and more.

This primer introduces the reader to accented areas of concern for effective, fruitful, and sustained ministry in the church and in the world, and it does so with so much more involved in the writing of each chapter than an apparent simplicity of presentation and understood brevity. Each writer has brought to her or his task a life that reflects the very principles being studied; each one has dipped a pen into the inkwell of his or her own experiences to set forth what has been explicated in their assignment.

Having known most of the writers since their student years in college, seminary, and graduate school, I have observed their course of life and labors since those years of preparation. I am pleased that many of them look upon me as mentor. I feel both privileged and proud to be the writer of the Foreword to this manual to which they have made timely and noteworthy contributions.

This book abounds in wisdom, offering information balanced with inspired guidance. For those readers taking their first steps to ministry, this primer sets forth with plainness the principles which underlie servant ministry in the spirit of Christ. This book also offers a refreshing read for those whose service years have been many, whose first steps to ministry lie well in the past, but whose heart and feet are still marching in glad service to the beat of the heavenly drum.

50

DOORS TO LIFE: GUSTAV JEENINGA

by James Earl Massey

Originally appeared as the "Foreword" to *Doors to Life:
The Stories of Gustav Jeeninga*, Barry L. Callen, ed.
(Anderson University Press, 2002), 9-10.
Used by permission.

Mention the name Gustav Jeeninga in certain circles of faculty, students, Old Testament scholars, and archae-ologists and hearts are warmed as memorable relation-ships are recalled. There is a host of his friends and associates from across the years at Anderson University and places far beyond, es-pecially in Holland and the Middle East. This is to be expected because Dr. Jeeninga has been one of the most distinctive, lov-able, and productive scholars, college teachers, and world travelers among the many who have served at Anderson University.

"Gus" and I have been friends across more than forty years. We first met in 1962. He was an Associate Professor in the Department of Bible at Anderson College when I arrived on campus that year to speak during Religious Emphasis Week. We met after the first chapel service in which I spoke. Gus, who loved humor, had espe-cially enjoyed a moment (the president had misspoken my name in his introduction). He voiced his appreciation to me for the way

I had humorously handled the matter. I never forgot the spirit of his comment and the way he responded to my additional speaking across that week.

Seven years later I was back on campus as a fellow faculty member, a colleague of Dr. Jeeninga, teaching courses in Bible and religious studies. As we explored ways to share with greater appeal the information of our required courses in Bible, Gus suggested, and I readily agreed, that we team teach. This inventive approach proved so popular that we continued it, and across each school year students rushed to find seats in our classes. It was an enviable joy we had across those years to see new students line up, seeking our signatures to be admitted after our class enrollment quotas had been filled!

In this autobiography, Gustav Jeeninga has reported on this team teaching and on so much more from his life and labors. It is a reporting done with his characteristic gusto, openness, honesty, and humor. This book honors God who opened the eyes of its writer to many "doors to life." I am confident that it will benefit many others whose hearts earnestly seek faith, hope, and meaning.

51

CHRIST COMPELS US!

by James Earl Massey

Originally appeared as the "Foreword" to Edward L. Foggs,
Christ Compels Us! (Warner Press, 1986), vii-viii.

T o treat the theme chosen for the 1996 International
Convention of the Church of God, *Christ Compels Us!*,
presents a responsible, thoughtful, and convictional statement that deserves an open and careful reading.

Henry Thoreau once commented that many a person has dated
a new era in their life from the reading of a seminal book. This
book, with its hearty and essential theme, can help to initiate a new
era for a believer, a congregation, or for the larger church.

Author Edward L. Foggs begins with an in-depth look into 2
Corinthians 5, the foundational biblical passage for the convention theme, and rightly accents the love of Christ for us and in us
as a compelling motivation parentheses (5:14). The credibility and
contagion of the Apostle Paul, writer of the passage, are described
as possible for our time and lives. The example and love of Christ
that the Apostle experienced are explained as worthy of our trust
and commitment.

The author of this book points clearly and effectively to what
being gripped and guided by the love of Christ can do within us

and through us. As one reads his statement about it all, one can even feel the urgency that leaves one no choice but to know and serve the Lord with a full openness.

Dr. Foggs has ably stated the case, and he has used many biblical sources in making it. That being "compelled" by Christ is not only our opportunity and privilege but also our only means of being effective in such a world has been clearly and persuasively illustrated.

After treating the passage from 2 Corinthians 5, Dr. Foggs has accented the areas of concern that Christian living addresses: holiness (chapter 2), witnessing (chapter 3), community building (chapter 4), prayer (chapter 5), worship (chapter 6), and the imperative to work at making a difference in the world (chapter 7).

The message in this book is amply and aptly illustrated, sometimes by an appeal to experiences reported by or about notable persons, and sometimes by the personal witness of the author. Now and again aspects of our church heritage come into focus through the pungent quoting of some strategic hymn stanza. Strategic questions are listed at the end of each chapter, which can be used as guides for personal reflection and group discussion.

René Descartes once commented that the reading of a good book is like conversing with a fine and helpful person. This book allows such an interaction and Edward L. Foggs is a leader who has moved far enough along the Christian path to share his insights and wisdom with a poignancy that we can trust. Having known and worked closely with him across many years, I know that he is a believer who travels with the enthusiasm of an adventurer in faith.

This book lets us travel in his gracious and thoughtful company. The witness he has given here is carefully worded and warmly shared. It could not be otherwise since he has written from his own experience of the love of Christ, whose compelling influence has been evident across his many years as pastor, evangelist, teacher, and agency leader.

CONCLUSIONS

52

A CONCLUDING TRIBUTE
*Offered on the Seventieth Anniversary
of Dr. Massey's Call to Ministry*

by Timothy George

Originally appeared on the web site *FIRST THINGS* as the
lead piece titled "James Earl Massey: Steward of the Story,"
by Timothy George, July 25, 2016. Used by permission.

I first heard the voice of James Earl Massey when I was a theological student at Harvard Divinity School and he was the stated preacher for the Christian Brotherhood Hour, a weekly international broadcast sponsored by the Church of God (Anderson, Indiana). In those days, homiletics was not a regular part of the curriculum at Harvard. As a young minister with a small pastoral charge, I was eager to learn all I could about the craft of preaching, especially in a multi-racial, inner-city congregation.

James Earl Massey was different from any other radio preacher I had ever heard. His diction was perfect, his command of the English language was superb, and his style was lively and compelling, though never marked by ostentation. He also had a way of getting on the inside of a biblical text, of unraveling it, so to speak, not the way a botanist would study a leaf in a laboratory, but like a great singer offering a distinctive rendition of a famous song.

Music is an apt analogy for Massey's preaching. Early on he received advanced training in classical piano and had all the makings of a refined concert artist. The modalities of music—rhythm, pitch, tone, phrasing, cadence, melody, mood—also apply to the work of the preacher, and Massey is a master of them all. When his career path turned from music to the ministry, the world lost a great pianist but gained a magnificent preacher of the Gospel. For Massey, though, preaching is never a mere performance, however well-honed and powerfully presented. The sermon is more a deliverance than a performance: What is said is more important than how we say it, though these two aspects can never be completely divorced.

Yesterday, July 24, 2016, marked the 70th anniversary of the pivotal event in Massey's life when, on a Sunday morning in 1946, God called him to preach. Seventy years is a long time to do anything in one human life, but to sustain a pulpit tenure of quality and depth for seven decades is truly remarkable. This year, Massey also celebrates two other important anniversaries: sixty-five years as an ordained Christian minister and sixty-five years of marriage to Gwendolyn Inez Kilpatrick, a beautiful and gifted woman from Alabama whom Massey met in Detroit when she moved there to live with her sister. James and Gwendolyn have shared a lifetime of love and ministry together in the service of the church.

Across the years, James Earl Massey has been a pastor, scholar, teacher, evangelist, theological educator, denominational counselor, and respected leader in the world Christian movement. These are all positions—influential positions—he has held in fulfillment of that prior calling he received in 1946 at a worship service in Detroit. In each of these roles, the task of preaching has been central. The desire to do pulpit work well, to the glory of God and for the blessing of all who hear, has ever claimed the deepest passion of James Earl Massey.

Massey is the heir of a rich heritage of faith. Brought up in a home marked by warm-hearted Christian devotion, he was spiritually formed by Wesleyan theology, the Holiness movement, and the African-American tradition. The rich spiritual resources of these cultural and church traditions have informed his approach to ministry and preaching. But there is a sense in which he transcends them all. The quest for authentic Christian unity is a major motif that runs deep through all of Massey's ministry; his work has been at once both evangelical and ecumenical. For twenty-two years he served as senior pastor of the Metropolitan Church of God in Detroit, a congregation he founded in 1954, the year of *Brown v. Board of Education*. His commitment to human dignity for every person made in the image of God and to civil rights for every citizen of the land was shaped by Martin Luther King Jr., his colleague and friend, and by Howard Thurman, his mentor and inspiration.

On three separate occasions, Massey has presented the William E. Conger, Jr., Lectures on Biblical Preaching at Beeson Divinity School. In the 2004 series, he spoke on the theme "Stewards of the Story." In Massey's depiction of "The Story," the definite article makes a particular point. Preaching is not merely about *stories*, understood as a disparate collection of personal experiences, memories, recollections, and intuitions divorced from the narrative unity of the Bible read as a whole.

The fragmentation and disconnection of much contemporary preaching is a reaction, or perhaps an overreaction, to certain totalizing and oppressive ways the Christian Story has sometimes been told in the past. But Massey calls the preacher back to a fresh encounter with the canonical shape of biblical revelation. The undeniable diversity found in the Scriptures does not obscure the fact that there is one *biblion*: a coherent account of God's purpose for the world and for each of us.

God-called preachers, Massey argues, are *stewards* of this amazing Story. There is great joy in such a stewardship, but it brings a burden as well. Story-stewardship implies a unique calling, a divine commissioning, a holy accountability, and a distinctive demeanor among those who would handle it well. The unifying center of the preaching moment remains the fidelity and clarity of the message on the one hand, and the passion and integrity of the messenger on the other. Stewards of the Story are preachers who speak the truth in love.

Stewards are trustees, those into whose care and responsibility something precious—in this case, something infinitely precious—has been entrusted. In the most basic sense, trustees are not "owners" of the prized bequest they have received. Rather they hold the bequest in trust, and they have a fiduciary responsibility to pass it on intact to those who will one day receive it in turn from them. To discharge this duty faithfully requires not only a knowledge of the Story's content, but also the kind of wisdom that comes only through the hard work of listening, praying, serving, loving, and representing the One in whose name we speak and for whose sake we do this work.

While many people seek greatness but only attain mediocrity, James Earl Massey has been lifted to greatness while seeking simply to be faithful to his calling. Beyond his many accomplishments, at the core of Dr. Massey's being there is an essential decency, humility, and spirituality that is compelling. Never one to give himself to minor absolutes, he has modeled, with courage and compassion, the burdensome joy of a herald whose life reflects the message he proclaims. In the words of the great Howard Thurman, his life has been "a great rejoicing!"

53

UNTIL I REACH MY HOME: THE FINAL THOUGHTS OF DR. MASSEY

by James Earl Massey

Originally appeared as the last pages of James Earl
Massey's autobiography, *Aspects of My Pilgrimage* (Anderson
University Press,2002), 450-452. Used by permission.

Until I reach my home,
Until I reach my home,
I never 'spect to give the journey over,
Until I reach my home.

The above words from a beloved Negro Spiritual bespeak the need for a settled commitment to fulfill the Christian pilgrimage. As for commitment, I have always been encouraged by Abraham's example. The writer of the letter to the Hebrews tells us: "By faith Abraham obeyed when he was called to set out for the place that he was to receive as an inheritance; and he set out, not knowing where he was going" (11:8). This does not mean that Abraham lack direction, but rather that in setting forth at God's call he would experience the new, the different, and the unfamiliar. His pilgrimage to gain Canaan would be a long and sometimes lonely journey into life, a journey with features and fatigue-points which would mark his body, burden his mind, tutor his spirit, and test his resolve. But Abraham sets out, open to travel lanes of test, but also prepared to become heir to ascending levels of truth and the living rewards of trust.

The beckonings of God also came to me, inviting me to pilgrimage in the Divine will. Like Abraham, I too have been on the way somewhere, not knowing the journey beforehand, but steadied by an assurance that God has been directing my steps. This is the meaning of pilgrimage for us all, and the demands of this unfinished journey keep exacting on our part an open ear, a steady step, and a resolved will. An open ear, a steady step, and a resolved will are the pilgrim's trinity for triumph, and they must remain well in place as we deal with the dust and grit of life's journey.

No human is ever privileged to understand in full the logic of his or her life, and whatever understanding one gains cannot be spoken with fullness. We humans cannot understand our individual paths except when flashes of light from God illumine crucial points along the way. As I view my life, my years hang together bound by a central thread called guidance.

My upbringing made me sensitive to this reality, my studies informed my thought about the meaning of this reality, and my experiences of moments of grace deepened my appreciation for this reality.

More than anything else, I have always wanted to be led into meaning, received into God's presence, and to be a servant whose life can help others experience that meaning and sense that presence. It is a sense of meaning and a sense of God's presence that bring a world of difference to our human condition. God is the one to satisfy our quest to know and understand as we journey, and God is the Other to satisfy our need for companionship and guidance in the loneliness of our pilgrimage. I have been steadied by the memory of certain days when a fresh beckoning came to me, and two of the earliest such days still stand out in my mind as fresh to my consciousness as the present hour.

There was that Sunday when during worship I was beckoned to ministry. But there was also that grand day, the final day of a period of fasting, when I heard that same Voice beckon again, promising aspects of meaning that became mine far later as I journeyed. I was still a teenager, a senior in high school. I had walked into a vacant classroom, purposefully alone, and seated myself to read the Scriptures during my lunch hour. As I read, the Voice spoke!

In a moment that was intensely real, that room became for me the center of the universe. The clarity of the message excited and exhausted me. As rich meanings gathered in my brain, I sensed the future unfolding. It was a mystic moment, a holy hour! On that day, in that room, in that way, I heard the Word and embraced the future, and ever afterward I would be undaunted by the human categories and constraints of race, region, or religious preferences.

Because of received meanings and the sense of God's presence, life for me has been an unfolding drama, a joyful pilgrimage, a sequence of guided steps as I have remained surrendered to the lure of what was held before me. What I experienced then, and in holy moments since then, still lures and holds me now.

God calls us into pilgrimage in his will. The crucial response is to give God our full consent, granting him freedom to guide our lives. With our consent, God will take us from where we are to where we ought to go, shaping and using us by his wiser plan.

Abraham did not choose the place from which he started in life, nor do we but, like Abraham, we too must choose the direction we will follow as we live. Abraham wisely trusted God, obeying as beckoned and directed. Following ever onward, he "stayed the course," and succeeding history keeps vindicating and validating his daring deed.

It is my intention to keep saying "Yes!" to God, whose wisdom shows the right way, whose strength helps us move with purpose, and whose direction keeps us assured. Having this, we need nothing more, while lacking this, any life is poor indeed.

> Until I reach my home,
> Until I reach my home,
> I never 'spect to give the journey over,
> Until I reach my home.

Editor's Note

Dr. Massey was once asked about the inevitable passing of great leaders of the faith. How should we think about the considerable vacuum their passing leaves behind? His response gives us hope for every tomorrow.

> In the economy of God, there has always been a plan to continue what has been started through Jesus Christ, and before him what God started in Israel's life and history. The passing of persons who are in current leadership does not mean that there is not provision for the future. There are those coming on who will take up the mantle when it is necessary. History grabs the person it needs at the moment. You can always trust God's providence.

EDITORIAL POSTLUDE

by Curtiss Paul DeYoung

As Dr. Barry Callen noted in his opening editorial comments, Dr. Massey invited us into this labor of love to edit this volume—a major compilation offering various perspectives from the Massey literary canon. Dr. Callen has long been Massey's colleague in ministry and the academy, and his trusted and dear friend. I am Massey's student and mentee. I first met Dr. James Earl Massey over forty years ago. He was my campus pastor and professor of biblical studies at Anderson University. We have grown close through the years.

I have had the honor of standing where he stood when I preached at Metropolitan Church of God in Detroit, many years after his tenure there. I have walked the hallways of the Mozarteum in Salzburg, Austria, where he refined his classical piano skills. I have sat at the desk in his personal office and library in Alabama called the "Outback." And I received an honorary doctorate at his beloved Anderson University when he was scheduled to give the commencement address in 2016—his final scheduled public speaking event which he had to cancel because of illness (the text to his planned remarks are made public for the first time in this book). The spaces that Massey has inhabited now have a special quality to them.

Since we first met, Dr. Massey has become my father in the ministry and personal mentor. He came to Washington, D.C., to lay hands in ordination on Rev. Mitchell Bettis and me as we served with his close friend Dr. Samuel G. Hines. Many others have been mentored by Dr. Massey. The people who would claim a spot in Massey's circle of influence are too numerous to count. His impact on parishioners, students, preachers, academics, activists, and pastors is legendary.

Howard Thurman wrote, "The willingness to be to another human being what is needed at the time the need is most urgent and most acutely felt. . .is to stand for one intimate moment in *loco dei* in the life of another—that is, to make available to another what has already been given us."[1] Dr. Massey has stood in my life and Dr. Callen's and passed on to us what has been given to him. It has been an act of amazing generosity on his part.

James Earl Massey often speaks of his own mentors. In his interview with Henry Mitchell found in this volume, he notes four preaching mentors. Yet in the many years that we have known him, there is one mentor who singularly impacted him at the deepest level. That was Howard Thurman. Massey once shared that Thurman was the human being he felt most at one with in spirit. I once lamented to someone that I was disappointed that I had not met Howard Thurman before he died. The reply was, "You have met Thurman. If you have met Massey, you have met Thurman."

Our connection to Massey links us to Howard Thurman—the mystic-activist and theologian who influenced Martin Luther King, Jr., and the Civil Rights Movement. Thurman passionately searched for the common ground of human community and the experience of knowing oneself to be fully human as God intended—something his grandmother, a woman freed from slavery, pined for.

Educator Mary McLeod Bethune was a mentor to Thurman during his youth. He attended her school in Daytona, Florida.

---

1   Howard Thurman, *Disciplines of the Spirit* (New York: Harper, 1963), 126.

Born to parents who had been enslaved, Bethune believed that education enables one to embrace her or his own sense of worth, respond to racism, and succeed in a country beset with racial injustice. Preacher activist Sojourner Truth's life inspired Bethune to develop leaders. She was born into slavery, escaped as an adult, and took the name "Sojourner Truth" to replace her slave name. She spent her life serving God as a trumpet of truth against racism and sexism.

By connecting to Massey, not only are we linked to Thurman. We also inherit a lineage of mentors. We have been enriched by aspects of the wisdom handed down from Sojourner Truth to Mary McLeod Bethune, from Bethune to Howard Thurman, and from Thurman to James Earl Massey. The Hebrew Psalmist wrote, "You have given me the heritage of those who fear your name" (61:5). Such a heritage helps us reach our full potential as human beings created in the image of God.

James Earl Massey is not as accessible as he once was. Now ill at age 88 years, he likely will not be able to take on new mentees. But this volume, alongside his own many books, becomes a corpus of knowledge that will continue to nurture and mentor us and future generations. This volume has presented Dr. Massey's timeless voice and wisdom. Re-read it; appreciate it; ponder it; share it . . . and embrace his secret to life. That secret, elaborated in chapter three of this volume, is:

> *After all, in the beginning, God.*
> *And in the end, God.*
> *And in between, God.*
> *That's the secret!*

APPENDICES

APPENDIX A

The Published Books of
James Earl Massey

1957   *An Introduction to the Negro Churches in the Church of God Reformation Movement.* Shining Light Survey Press.

1960   *When Thou Prayest: An Interpretation of Christian Prayer According to the Teachings of Jesus.* Warner Press. Second edition 1978.

1961   *The Worshiping Church: A Guide to the Experience of Worship.* Warner Press.

1967   *Raymond S. Jackson*: A Portrait. Warner Press.

1970   *The Soul Under Siege: A Fresh Look at Christian Experience.* Warner Press.

1972   *The Hidden Disciplines.* Warner Press.

1974   *The Responsible Pulpit.* Warner Press.

1976   *The Sermon in Perspective: Study in Communication and Charisma.* Baker Book House.

1979   *Concerning Christian Unity: A Study of the Relational Imperative of Agape Love.* Warner Press.

1980   *Designing the Sermon: Order and Movement in Preaching.* Abingdon Press.

1982   *Interpreting God's Word for Today: Inquiry into Hermeneutics from a Biblical Theological Perspective,* co-editor with Wayne McCown. Warner Press.

1984   *Educating for Service: Essays in Honor of Robert H. Reardon,* editor. Warner Press.

1985   *Spiritual Disciplines.* Francis Asbury Press/Zondervan Publishing House. Revised edition of *The Hidden Disciplines* (1972).

1987   *The Soul Under Siege: Dealing with Temptation,* revised edition of the 1970 book. Francis Asbury Press/Zondervan Publishing House.

1988   *A Bridge Between: A Centennial History of Campus Ministry at Tuskegee University, 1888-1988.* Tuskegee University Press.

1998   *The Burdensome Joy of Preaching.* Abingdon Press.

2000   *Sundays in the Tuskegee Chapel: Selected Sermons.* Abingdon Press.

2002   *Aspects of My Pilgrimage: An Autobiography.* Anderson University Press.

2005   *African Americans and the Church of God: Aspects of a Social History*, Anderson University Press. Awarded the 2006 Smith-Wynkoop Book Award of the Wesleyan Theological Society.

2006   *Stewards of the Story: The Task of Preaching*, Westminster John Knox Press.

2009   *Spiritual Disciplines: A Believer's Openings to the Grace of God.* Third edition of *The Hidden Disciplines*, 1972. Warner Press.

2009   *Our Sufficiency Is of God: Essays on Preaching in Honor of Gardner C. Taylor*, co-editor with Timothy George and Robert Smith, Jr. Mercer University Press.

2012   *The Pastoral Letters*, Immersion Bible Study Series. Abingdon Press.

2013   *"Learning and Labor": African-American Graduates of Oberlin College's Graduate School of Theology, 1853-1966.* Outback Press.

2014   *Preaching from Hebrews: Hermeneutical Insights and Homiletical Helps.* Warner Press.

2018   *Tradition and Engagement: Essays in Honor of Timothy George.* Co-editor with David Dockery and Robert Smith, Jr. Pickwick Publishers.

2018   *Remembering William Levi Dawson: Composer, Conductor, Music Educator.* Tuskegee University Press.

Editor's Note

There, of course, also are numerous journal articles by James Earl Massey and contributions of his to numerous books of others, many referenced and sampled in this book. There also is *Sharing Heaven's Music*, a 1995 book in Massey's honor edited by Dr. Barry L. Callen and comprised of original essays by the top professors of preaching in today's universities and seminaries. In addition, there is a doctoral dissertation inspired by Massey's many insights, *Incorporating Perspectives from the African-American Homiletic Tradition in Order to Increase Socio-Political Awareness and Activism Among Evangelicals* (Wesley W. White, D. Min., Denver Seminary, 2000).

APPENDIX B

Appreciation for Those Who Helped
Make This Volume Possible

Barry L. Callen and Curtiss Paul DeYoung, volume co-editors, wish to make clear that a volume of this nature could not have been accomplished without the financial assistance and range of expertise and time investment of many people. The help began with Dr. Massey himself who suggested a selection of his past writings that he judged most appropriate for this book. That body of potential entries was refined and supplemented by the co-editors with the awareness and approval of Dr. Massey. Clearly, we and all readers are in his debt.

Once the list of approved entries was set, a series of necessary tasks began. Overall themes had to be identified, an organizational pattern for the book established, and prominent individuals recruited to function as section editors. Beyond ourselves as the co-editors of the whole volume, we became indebted to Drs. Cheryl J. Sanders, Edward L. Foggs, and Ronald J. Fowler. In addition, all material had to be digitized, edited, and permissions gained for re-use from the original publishers.

A publisher for this volume had to be found. I (Barry Callen), as Editor of Aldersgate Press, turned to my Publications Team with a detailed publication proposal. All members readily agreed on the unusual worth of this project and affirmed my proposal that it be accepted as an Aldersgate publication. For their ready support, deep gratitude goes to Kevin Mannoia, Bernie Van De Walle, Don Thorsen, Brett Burner, and Marlene Chase.

Because of the strong identification of Dr. Massey with Anderson University, John Pistole, its president, was contacted. He was presented with the possibility of Anderson University Press acting as a collaborating publisher with Aldersgate. His affirming of this possibility was immediate. With that collaboration came the time and skills of librarian Trish Janutolo and archivist Nick Don Stanton-Roark, soon supplemented by Joe Allison, retired book editor of Warner Press, and Rachel DeYoung who typed some of the previously unpublished pieces.

The graphic skill of Brett Burner is now obvious by looking at the book's cover and internal layout. More in the background but no less significant was the practical assistance of Fawn and David Imboden. To assist with the financial viability of a publication of this magnitude, I (Barry Callen) sought and gained pre-publication purchase agreements from a range of institutions and individuals. Here are a few of them, with thanks expressed for the generosity of each and their belief in this project long before it became reality.

Institutions

- Aldersgate Press
- Anderson University
- Anderson University Press
- Asbury Theological Seminary, Orlando campus
- Association of Church of God, Southern California/Nevada
- Beeson Divinity School, Samford University
- Church of God Colorado Conference
- Church of God Ministries, Anderson, IN

- Crossings Church, Oklahoma City
- Eastern New York General Assembly of the Church of God
- General Assembly of the Church of God in Michigan
- Illinois Ministries of the Church of God
- Indiana Ministries of the Church of God
- Leadership Focus of the Church of God
- Mid-America Christian University
- National Association of the Church of God
- Ohio Ministries of the Church of God
- Park Place Church of God, Anderson, IN
- Tennessee Ministries of the Church of God
- Warner Pacific University
- Warner University
- Wesleyan Holiness Connection

Individuals

- Banarsee, Harold
- Booker, Demetrius
- Callen, Barry
- DeYoung, Curtiss Paul
- Dwyer, Timothy
- Flynn, Jeannette
- Foggs, Edward
- Fozard, John
- Frymire, Jeffrey
- George, Timothy
- Grubbs, Marty
- Jones, William

- Livingston, Eric
- Myricks, Charles
- Odell, Bob
- Pistole, John
- Rennick, Steve
- Smith, Handel
- Smith, Obadiah, Jr.
- Talley, Doug
- Winn, David

Of special note is Marty Grubbs. Out of his profound appreciation for Dr. Massey's friendship with and ministry to his family, he purchased enough copies of this book to supply one as a gift to ministerial credentials candidate in today's Church of God movement (Anderson) in North America (350). Dr. Massey was overwhelmed when told of this gift, the placing of his accumulated wisdom in the hands of the next generation of leaders for the church fellowship he has loved and served so well.

It indeed does "take a village." Since Dr. Massey is so well-known and deeply respected and loved, gathering the needed village was easily possible. Thanks be to God!

Co-Editors
Barry L. Callen and
Curtiss Paul DeYoung

APPENDIX C

Endorsement Statements by
Appreciative Colleagues of Dr. Massey

I think it timely and significant that this publication—highlighting and celebrating much of the ministry and prolific writings of Dr. James Earl Massey—has been compiled. It will benefit present and future generations of leaders. He has distinguished himself as a multi-gifted leader: pastor, preacher, teacher, scholar, communicator, and ambassador for our Savior and Lord, Jesus Christ. I have been privileged to know him as a brother, personal friend, and colleague for more than six decades. I salute him as a stellar and humble servant, always advancing the Kingdom at its Biblical best.

Edward L. Foggs, General Director Emeritus,
Church of God Ministries (Anderson)

Rarely does one man possess both the highest of intellects and exceptional preaching ability, shepherding acumen and scholarly prowess, a head and heart for the most demanding of tasks. Dr. Massey is rare. Often I have wondered how an individual so catholic in his living, so open to the world, could have survived and even flourished in cultural and church environments that sometimes are so provincial in outlook. This is one of the mysteries of this man!

Calvin S. Morris, former Dean of the
Interdenominational Theological Center,
Atlanta, Georgia

James Earl Massey was my predecessor as Dean of Anderson University School of Theology. It was impossible to fill his shoes but his supportive words and deeds made my seminary transition smooth. Wherever I would travel in church or academy, his reputation and scholarly wisdom opened doors of service. This compilation of Dr. Massey's works will allow us to once again sit at the foot of the mountain and learn from a scholar and friend who has heard from God.

David L. Sebastian, retired Dean,
Anderson University School of Theology

The modalities of music—rhythm, pitch, tone, phrasing, cadence, melody, mood—also apply to the work of the preacher, and Massey is a master of them all. When James Earl Massey's career path turned from music to the ministry, the world lost a great performer but gained a magnificent preacher of the gospel of Christ.

Timothy George, Dean of Beeson Divinity School,
Samford University

Absorbing his seminary lectures certainly enriched my understanding and knowledge. But the greater impact on me was the dignity of Dr. Massey's words and life, even when life in the church didn't always treat him with dignity. It was the way he honored every person who came into his presence. He never opted for position or fame, it just kept coming his way.

Jeannette Flynn, Director of the *Leadership Focus*
program of the Church of God (Anderson)

As Editor of *Preaching Magazine*, I have a wonderful opportunity to hear many of the finest preachers of our day. Frequently I am asked to provide a list of the "best" preachers in America. The list varies from year to year, but one name appears every time: James Earl Massey.

> **Michael Duduit,** Editor of *Preaching Magazine*,
> Professor of Preaching,
> Southern Baptist Theological Seminary

I suspect that the signal place of James Earl Massey in the academy and church has been maintained through the integrity of his being and living. He has sought to live the life about which he has taught, preached, and written. This he has done, leaning on the Lord, with elegance, eloquence, and grace.

> **Robert H. Reardon,** longtime president
> of Anderson University

Rev. Dr. James Earl Massey has had a very distinguished career as the seminal preacher in the nation. Following his many years as Dean of the Anderson School of Theology, I came to appreciate the uniqueness of his scholarly gifts and pastoral wisdom. More than anything, I count it all joy that he proves himself at difficult times. I now break a vow to share this story of Brother Massey's personal care in my own life. Due to circumstances out of my control, I was late in meeting the deadline for my submission to the *New Interpreter's Bible*. Dr. Massey called me, assessed the challenge, and offered to finish my submission. He proved himself a true colleague, dear friend, and ghost writer! I am honored to add my voice in tribute to James Earl Massey.

> **Cain Hope Felder,** Emeritus Professor of
> New Testament Language and Literature,
> Howard University School of Divinity

James Earl Massey, through love, patience and truth-telling, helped me finally make the long step from boyhood to manhood. The road was not easy. Having my own father die when I was 20 years old, and facing American racism at every turn, I resisted the notion of "a better world" through hard work and perseverance. But Dr. Massey would not let me fail. He challenged me to reach beyond my grief, beyond my pre-conceived notion of defeatism, to a place worthy of a child of God. For him, I am eternally grateful.

Al Miles, Lead Chaplain, Pacific Health Ministry at The Queen's Medical Center in Honolulu, Hawaii and author of *Domestic Violence: What Every Pastor Needs to Know*

Dr. James Earl Massey is a son of the National Association of the Church of God. While led to Christ and discipled by members of the Church of God movement, his ministry has been ecumenical, ultimately reaching wide into the body of Christ. His love for all people and his gracious friendliness have made him a brother to many. His legendary scholarship, prodigious productivity, and tireless mentoring now have made him a father to us all. We rejoice to see his legacy preserved and made available to inform and inspire the coming generations of God's people. Dr. Massey—son, brother, father. To God be the glory!

Charles Myricks, Jr., Chief Operating & Development Officer, National Association of the Church of God

This wonderful anthology of the lifetime writings of James Earl Massey is certainly recommended reading church-wide. Written with academic integrity and theological clarity, it reveals the numerous dimensions of the life of Christian holiness as it confronts the religious and racial struggles of today's culture. To read this book is to experience applied theology at its best.

Arlo F. Newell, Editor in Chief, Warner Press, retired

APPENDIX D

The Co-Editors of This Volume:
Rev. Dr. Barry L. Callen
&
Rev. Dr. Curtiss Paul DeYoung

Rev. Dr. Barry L. Callen is University Professor Emeritus of Christian Studies, Anderson University, former Dean of Anderson University's School of Theology, and Anderson University's Vice-President for Academic Affairs. Currently he is Special Assistant to the General Director of Church of God Ministries, Corporate Secretary of Horizon International (AIDS orphans ministry in six African nations), former editor of the *Wesleyan Theological Journal,* and current editor of Aldersgate Press of the Wesleyan Holiness Connection. Ordained minister of the Church of God movement (Anderson, IN), Dr. Callen holds graduate degrees from Anderson University, Asbury Theological Seminary, Chicago Theological Seminary, and Indiana University. He has authored, edited, and published dozens of books, including Dr. Massey's autobiography, *Aspects of My Pilgrimage,* his *African Americans and the Church of God,* and the book of essays in Dr. Massey's honor, *Sharing Heaven's Music.*

Rev. Dr. Curtiss Paul DeYoung is the CEO of the Minnesota Council of Churches. Previously he was the Executive Director of the historic racial justice organization Community Renewal Society in Chicago and the inaugural Professor of Reconciliation Studies at Bethel University in St. Paul. He has served congregations in Minneapolis, New York City, and Washington, DC. Dr. DeYoung earned degrees from the University of St. Thomas, Howard University School of Divinity, and Anderson University. He is an ordained minister in the Church of God movement (Anderson, IN) and author and editor of ten books on reconciliation, multi-racial congregations, social justice activism, and multi-cultural perspectives on the Bible. DeYoung was a student of Dr. Massey at Anderson University and Anderson School of Theology.

INDEX

V

W

Y